B
M8209L **Morgan, Charles,** 1894–1958.

Selected letters; edited and with a memoir by Eiluned
Lewis.   London, Melbourne, Macmillan, 1967.

[11], 235 p.   front, 6 plates (incl. facsims., ports.).   22½ cm.   42/–

(B 67–6669)

I. Lewis, Eiluned, ed.

PR6025.O645Z53   1967

SELECTED LETTERS OF
CHARLES MORGAN

Charles Morgan on Llangorse Lake, Breconshire, 1940
Photograph by Rache Lovat Dickson

SELECTED
LETTERS OF
CHARLES MORGAN

Edited and with a Memoir by
Eiluned Lewis

MACMILLAN
LONDON · MELBOURNE

1967

MACMILLAN AND COMPANY LIMITED
Little Essex Street London WC2
also Bombay Calcutta Madras Melbourne

PRINTED IN GREAT BRITAIN BY RICHARD CLAY (THE CHAUCER PRESS), LTD.,
BUNGAY, SUFFOLK

This book is dedicated to
the memory of two of his devoted friends,
CHRISTOPHER ARNOLD-FORSTER
21 July 1965
and
PATRICK MURPHY MALIN
13 December 1964

Si nostre vie est moins qu'une journée
En l'eternel, si l'an qui faict le tour
Chasse noȝ jours sans espoir de retour,
Si perissable est toute chose née,

Que songes-tu, mon ame emprisonée?
Pourquoy te plaist l'obscur de nostre jour,
Si pour voler en un plus cler sejour
Tu as au dos l'aele bien empanée?

La est le bien que tout esprit desire,
La, le repos ou tout le monde aspire,
La est l'amour, la, le plaisir encore.

La, ô mon ame, au plus hault ciel guidée,
Tu y pourras recongnoistre l'Idée
De la beauté, qu'en ce monde j'adore.

JOACHIM DU BELLAY
1522–60

ACKNOWLEDGEMENTS

CHARLES MORGAN was a copious writer of letters. The ones printed in this book are a comparative few chosen from the very great number which it has been my privilege to read. For the ready help given by his friends and relatives, I am deeply grateful, wishing only that more of his letters to them could have been included. Many of the letters have been shortened and passages irrelevant to the theme omitted. For ease of reading, omission marks at the beginning and end of letters have been left out.

The debt that I owe, to both the living and the dead, is inadequately shown by the following list of those who have lent their letters and shared their memories: the Marchioness of Anglesey, Miss E. M. Almedingen, the late Commander Christopher Arnold-Forster, the late Sir Carleton Allen, Mr. Peter Alchin, Mrs. Robert Barrett, Professor Louis Bonnerot, Mr. Vernon Barlow, the late W. Bridges-Adams, Mr. Archibald Black, the late Maurice Colbourne, Mr. Lovat Dickson, Mr. W. A. Darlington, Mr. Alan Dent, Mr. St. John Ervine, the Hon. Mrs. Christopher Fremantle, Mr. Hugh Giffard, Admiral J. H. God-frey, C.B., Mr. Walton von Hemert, Mrs. Helen von Hemert-de Pallandt, Mrs. Stephen Hobhouse, Colonel Robert Henriques, Mr. Richard Hughes, Mr. Stewart Hunter, Mr. Philip Hope-Wallace, Mr. Christopher Hussey, Mr. Rupert Hart-Davis, Mr. Hamish Hamilton, Miss Kitty de Josselin de Jong, Mme Christine Lalou, Mr. F. W. H. Loudon, Lady Lenanton (Carola Oman), Mr. Laurier Lister, Mr. Roger Morgan, the late Mrs. Jack Morant (his sister Marcie), the late Miss Mildred Morgan, the late Mrs. Robert Mennell, Mr. Hugo van Manen, Mr. and Mrs. Christopher Medley, Mrs. Elma Napier, Mr. Bruce Oliphant, Mrs. Ruth Pitman, Dr. Stephen Pasmore, Miss Margaret Storm Jameson, Mme Sauzey (a grand-daughter of Jacques Delamain), Mrs. Hilary St. George Saunders, Miss Veronica Wedgwood, Dr. Orlo Williams and Mr. Charles Williams. Finally, a word of love and gratitude to my husband, Graeme Hendrey.

E. L.

ILLUSTRATIONS

CHARLES MORGAN

Chief events and publications

Born 22 January 1894
Entered Royal Navy 1907; resigned 1913
Rejoined Navy, August 1914
Interned in Holland 1914–17
The Gunroom 1919
Brasenose College, Oxford 1919–21
Joined editorial staff of *The Times* 1921
Married Hilda Vaughan 1923
My Name is Legion 1925
Principal dramatic critic of *The Times* 1926–39
Portrait in a Mirror 1929
The Fountain 1932
Epitaph on George Moore 1935
Sparkenbroke 1936
The Flashing Stream (play) 1938
Served at the Admiralty (with intervals) 1939–44
The Voyage 1940
The Empty Room 1941
Lectured in the U.S.A. 1941–42
Ode to France 1942
The House of Macmillan 1943
Reflections in a Mirror (First and Second Series) 1944 and 1946
The Judge's Story 1947
The River Line (novel) 1949
Elected Membre de l'Institut de France 1949
Liberties of the Mind 1951
A Breeze of Morning 1951
The River Line (play) 1952
The Burning Glass (play) 1953
President of International P.E.N. 1953–56
Challenge to Venus 1957
Died 6 February 1958.

CHARLES MORGAN

(Life, events and publications)

Born 22 January 1894
Entered Royal Navy 1907; resigned 1913
Released from Navy, August 1914
Interned in Holland 1914-17
The Gunroom 1919
Brasenose College, Oxford 1919-21
Joined editorial staff of *The Times* 1921
Married Hilda Vaughan 1923
My Name is Legion 1925
Principal dramatic critic of *The Times* 1926-39
Portrait in a Mirror 1929
The Fountain 1932
Epstein (engraved essay) 1932
Sparkenbroke 1936
The Flashing Stream (play) 1938
Served at the Admiralty (until his death) 1939-41
The Voyage 1940
The Empty Room 1941
Banned in the U.S.A. 1941-42
Ode to France 1942
The Flashing Stream 1947
Reflections in a Mirror (First and Second Series) 1944 and 1945
The Judge's Story 1947
The River Line (novel) 1949
Elected Membre de l'Institut de France 1949
The Voyage... 1950
A Breeze of Morning 1951
The River Line (play) 1952
The Burning Glass (play) 1953
President of International P.E.N. 1953-56
Challenge to Venus 1957
Died 6 February 1958

CHARLES MORGAN : A MEMOIR

THESE letters do not claim to be the portrait of a whole man; but what portrait is complete? Voltaire's definition of a bore is someone who cannot leave anything out. In this case almost everything has been left out except that which concerns the writer at work — the habit of his creative imagination, the manner in which it crystallized into stories and plays, the technique (even the physical technique) of his writing, and the philosophy of the writer's life and task. The other exceptions are his love of France and his mysticism. Thousands of his letters, many in his own hand — dutiful family letters, love letters, letters of congratulation, sympathy and patient advice, and letters dealing with matters of national and international interest — were read before this selection was made.

More than most people in his dealings with the world Charles Morgan wore protective armour. The greatest of his French friends has said that he found it almost impossible to recognize in the austere and often suffering critic at a London theatre the man who had been his gay companion in the streets of Paris and the French countryside. Some people thought him arrogant and self-centred. In a letter (23 November 1948) there is a comment on Chateaubriand — incidentally a Breton and a romantic — that seems singularly fitting to Morgan himself:

> Everyone who writes about Chateaubriand says he was egotistical and ambitious, generally with the implication that he was cold-hearted and false. . . . He was, in his style, true to himself. . . . Even more important is the fact that the defect in his character is not cynicism or cold-heartedness, but a shy, sentimental desire to be loved. A dangerous desire . . .

There are friends of Charles Morgan still alive to refute any notion of cold-heartedness. 'He was, in his style, true to himself'; grave, witty and compassionate with a warm humour, at once quizzical and exhilarating, which delighted the circle of his intimates. To be in his company was to taste the wine of friendship.

By origin on both sides of his family Morgan was of Welsh stock, but the roots had been severed and his upbringing was English. He was therefore a 'displaced Celt', or as he himself put it 'a Celt trained down'.

B   I

Touching the purpose and intention of his life, he was single-minded; in other ways contradictory.

'All my life I've been a queer mixture of pride and humility,' he wrote, and other contradictions will appear to the reader of these letters. Here can be found a young revolutionary who later remodelled himself as a conformer; the author of *The Gunroom*, running his head against the Establishment, but all his life proud of his naval training; a contemplative who hated crowds, yet dreaded solitude and never took a country walk if he could help it; a mystic with an intense interest in money; an Englishman homesick for France; a Platonist who never lost his love of the Church liturgy, but wrote some of his most revealing letters to Quakers.

There were basic tensions in his character which were all important, for in his own words, 'a character which has lost its warming and light-giving tensions will not produce art at all'.[1] Causes for some of these tensions can be traced to his heritage of blood. Even more perhaps to his family history, for Charles Morgan the artist was grafted on to a striving and very persistent stock.

William Morgan, his grandfather, shared with the poet William Collins the distinction of being a hatter's son, but of Mark Morgan, the hatter, little is known save that he is buried in the village of Bitten, near Bath. William Morgan (Charles's grandfather) worked as an engineer in Pembroke Dock in the 1840s and there made friends with a young Welshman, William Watkins (originally Gwatkin), born in Pembroke in 1822 and already a foreman and overseer at the age of twenty-one. The forties were a lean time in rural Wales; the dockyard did not provide scope for ambition, and presently Will Watkins, having married his Pembrokeshire cousin, Martha Dally, sailed for Australia.

In New South Wales there were bridges and railways to be built. Watkins reported the good news to Morgan, and he likewise took ship for Sydney, accompanied by his wife and young family. The two worked together as contractor and engineer, and their children — sharing the hardships and hazards of pioneering life — were eventually linked by marriage.

Will Morgan had married Sophia Langbridge (of Irish descent and 'strikingly beautiful', according to family legend). She had another claim to interest for, as well as becoming Charles Morgan's grandmother, she was aunt to William John Wills, the explorer and

[1] 'Ivan Turgenev' in *Reflections in a Mirror*, First Series (Macmillan, 1944).

companion of Robert O'Hara Burke. The story of how these two traversed Australia from south to north in 1861, and perished on the return journey, is a classic event in Australian history. Their statue stands in Melbourne today.

Wills joined the exploring party as astronomer and surveyor. He was twenty-seven when he died of starvation in the Australian desert, and is described as 'an excellent and reliable young man, studious and eager to get on'. His portrait — above and behind his mid-Victorian beard and side-whiskers — bears a marked resemblance to Charles Langbridge Morgan, writer of these letters.

Meantime, at Lithgow in New South Wales, the young Charles Morgan (son of William and Sophia and father of our Charles) walked eight miles to school every day. He returned to England at the age of sixteen to be apprenticed to an engineering firm, and from his lodgings at Hampstead walked daily to and from his work at Blackfriars, a distance of about seven miles.

In 1883 he sailed once more for Australia in order to carry away his bride, Mary, one of the seven children of William and Martha Watkins. They had waited for each other for nine years. Without surprise one learns that Charles Morgan (senior) rose to the top of his profession and ended his career as a highly esteemed President of the Institution of Civil Engineers. He was knighted in 1923.

The Watkins stayed on in New South Wales and bought property. Years later William Watkins returned to his native Pembroke. He had promised his mother that one day he would drive her round that pleasant countryside — among the castles and famous houses and along the wooded, winding shores of Milford Haven — and he did it. The legend hesitates between two and four horses to draw the carriage, but is precise as regards the liveried coachman and footman. No doubt, Will Watkins had panache.

For neither family was there any abiding background. The Morgans mislaid theirs in an earlier generation; the Watkins never lived again in Pembrokeshire. It is both the strength and the weakness of Welsh people to be rooted in their own land, and all his life Charles Morgan, the writer, knew the handicap of rootlessness. While in his mid-fifties, and six years after his father had died, he could write: 'I still feel by his death terribly cut off from my childhood and my origins' (February 1947). When Lewis Alison in *The Fountain* sees himself 'a solitary and adventurous figure, travelling through a virgin landscape from birth to death',[1] there is an uneasy reminder of William John Wills, perishing in the homeless desert of another continent.

Charles Morgan the engineer remained the yardstick by which his son throughout his life measured a man's integrity and application. There is a sketch of him in *A Breeze of Morning* as the father with 'his freedom from self-indulgence, his unswerving advance in his own profession', but a subtler picture in *The Judge's Story* in the unsentimentalized portrait of a good man, as well as of a 'very solid, very unpretentious Victorian'. His wife, Mary Morgan, died when Charles (youngest of her four children) was twelve years old. There was a deprivation here which could not be remedied — even by the devoted elder sister, the Marcie of these letters.

The elder brother, Will, went to Marlborough and Trinity Hall, Cambridge. His portrait can be found in the handsome, gifted Howard of *A Breeze of Morning*. 'Scholarship after scholarship. First at Cambridge. First in his Bar Exams.' He had chosen law, and his younger brother never doubted but that one day Will would be Lord Chancellor or Lord Chief Justice. Instead, he was killed at Gallipoli in 1915.

Charles, as a small boy, pretending to write in his sisters' old exercise-books even before he had learnt the art, also knew what he wanted to do. He would be a writer. Why then the Navy? There were, apparently, several reasons. In ceaseless conflict with the desire to write was the Morgan view of life 'as a huge ladder to be climbed step by step'. Below the ladder were the failures, the ne'er-do-weels into whose company one might slip back if a rung were missed. To be *only* a writer was dangerous. 'The Death of Chatterton', painted by a lesser pre-Raphaelite artist Henry Wallis, which Charles was shown one day in the Tate Gallery by his father, was an example of what might happen to the writer who failed.

There were other reasons. It was a highly honourable profession. Boys who joined the Navy saw the world; how could a stay-at-home learn enough of life to write about it? There was, too, an odd and sadly mistaken notion that a ship at sea would provide leisure and silence for composition.

The letters to his family from his cadet ship, H.M.S. *Cumberland*, are ordinary and dutiful. Those to his father give details of mechanical operations likely to interest a distinguished civil engineer. It is clear that at the time Charles was fairly content and as yet uncritical of

[1] *The Fountain* (Macmillan, 1932), p. 79.

conditions at sea. Of his service as a midshipman in his next ship, H.M.S. *Good Hope*, with the Atlantic Fleet, there is no record in any letters. The history of that unhappy period lies between the covers of *The Gunroom*, his first novel, written during internment in Holland. In this memoir the story of its chequered fortunes is included later in the account of those years.

In his third and last ship, H.M.S. *Monmouth*, Charles had the supreme good fortune to encounter the man who became his life-long friend, Christopher Arnold-Forster, at that time Senior Sub-Lieutenant and the autocrat of the gunroom mess. Under his civilized rule there was a firm suppression of those barbarous 'time-honoured' customs suffered by the midshipmen of the *Good Hope*.

I am indebted to Commander Arnold-Forster for this account of their first meeting:

The officers and crew that were to relieve those serving in the *Monmouth* on the China Station took passage in H.M.S. *Euryalus* and joined the latter at Devonport.

On the morning of 'joining ship' the Senior Sub-Lieutenant was officer-of-the-watch, and the strict protocol of the quarter-deck was being observed. An unusual incident occurred. The midshipman-of-the-watch approached the Sub-Lieutenant, saluted and asked permission to leave the quarter-deck and go to the gunroom for a short while. The officer-of-the-watch asked for what purpose he made this request to go off duty. The midshipman replied that he had 'left some papers sculling about in the mess', and wished to clear them up. Would not the other midshipmen see to this he was asked. Yes, that was what he wished to forestall. 'What then are these papers?' And to his question came the surprising reply, 'Sonnets, sir.'

The midshipman was given the leave he sought, but on the condition that he reported to the Sub-Lieutenant's cabin that evening with two whiskeys and soda — and the sonnets.

The midshipman, the drinks and the sonnets duly arrived, and that was the first of very many occasions on which Charles claimed the refuge of that cabin (and the interest of its tenant) in which to read, to write, and finally to choose a new way of life.

Twenty-three years later *Sparkenbroke* was dedicated 'To Christopher Arnold-Forster, who lent me courage to seek my trade, and to my father, Charles Morgan, who gave me freedom to ply it'.

No letters survive from the time in the *Monmouth*. In *Liberties of the*

Mind, a book of essays published in 1951, there is a vignette of a boy's first encounter with Keats's 'The Eve of St. Agnes', read in a ship's cabin in the China Seas. *The Gunroom* (now become a collector's piece) gives a vivid picture of conflict in the boy's mind, summed up by Charles as 'a very accurate self-portrait'.[1]

> He would banish poetry from him as men banished a drug. . . .
> Keats should go; and Blake, and Milton's prose, and Burke's
> speeches. One afternoon of resolution he piled them together and
> carried them off. . . . From his sea-chest he disinterred battered
> notebooks on Mechanics and Heat and Steam.

By the beginning of 1913 the decision was taken. Mr. Charles Morgan wrote to Sir Graham Greene, K.C.B., Secretary of the Admiralty:

> It is with regret that I have to inform you that my son Mr. C. L.
> Morgan who is now serving as a Midshipman in H.M.S. *Monmouth*,
> on the China Station, is desirous of retiring from the Service. . . .
> It appears he is happy in his present work, and all his surroundings;
> the reason he gives for desiring to retire from the Service is that he
> wishes to follow a literary career.

Permission to withdraw from the Navy being granted, within a few months Charles took his examinations for Oxford and was entered at Brasenose College for the following autumn. But the year was 1914. With the outbreak of war in August he volunteered for Service and was given a commission as sub-lieutenant in the R.N.V.R. and appointed to one of the newly formed Naval Brigades.

In the first critical weeks of the war the volunteer officers of the future Naval Brigade were summoned to the Admiralty and addressed by the First Lord. Churchill, who had been without sleep for nights, spoke to every officer individually, having concerned himself to know something of the background of each one. For Charles this meeting with the man whom he so greatly admired was 'magical'. With the men still largely untrained and not fully equipped, they were drafted to the expedition for the defence of Antwerp, described in Churchill's history as 'the sole stronghold of the Belgian nation; the true left flank of the Allied front in the West'.

Its capture was an urgent necessity for the German army. Thirty years later Charles wrote: 'This Naval Division must have been the first volunteer division to go into action — two months training, one

[1] Letter to Louis Gillet, August 1933.

machine-gun to a battalion, no ambulances — just rifles and, for those of us who were officers, swords! But we *felt* that we were a crusade . . .'

For five days the defence of the city was prolonged, while the Belgian Field Army and its brave king safely extricated themselves. But nothing could silence the German siege guns. On 8 October Antwerp was 'considered to be untenable', and the retreat began towards Ghent and Ostend. One letter only from Charles survives to describe these events. It was written on 15 October from a prison camp in Groningen to his Oxford tutor.

> The end of our twenty-one-hour retreat from the trenches outside Antwerp found us at St. Gilles where we should have found a train to take us to Ostend. On our arrival there — some 500 men — we found that the rest of the Naval Division had retreated earlier and left us, so that we had neither trains, nor support, nor ammunition for that had all been thrown away somewhere on our nightmare march of 45 miles. There was no course open to us but that of laying down our arms in Holland, and as a result I find myself in Groningen, a prisoner of war on parole.

Early in 1915 the barracks at Groningen were exchanged for a fortress between Leyden and Utrecht; from then onwards, for nearly three years, the background of Charles Morgan's life, with some vital differences, closely resembled the scene of *The Fountain*. The opening words of the novel state exactly what befell the officers of the Naval Brigade.

> On an afternoon of January 1915, a small train dragged itself across the flat Dutch countryside in the neighbourhood of Bodegraven, carrying a group of English officers under guard. . . . Separated from their men, with whom they had been living in an internment camp at Groningen, they were now being taken to closer imprisonment in a fortress.

The Fort of Wierickerschans stands today. Built by William of Orange (William III of England), it is a dry strategic point — one of many — in that watery region defending the heart of Holland. Tall trees still grow below the grassy ramparts; the earthen bastions are guarded by a wide moat, and beyond the moat an arm of the Rhine — the 'Old Rhine' — meanders towards Leyden. The flat country around is as placid and sky-filled as a picture by Ruysdael, and so it was when Charles watched 'the brown sail of a barge, whose hull was concealed by the deep canal-banks, rise out of the meadows and dwell long in the great landscape, seeming to have fallen asleep in anticipation of dusk'. The scatter of neat red houses may have grown since 1915, but in the fat water-meadows it is the black and white Friesian cows and the wheeling flocks of plovers that take the eye.

In this place the imprisoned officers of the Naval Brigade were confined for a year, and Charles spent his twenty-first birthday in the custody of a Dutch commandant, the 'man of genial disposition'. Thence, as told in the novel, they attempted to escape by the laborious digging of a tunnel to the inner edge of the moat. The mouth of the tunnel, concealed beneath an officer's bed, was discovered by a Dutch orderly. With the granting of parole, captivity ended, and Charles Morgan's particular story moved eastwards, almost across the breadth of Holland, to a cottage beside a castle.

The Castle of Rosendaal stands among the deep woods and solitudes of Guelderland; Arnhem, where another forlorn hope foundered in another war, lies a few miles away. Rosendaal is still today the home of the Baron van Pallandt. With his family one of Morgan's fellow-prisoners, Hugh Giffard (a friend of Osborne days), was acquainted. Through this happy chance a cottage on the castle estate was offered to him, Charles and Robert Barrett.

Hugh Giffard, nicknamed 'Tiny', who had left the Navy to study agriculture, has clearly much in common with Ballater in *The Fountain*. Robert Barrett (known as Roger to his naval friends) does not appear in the novel. Perhaps the writer felt that any portrait, or half-portrait, might spoil their deep friendship, which lasted as long as they both lived.

There could scarcely be a sharper contrast than conditions in Holland during the two wars. Starvation and the ignominies of enemy occupation were the common lot of the Second World War; during the First World War, but for some scarcities, it was still possible to maintain a 'civilized' way of life. The moment in time which found Wilfred Owen writing from the front to describe 'the universal pervasion of UGLINESS: hideous landscapes, vile noises, foul language, everything unnatural, broken, blasted; the distortion of the dead', discovered Charles Morgan and his companions among the dignified beauties of an old estate, in a charmed circle of friends, with seamen servants — sent up from the Groningen camp — to tend to their needs.

For eager, ambitious youth it was a strange fate. Roger Barrett, perhaps the most selfless of the three, said long afterwards: 'We are men who ought to have died.' In an essay published after his death, Charles has described his own response. 'The fates had suddenly given me Time Out — infinite time as far as I could tell . . . there was, in effect, no time. Until the moment should come in which the Germans decided to go home again, there were no calendars, even of the years.'[1]

He compared his Time Out to the traditional Grand Tour of fortunate youths — a long and leisurely journey through Europe coming at an age when it was most precious. 'Its value was not only that it enabled them to see the world and civilize themselves by contact with European society, but it took them away from home and from the too familiar stresses, emotional and intellectual, which beset us when we are twenty-one.' It was, he said delightedly, 'freedom such as I had never known before'.

None of this would have been experienced without the 'European society' of Rosendaal and its library of which he was given the freedom. The Pallandts had been hereditary marshals of Cleves in the fourteenth century; there were Pallandts of Keppel, Rosendaal and Neerijnen at the beginning of this century, still owning a dozen major houses and castles. Most of the family spoke four languages, and they bear no likeness to the characters of *The Fountain*, as Charles was careful to point out. Two of them played a notable part in his education.

One was Madame Loudon, née *de* Pallandt (as she would have called it) widow of a roaming Scot whose forebears had served under Sir Stamford Raffles in Java. When the young Englishmen came to Rosendaal she was eighty-six years old and blind. High society in the Holland of her youth was largely French speaking, and she had lived for a time in France. Thirty years later Charles wrote that 'he first loved France for her sake'. In her presence he felt that he was on a stage, 'playing a part in a very great play'. Through her he lived imaginatively in the France of the mid-nineteenth century. 'She had danced to Chopin's waltzes with, as she said, "Monsieur Chopin playing them" . . . She had the gift of the great saying.'

One of her two daughters, having married her cousin the Baron van Pallandt, lived at the castle. The other, Helen, was the widowed Madame Elout van Soeterwoude — witty and elegant, an artist and well read in four literatures. Speaking of her afterwards Charles once

---

[1] 'Time Out', in *The Writer and his World* (Macmillan, 1960), p. 73.

said that Julie in *The Fountain* was 'as he imagined Madame Elout in her youth'.[1]

The castle of Rosendaal still exists, and opposite its gates is the eighteenth-century dower-house where Charles would sit reading aloud the letters of Madame de Staël and Macaulay's history to his blind hostess. One unchanging sound in those quiet rooms is the soft rushing of a waterfall as it runs over the stones into the castle lake. (Had Charles this in mind when he so often chose the sound of water in the titles of his books?) There are three lakes at Rosendaal and the lowest washes the foot of the thirteenth-century tower, 'a great-girthed cylinder of ancient brick'. Le Nôtre designed the garden with its Neptuned fountain and tree-lined vistas; William III and Mary Stuart built the garden pavilion,'a little pillared building with a flattened dome'. The orangery above the rose garden was smashed by Canadian gun-fire in 1944, but the wooded eyot, the chain-ferry and stepping-stones are still as they were when Lewis Alison in *The Fountain* first saw them.

Within the castle today most of the rooms are empty, the tapestries and pictures are gone, and the staircase in the tower 'built into the thickness of the wall' ends in the locked door of the library above the banqueting hall, where once the dancers moved beneath the light of many candles. 'Their timelessness would take my breath away,' said Charles of the van Pallandt circle. With them he first discovered that in true understanding there need be no frontiers of time or nationality. Perhaps too in Rosendaal, silent among its trees like a castle in a tapestry, he gained some lasting apprehension of 'the innermost court of quietness itself', where a fountain of the spirit may rise.

If these impressions were the ultimate fruit of Charles Morgan's internment, the book that he immediately set about writing was *The Gunroom*. His companions, Barrett and Giffard, had both been trained at Osborne and Dartmouth, and Morgan's memories of the unhappy *Good Hope* were reinforced by Giffard's experiences in H.M.S. *Britannia*. In the latter ship the treatment of midshipmen resulted in a Court of Enquiry and subsequent Court Martial.

A certain mystery surrounds *The Gunroom*'s reception. It was published by A. & C. Black in 1919, and reviewed by Edgar Wallace in the *Sunday Chronicle* under the heading 'The Midshipman's Hell: Amazing Charges in a Remarkable New Naval Novel'.

The *Nautical Magazine* commented cautiously: 'Mr. Morgan has a

[1] See also letter to Roger Barrett (No. 30), 3 May 1929.

gift for writing. We hope this book will effect good and that he will find time to develop and expand his literary tastes.'

The story of what happened to the book is told in a letter to Louis Bonnerot (1 March 1932) given here. Certainly it was not 'officially suppressed', and Mr. Archie Black, the present head of the firm, has found nothing in his archives to alter this opinion. Strangely, he received a letter from Charles on the subject, dated January 1958, within a few weeks of his death:

> Your father [Adam Black] felt sure then, and I had ample confirmation afterwards, that the Admiralty, having considered prosecution and thought better of it, had provided for the suppression of the book by more subtle means. . . . Anyhow it is certainly true that bookshops which had little piles of *The Gunroom* on Monday replied on Tuesday that they had never heard of the book. Very odd and very interesting.

The Gunroom was never reprinted. 'It was deadly true about the Navy as I knew it,' he wrote more than thirty years afterwards, but he 'deliberately refrained' from republishing it. All his life he was proud of having served, and it was for Naval Service that he hastened to volunteer in both wars. The final word on the affair lies with his chief in the Second World War, Admiral John Godfrey, Director of Naval Intelligence (1939–42). Asked his opinion, he replied: 'Charles didn't like *The Gunroom*, but it was true.'

Late in 1917 came the sudden ending of the Dutch interlude. Charles was granted leave to return on parole to England, and sailed in convoy from Amsterdam on 11 November. His ship, the *Lapwing*, struck a mine and sank in seven minutes within an hour of the English shore. He was picked up by a British destroyer, but lost all his possessions, including the manuscript of *The Gunroom*.

The Dutch authorities agreed to waive his return. There was still a year to go before the Armistice, and Charles, who was neither escaped prisoner nor serving officer (so that even his wartime food-ration was difficult to obtain), spent it rewriting his novel. In the words of his sister Marcie, 'he was ill and terribly thin'. He had lost his book and his baggage, but still carried a full cargo of ideas.

Like so many of his generation who returned from the wars (such as did return), these ideas were out of tune with civilian life in England: '. . . what *are* we fighting for? Not for freedom surely, not for peace.

All that has been forgotten long enough ago.' He writes that to a Quaker friend (Mrs. Robert Mennell), and on the day after the signing of the Armistice tells her that he is 'oppressed by this intolerable sense of the unreality of victory'. Meanwhile he wrote in *The Gunroom*, 'It can't go on like this. We must substitute the motive of Sharing for the motive of Gain. It's the only way to stop the cruelty everywhere . . . I suppose it does mean a Revolution for Christ. . . . Some day the young men will break free.'

As it turned out, Charles Morgan was not one of the young men who broke free; on the contrary, he conformed. When in May 1919 he went up to Brasenose College, Oxford, he joined a generation that was determined, above all, to lose no more time.

'After the darkness and negation of universal war', wrote a correspondent of the *Morning Post* who had visited Oxford, 'there has come a Renaissance, a re-birth of every form of intellectual activity.' Politics had become 'a matter of thoughtful study and consideration. The Union and University clubs have an importance which in the past they lacked.' Charles read history and had 'never been so busy' in his life.

'The key to Charles Morgan, when I knew him as an undergraduate', writes a friend of those years, 'was his overwhelming ambition. . . . He told me that he had to choose between becoming (as he hoped) President of the Union or President of the O.U.D.S.' He chose the latter and the choice proved decisive.

The O.U.D.S., which had fallen into decay, was forthwith revived by their first post-war president, Maurice Colbourne, future actor-manager. He and Charles (who followed him as President), born in the same year and kindred spirits, joined in producing Thomas Hardy's epic play, *The Dynasts*. The choice and organization were entirely Charles Morgan's. He considered Hardy the greatest of English writers then alive and the only one certain of immortal fame. Tribute must be paid while he still lived.

Without doubt 1919 and 1920 were vintage years at Oxford, and the list of 104 members of the cast — Charles took the part of Sir John Moore — include some resounding names. Carola Oman, also in the play, comments that 'as an undergraduate Charles showed marked signs of having been a naval officer — organisation first class.' 'A mixture of force and courtesy,' was Maurice Colbourne's description.

Thomas Hardy and Mrs. Hardy were persuaded to come up from

Dorset to attend the first night of an undoubted triumph. 'Such a delightful break in the long winter,' wrote Hardy afterwards from Max Gate. He was in his eighty-first year.

As You Like It, performed as a first open-air summer play in the garden of Wadham, and a notable production of *Antony and Cleopatra* took place during Morgan's presidency. They are worth remembering for several reasons. It was then he came to know two of his lifelong friends — Gordon Alchin and Hilary St. George Saunders, 'the one invaluable man' to whose memory thirty years later he dedicated his play *The River Line*. For *As You Like It* Claud Lovat Fraser designed the costumes, and a future Lord Chancellor (Gerald Gardiner) played Orlando. Bridges-Adams, another lasting friend, produced *Antony and Cleopatra*, and a fateful supper party took place on its last night.

A. B. Walkley, dramatic critic of *The Times* and chief guest of the occasion, sat next to the President. In the course of the evening he remarked that he was looking for a young assistant to help him cover the London plays, and invited his host to apply for the position. By the end of that year Charles was writing for *The Times* theatre page. He joined the editorial staff in 1922, and when Walkley died four years later Morgan succeeded him as dramatic critic.

So far the time at Oxford appears to lead directly to a comfortable niche in a top establishment. But there are contradictions. 'Charles never intended his post on *The Times* as a permanency,' writes Sir Carleton Allen, who knew him then. 'It was all practice in writing, to which he had devoted himself.' Before that resolve was made there came other distractions.

There is a story of him defending a newly found society for the appreciation of 'Beauty and Culture', inaugurated by Vernon Barlow, a younger member of his College. Rumour went round that a meeting of the Club would be broken up by the 'toughs' of Brasenose. On hearing this, Charles organized a bodyguard of like-minded friends, who quietly took their places round the room and showed the opposition that they too meant business. When Barlow thanked him, Charles replied briefly, 'I always fight for liberty. If we can't get it at Oxford, what's the use of anything?'

Then there was politics.

'There's rather an amusing political situation in Oxford,' Charles told his father (May 1920). 'The Liberal Club has split on the fusion question.'

This was a move to get the Independent wing of the Liberal Party —
the 'Wee Frees' — to join with the Coalition Liberals who followed
Lloyd George. At the University Charles Morgan was speedily involved
in the New Reform Club, founded by Gerald Howard of Balliol,
eventually to become Conservative M.P. for Cambridgeshire and one
of Her Majesty's judges.

The 'amusing political situation' occupied a great deal of Morgan's
time that summer of 1920 although, like the Navy, it proved another
false start. He was too vulnerable for the ruthless political life.

At the end of May he wrote to his father:

On June 10th I am coming to London to a lunch of the Government
M.P.'s etc. at the Connaught Rooms, and there I have to speak as
representing Oxford and the New Reform Club. Rather an ordeal,
I'm afraid. Yesterday I lunched with Maurice Colbourne. Lillah
McCarthy[1] and her husband were there and Mary Mond — who is
a girl undergraduate at Lady Margaret Hall and the daughter of
Brunner Mond & Co. She's a pretty girl with any amount of brain
and, I should think, common sense. . . .

We went on to the river afterwards. I want to secure Mary Mond
to assist the New Reform Club.

Mary's father was Sir Alfred Mond (later Lord Melchett) one of the
leading members of the Liberal Party.

In the long vacation Charles and other members of the New Reform
Club undertook to conduct a political campaign 'in the constituencies
of Suffolk, Norfolk and thereabouts'. 'We are booked to speak in the
Market Place at Norwich,' he wrote. 'There are 5,000 unemployed in
the town who are causing no end of trouble and we are being put up to
state the Government case.'

Next day, 'I spoke last because I am supposed to be the "manful
mob orator" who goes into the breach when there's trouble. . . . Then,
as I always do when there's a mob, I got carried away and had a tremendous innings.'

That Charles was presently to be carried away by a force more
potent than oratory is clear from the letters of that autumn. He and
Mary Mond were in love. 'I do believe this fairy-tale will come true,'

[1] Actress, b. 1875. She had divorced her first husband, Harley Granville-
Barker, in 1918, and was married to Professor Sir Frederick Keeble of Magdalen
College.

he told Roger Barrett. By Christmas they were engaged and Charles 'almost sickeningly happy'. Lady Megan Lloyd George remembered seeing them dance together and their air of happiness. Mary was 'quite lovely and very attractive and intelligent'.

The fairy-tale lasted for no more than a chapter. Neither politics — the opportunist, materialist politics of England in 1920 — nor the plutocratic circle of the Monds could provide Charles with a spiritual home. His letters show the conflict between a young man with his foot on the ladder; the captive who had found liberty in his Dutch prison, and the far-off boy in the *Monmouth* cabin weaving dreams.

Was this the chance for which he was looking? 'He [Sir Alfred Mond] and Mary apparently are in favour of my writing only — at any rate for a time,' he confided to Roger Barrett. 'It's the hell of a temptation. It's what I want to do. I'm simply bursting and bursting to write nowadays. And yet it would be difficult to sit down and live on one's wife's money.'

It was Lady Mond who removed the temptation. She had other ambitions, in which Charles Morgan found no place as a suitor to her second daughter. Desperately he planned a runaway marriage with Mary. 'She is a minor. Can you find out for me whether it is possible to make an irrevocable marriage with a minor?' he asked Roger Barrett whose father — origin of the learned clergyman in *Sparkenbroke* — was to conduct the wedding ceremony in this day-dream.

Lady Mond won the day. The engagement was broken and Mary, first sent away to India to stay with her Reading connections at Viceregal Lodge, married in the following year Sir Neville Pearson, Bt.[1]

'The fight for Mary is over and I've failed,' wrote Charles. It was a fight that cost him for a time his health and even his mental powers. 'At first the blow and horror of it nearly killed me. I couldn't eat or sleep for days. . . . I didn't know that evil and corruption went so far.'

Somehow he managed to take his degree, a Second, instead of the confidently expected First. ('I used to know it once, but all the facts have gone,' he wrote in the midst of his Schools.)

The letters of this period are despairing. When he turned to his second novel, the writing of it was a necessary purge. *My Name is*

---

[1] This marriage was dissolved six years later. She subsequently became the wife of C. Willoughby (Peter) Hordern. She died in 1937.

Legion, is a tormented and chaotic book. Years later to his friend and critic Louis Bonnerot, Charles gave this explanation:

> I took more than four years to write it. During that time . . . I went through periods of profound personal bliss and misery. These experiences changed my whole attitude to life and threw me into emotional turmoil, with this consequence — that the man who finished *My Name is Legion* was not the same as the man who began it.

The man who finished this uneven book had achieved security, work after his own heart and the fulfilment of marriage. Certainly the novel's happy ending has little connection with the rest of the story.

On leaving Oxford Charles did not immediately find a full-time occupation. Prudent family counsel suggested 'something solid', such as publishing, and presently he obtained a post in the old-established house of A. & C. Black, which two years before had accepted *The Gunroom*. This dignified firm, one-time publisher of the *Encyclopaedia Britannica*, were looking for 'a likely young man'; but for the young man, however likely, who wished only to write, it was another sojourn in a strange country.

At the end of that same year (1921) came the desired offer from Printing House Square. 'By the Grace of God I've just been appointed No. 2 Dramatic Critic of *The Times*,' he wrote to his Oxford friend, Eric Oliphant. The salary was £650 a year for 'Walkley articles, book reviews, leaders and theatre notices'.

Rumours of his lost love still occur in letters of this period. Mary had not yet married another; there was still a chance of mending the broken pieces. 'They've smashed Mary again and life's bloody and the Christmas rush of theatres is the Devil of a strain,' he writes to Roger Barrett. 'Don't write about Mary. It may not be all over even yet.'

But early in the spring of 1922 Mary Mond was married to Sir Neville Pearson, and on the evening of her wedding day Charles Morgan and Hilda Vaughan met at a dance in London. Gordon Alchin, with kindly concern for his friend's misery, had persuaded him to come, although unwillingly, to the dance. Hilda's escort was a naval cousin who disapproved of *The Gunroom*.

Hilda's immediate impression was of a man of extraordinary quality turned to ice. Her first warm instinct was to come to his help. She was the daughter of Hugh Vaughan Vaughan of Builth, Breconshire, of Welsh blood sprung from the borders of Brecon and Radnor. The family, being by legend and tradition connected with the Vaughans of Tretower, could lay some claim to descent from Henry Vaughan, the seventeenth-century 'Silurist' and poet. In Charles Morgan's words, 'Hilda had read a lot and against the wishes of her family had begun to write novels.' With her beauty and social gifts, her country upbringing and, above all, her ardent interest in writing, she brought fresh and living warmth into his life. Truly he could say of her, as Lewis Alison said of Julie, 'You are the death of another winter in me.'

Charles admired her gift of narrative, an ability 'to get on with the story', which was always his difficulty. Often in the years that lay before them she would suggest a course of action for the characters in his novels, and at times help to supply the actual plots.

'You have your finger on the nerve of the problem,' he wrote once to her. On his side he gave to everything she wrote the passionate care of a perfectionist. 'It's not a question of doing one's best. It means that you must always do a little more than seemed your best', he told her. The process of putting everything 'through the sieve' of Charles's mind — a selfless mind where a question of art was involved — was a guarantee of good craftmanship.

'I am a fanatic on the subject of writing,' he wrote two years after the publication of *The Fountain*. 'Nothing seems to me good enough.' He had an 'inhuman patience' with his own work, and a most human patience and generosity with the efforts of others.

They were married in June 1923. Charles had been sharing rooms in the Temple with Gordon Alchin. The home that he and Hilda chose for the first nine years of their wedded life was in More's Garden, Chelsea, close to the river, a flat with a small writing-room for Charles overlooking the plot of grass beside Crosby Hall, once the house of Sir Thomas More.

Both writers foresaw the future as a joint venture, 'a happy thing of work and imagination'. There would be, he envisaged, long, quiet mornings with no other sound 'but the flicker of flame and the scratch of a " going " pen' — in fact, two going pens.

But flames have to be tended, and tradesmen call in the mornings (as even Charles pointed out) and sometimes the noise of the traffic along the Embankment became unendurable. A daughter and a son were born to them within the first three years of marriage. Charles, tied by his

c

occupation, could not leave London, while Hilda, used to the silences of the country, found it difficult to write at all in a city.

Stresses of domesticity and the isolation required by an artist are not easily reconciled. He could write: 'O the joy of not being interrupted — of being left alone with the struggle.' Yet he had never really liked being left alone. When Hilda was away finishing a book or in attendance on an invalid father, Charles wrote of his own work, 'What an odd, exciting game it is when it flows', knowing that she would understand. But there are too many letters of separation — even for the habitué of a fort or a moated castle — and one ends by wishing that Breconshire were not, in Charles's own words 'so damnably far away' from Chelsea and the grind of the London theatres.

Yet nothing can destroy the rapture of those years. At long last the work was 'all happy work', and the streams flowed together in one direction. The false starts of the Navy, politics, publishing; even the ambitions of journalism, which might have led to an editorship, could be regarded as so many interruptions.

An incident of a rejected leader in *The Times*, a month before his marriage, had shown Charles that he was unsuited to political journalism. He poured out his troubles to Hilda.

I remember a coast-guard, when I was a small boy, telling me — when I was contemplating the Navy — that what was needed at sea was a thick skin. I disregarded him and failed to stick the Navy. . . .

From now on journalism shall be a necessity to be disregarded if ever the necessity for it ceases. . . . That part of ambition is all dead sea fruit. . . . I've rediscovered our own territory, and in that we'll live, safe from all hurts while we're together in the faith you've always held firm and which shall be ours and a single, indisputable faith from today.

It was a faith in the high calling of the writer, which he would keep intact until the end.

Meantime *My Name is Legion* was somehow finished, Hilda helping with the last chapters. To return to it, Charles confessed, was like putting on dirty clothes after taking a bath. Surprisingly, Heinemann accepted the book and published it in 1925. It was his last piece of apprentice work. Four years later, in his thirty-fifth year, when the well-tempered steel was forged, came his third novel, *Portrait in a Mirror*.

The mistakes of publishers are notorious and hard to explain afterwards. On an April evening in 1928 Charles Evans, the chairman of Heinemann, met Charles Morgan in a theatre and remarked that he would be taking away with him the new novel, *Portrait in a Mirror*, then called 'First Love', to read at Easter.

Confident that all would be well, for the book had already been announced by Heinemann as forthcoming, Charles and Hilda set out for an eagerly awaited holiday at Pardigon, near Cavalaire, in the south of France. From a deck-chair in the sunshine he wrote in high spirits to Roger Barrett in Hong Kong about another story he had just begun, a kind of 'undated morality on the adventures of the liberated human soul'.

> The point is, of course, 'The Kingdom of God is within you'. And what liberty to write! What a gigantic freedom from cup and saucer and my lady's chamber!

Then, like a thunderbolt from the cloudless May sky, came a letter from Charles Evans turning down the novel 'First Love'. 'We don't want to lose you,' wrote the chairman of Heinemann, 'but this new book does not fulfill the atmosphere and promise of the early chapters of *My Name is Legion*.'

This pronouncement — never wholly explained by Evans himself — was a severe shock. Instead of hopes and dreams, here were anguish of spirit and a dismayed loss of confidence. Pacing the shore where, five years before, Conrad set his tale of *The Rover*, Charles was tormented by doubt and depression. 'I shall destroy the book when I get home,' he told Hilda. She suggested a different course, which he still remembered gratefully many years later and commended to another distressed writer. It was to begin at once another book — a comedy with a naval setting, never finished, which lifted the evil mood from him, like a shout of laughter after a blow.

Back in London, once again a benign elder woman played a decisive part in Charles Morgan's life. She was Mrs. W. K. Clifford, widow of William Kingdon Clifford, mathematician and philosopher. Mrs. Clifford, herself a writer, had 'an intuition for literature', and to her dark little drawing-room near Paddington came some of 'the great survivors of the Victorian age' — they included Sir Frederick Macmillan, then nearly eighty — as well as young writers beginning to make their way. Macmillan's had good reason to revere Mrs. Clifford's advice, for she had brought them both Kipling and Maurice Hewlett.

Some time after the Morgans' return from France she learnt of the catastrophe over 'First Love', and read the book. She noted its quality and remarked: 'I shall see that Frederick reads it.'

The sequel is known. Macmillan's took the novel. Published under a new title, *Portrait in a Mirror*, it won immediate and resounding praise from both critics and public. This was the first of Morgan's books to be translated into French. It gained the Femina-Vie Heureuse prize in 1930.

By chance, the editor of these letters was at More's Garden on the evening that brought Macmillan's letter of acceptance by a late post. Charles, in a dressing-gown, danced round the room, then paused to say with sudden gravity: 'Suppose one became a best-seller! If ever I do, I'll know there's something *wrong* about the book!'[1]

Portrait in a Mirror had 'broken through' and carried its author into the ranks of accepted novelists. From his own point of view the book had a special importance, for in it he sought to explain beliefs that were at the root of his artist's creed. While working on the proofs he wrote to Hilda of a difficulty over one paragraph, 'my particular paragraph about the nature of artistic inspiration. I wasn't satisfied with it and spent nearly the whole day on it, typing and correcting and re-typing and correcting again. I think I have it right now.'

The long passage occurs in the second chapter of the book, and the echoes of Charles's voice still haunt the carefully turned phrases. It is the key to a great deal of his thought. The spirit of man alone is real, he says, and 'art is news of reality'.

The joy of the artist is here described as a *receptive*, rather than creative joy. There is a reminder of Wordsworth's 'wise passiveness', but still more of Keats's simile of bee and flower ('The flower, I doubt not, receives a fair guerdon from the Bee — its leaves blush deeper in the next spring — and who shall say between Man and Woman which is the most delighted').[2] It is an idea that was to appear often in his writing, but is never stated more clearly and freshly than when Nigel Frew, the boy artist in *Portrait in a Mirror* says, 'My mind leapt and sang; it was filled with a sense of renewal, of a flowering and impregnating wisdom not my own.'

[1] Perhaps he changed his mind. In 1943 he wrote: 'Daniel Macmillan knew as well as any man that popularity was not a proof of merit, but he did not make the opposite error, now fashionable, of supposing that it was a proof of demerit.' *The House of Macmillan* (Macmillan, 1943).

[2] Keats, in a letter to Reynolds, 1818.

That Charles should have chosen to explore a painter's mind is not surprising. When time allowed he liked to work in the studio of his friend, Fred Stratton, 'delighted when a drawing succeeded and sad when another failed'.[1] The bearded Henry Fullaton in the novel is a half-portrait of Stratton. In his studio Charles made the acquaintance of Henry Tonks and Wilson Steer; his first meeting with George Moore, of lasting importance, took place in this circle of friends.

The writing of *Portrait in a Mirror* had proved that the writer was a poet and a craftsman, but for the next book, as is plain from the letters chosen here, he felt that he must go beyond into much deeper water, 'wherein, God knows, I may drown'. He was far from drowning. The three years spent in Holland, the 'life within a life — a sort of spiritual island', provided him with an incomparable scene for *The Fountain*.

About this novel hangs a 'brilliant lightness of spirit', such as its chief character, Lewis Alison, imprisoned in a fort, discovered to be the reward of long meditation. Both fortress and castle are delineated with the clarity of a Dutch landscape painting; numerous portraits throughout the book are drawn with care and delight. Lewis Alison, the central character, has much in common with his creator — 'part of him's a plain man of business; part of him's as wild as a martyr who'd go to the stake singing at the top of his voice. Part of him's a hermit.' And part very far from being a hermit, since the passionate love of Lewis and Julie, and Julie's betrayal of Rupert von Narwitz, her German patrician husband, are the theme of the book.

Yet the pulse of the story is Lewis's conviction that life is an inward and secret experience, that 'within the apparent form of all things is another form. . . . Within stones another stone; within the vitality of trees a secret and ghostly sap.' And that of these mysteries, 'the most fruitful are love and death'. Much of the book is suffused with the thoughts of the seventeenth-century English mystics. It was the age in which, above all others, Charles would have chosen to live; an age loved by his chief character, Lewis, who is shown reading *Silex Scintillans* in a window of the Castle library.

Sometimes, when he raised his head that a thought might resolve or a cadence declare itself in his mind, he heard the waterfall, but soon the external world fell away and the genius of Vaughan spread wings between him and the passing hours.

[1] 'On Learning to Write', in *The Writer and his World*.

In the poetry of Henry Vaughan Charles discovered those paradoxes of Light in Darkness, Love and Death, which became more and more his preoccupation. Nothing in *The Fountain* was so important to the author as the death of his character Narwitz.

During the writing of this long book George Moore once asked Charles Morgan what in life interested him most. As the two men walked together one evening up South Eaton Place, Morgan replied, 'Art, Love and Death', to which Moore objected that it sounded like a picture by Watts, and 'One cannot go through life being interested in a picture by Watts.'

He then asked Charles (who relates the story in his *Epitaph on George Moore*) why he chose these three experiences.

> 'Because', I said, 'I think of them always as three aspects of the same impulse.'
> 'Of what impulse?'
> 'The impulse to re-create oneself.'

Charles was astonished at the huge triumph of *The Fountain*. 'It is sure to live on the lips and in the hearts of men if anything of our time survives,' wrote Sir Edward Marsh. Sales soared in England and on the Continent, and America seemed 'to have gone mad'. The 'hermit' in its creator marvelled that a book largely devoted to the contemplative life should have touched so many readers; the man of business calculated that he could be certain of a 'minimum of £3,000' for any fiction he wrote, and could now, if he wished, be independent of journalism.

In June 1933 Charles Morgan received the Hawthornden Prize for *The Fountain*, and in the same month he and his family moved from the Chelsea flat to a tall house in Campden Hill Square. 'We have ripped off the roof and built a new storey on top,' he wrote to Roger Barrett. It contained two workrooms for him and Hilda, 'according to their own whims'. His was 'gloriously empty', with a touch of a naval cabin about it. It looked north and west over 'miles and miles of town and country'.

The way was clear for work on *Sparkenbroke*, his next novel, already one-third written. Could he find again his fortress of the mind, his 'spiritual island'? Not, it seemed, in the thirties, or perhaps ever again. 'The world is in an upheaval infinitely worse and more confused and more perilous than the war,' he wrote to Hilda. 'We happen to live in a chaos worse than that of the Dark Ages, and at the end of a civilization which will carry away all our works in it in the final slide.'

Early in the summer of 1934 Morgan was sent by *The Times* to write on the Passion Play at Oberammergau, and to report on the theatres of Munich, Vienna, Prague and Paris (twenty-three plays in twenty-one days). He 'learned a lot of politics, and enjoyed Vienna and loathed Munich, which is like a prison camp'. The Germans, he told Roger Barrett, 'desire conquest as an end in itself'.

It is this that makes them formidable and war, sooner or later, certain. Not yet. They aren't ready. But still, it's coming . . . A clear alliance between us and France would postpone it . . .

Earlier that same year he wrote:

Of course the only way to live until the crash comes is by pretending that it isn't coming. For this reason I continue to write with the passionate care and patience that is, in truth, only justifiable if one believes in posterity.

But for Charles Morgan there was no other 'way to live'. It was fundamental, and perhaps best explained by a question and answer taken from *Sparkenbroke*:

'Is this what you care for most in life? What do you want out of it — fame?'
'To do it,' Piers said.

And to do it in only one way, with fanatical patience, care of detail and the single-mindedness that was so often the theme of his writing. It was a rigid discipline, never relaxed from the early days of anxious apprenticeship to the accomplished mastery of later years.

To Philip Hope-Wallace I am indebted for this picture of Charles Morgan as *The Times* dramatic critic in the thirties:

He was an awe-inspiring performer for a tyro to watch. He would come into the office late, after a play, and sit for a full two-thirds of the precious minutes before edition time (even then we had only up to midnight, and theatres often began later than now). He would sit in silent meditation looking like a statue of some great French poet on a monument, his finger to his brow; then quite suddenly he would take a 'push pen' and block of paper and begin to write his notice with an even unbroken flow, line after line; and the copy boy could take them right to the printer, for there was never a comma out of place.

As to the quality of his criticism, an entry in one of James Agate's diaries (*Ego 2*, 4 April 1935) sums it up:

> When Charles is in his best form, he has us all whacked. *The Times* is happy to have a critic who is, when not insisting that sow's ears shall be silk purses, indisputably first-rate.

Yet he was a pupil all his life, writing as late as 1954 to his French translator. 'On January 22nd I shall be sixty. So many years, so little wisdom gained.'

To anxious apprentices, asking for help, he gave unstintingly. There was, I remember, a sultry evening in 1931 outside the little Gate Theatre, with the critics standing around in search of a breath of air blowing up Villiers Street. The play was Wilde's *Salome*, to which, in Agate's place, I had been sent by my newspaper. Not an easy beginning, and because Charles was a friend I asked him, 'How do I become a dramatic critic?', as one might ask how to attain eternal life. He answered lightly. But next day there reached me a long letter crammed with wisdom, written in *The Times* office after midnight when his copy had gone to the printer. Fortunate youth indeed to have such an adviser at hand! When A. E. Housman died unexpectedly and I was told to write on him, it was to the tall house on Campden Hill that I sped for counsel. Which poem, if any, would be best quoted? And Charles, taking down Housman's last slim book from its shelf, read aloud to Hilda and me, ending with the 'Epitaph on an Army of Mercenaries':

> *Their shoulders held the sky suspended;*
> *They stood, and earth's foundation stay;*
> *What God abandoned, these defended,*
> *And saved the sum of things for pay.*

I recall the beautiful voice reading steadily, and then faltering on those last lines. It was as though the ghosts and griefs of the First War had filled his quiet room.

While *Sparkenbroke* was still on the stocks, Charles Morgan wrote his *Epitaph on George Moore*, a brilliant, concise essay, which reads 'like milk'. It took the place of the full biography that Moore had intended him to write. The story of how Moore's letters to a single correspondent, Lady Cunard — knowledge of which he regarded as essential — were refused to his chosen biographer, is told in these letters. For Morgan, in spite of his admiration for Moore, it was a way out and an escape from a long and complicated task no imaginative writer would gladly undertake.[1]

Finished at last, *Sparkenbroke* appeared in 1936. No novel of his ever meant a longer struggle, so long that Charles Morgan sometimes wondered if there were something wrong with it; it had 'gone heavy'. Yet in some ways it is the most rewarding of his books; no other so admits the reader to an artist's mind. The great organ-notes of its theme are love, death and poetry. Here besides are brilliant evocations of English and Italian scenes; and a tender understanding of a girl's thoughts. The tomb, so evident in the story, becomes a symbol of release, and the book is 'filled with assurances of a springing virtue and reason in creation'.

Sparkenbroke was acclaimed by the public and the majority of critics. In France a fresh wave of enthusiasm rolled in. If French appreciation of *The Fountain* had been tinged with regret that a German should be given *le beau rôle*, the Byronic Shelley-like figure of Lord Sparkenbroke won all Gallic hearts. Then, too, the lucid prose lent itself flowingly to the French idiom.'It made me feel', Charles wrote, 'as if I had a mental lucidity to which no-one who does not use the French language can ordinarily pretend.'

When in May 1936 he received the Legion of Honour, the occasion was marked by a gathering at the French Embassy in London, and among the guests were Jacques and Germaine Delamain. Germaine was already the French translator of his novels; how soon the character of Barbet in *The Voyage* — then beginning to take shape — became identified with Jacques is not known. Two months later Charles wrote to Bonnerot that his new book would be 'a fantasy about a "fool of God"'.

Certainly no-one was further from an ordinary fool than Jacques Delamain, with his country skills and knowledge, both as a wine-grower and a brilliant ornithologist. This Protestant from the Charente was an unusual character. The author of several books on birds, he was a Frenchman who bore some resemblance to our English Gilbert White, but he was no bachelor. Jacques and Germaine Delamain were devoted lovers all their married life. A year after Jacques's death, Charles urged Germaine to begin a 'wonderful long-distance book' of

[1] An excellent biography of George Moore (without benefit of the Cunard letters) was written by Joseph Hone.

memoirs. 'No-one writes a happy book which is also a true book. YOU
COULD.' He stayed with them both at La Branderaie de Garde Epée —
in their home and in the village near by — while making his careful
study of the ways of the Charente. When *The Voyage* was published in
the tragic summer of 1940, he dedicated it —

> . . . to a French man and woman who have deepened my love for
> their country and given me an insight into human goodness that
> springs in them from singleness of heart.

There was more than the half-unreal envy felt by a sedentary urban
writer for an active countryman in his admiration. A new freshness and
freedom pervade the novel; the writing of it proved a tonic change
from the inward-looking toils of *Sparkenbroke*. For a time a door
opened for Charles (as it did for Thérèse in the story, whenever she
was with Barbet) to 'a natural and because natural, a miraculous
world'. Barbet, who could perceive 'innocence overlaid', and the
essences of men 'like birds and trees and night and morning' is the
touchstone of the book. If Jacques Delamain had not existed, *The
Voyage* would never have been written.

With *The Voyage* still brewing, Charles Morgan turned playwright
and wrote *The Flashing Stream*. 'I think of it only as a swerve from my
novels,' he told Hugh Walpole, but for a time it was all-absorbing. He
even offered to resign his post on *The Times*, on the ground — as he
wrote to the Editor, Geoffrey Dawson — that his association with the
theatre 'might be regarded as incompatible with the absolute detachment necessary' in a dramatic critic. His resignation was refused.

His reasons for writing the play are set out in a letter to Louis
Bonnerot (Christmas Night, 1937). For the published edition he wrote
a long and regrettable preface, criticized by his two good friends,
Bonnerot and St. John Ervine. His replies can be found here.

The Flashing Stream was produced in September 1938 with Godfrey Tearle and Margaret Rawlings in the leading parts. Miss Rawlings
is the actress for whom he shaped the part of Karen, the rare mathematician, and he dedicated the play to her. It prospered immediately —
'Box Office sizzling' — and weathered the Munich crisis, almost alone
among London plays. After the war it held the stage in Paris for over a
year. For its author it had been 'a swerve' and he was eager to get back
to *The Voyage*, 'to meet Barbet again' and Thérèse, the French *diseuse*
of the story. Set in their very different backgrounds, the English naval

station of *The Flashing Stream* and the French music-hall of *The Voyage*, the rôles of Karen and Thérèse show similar qualities of vitality and miracle-mindedness. As always with Morgan's characters Thérèse cannot be equated with one person. Some of her features suggest Yvette Guilbert, the famous *diseuse* whom he much admired, as well as Margaret Rawlings, the leading lady of his first play.

New and terrible interruptions came before the novel was finished. Certain of calamity, Charles offered his services to the Admiralty in February 1939, 'in the event of war'. They were accepted, and by the time war was declared he and Hilary Saunders were editing a Weekly Intelligence Report for the Navy, and Charles had bought a bicycle.

'Tell me even dull, small, peaceful things,' he wrote to Hilda. 'Here we have only one inhuman subject.' It was a long time before life would be dull and peaceful again. Charles, always expecting the worst, sent his wife and children to America,[1] to the care of his Quaker friend Patrick Malin. 'I think we can still beat them,' he wrote to Louis Gillet in Paris, but he was at times overwhelmed with melancholy foreboding, dreading chiefly the corruption of life by the enemy, the loss of human personality; a world turned into 'a loathsome prep. school'.[2]

Thanks to his percipient chief, Admiral Godfrey, he was released from his duties to finish *The Voyage* ('The public was starved of good reading matter during the war. *The Voyage* was needed,' wrote Admiral Godfrey.) So the warmest, most earth-rooted of all his novels appeared in 1940, while Charles himself was frozen in unhappiness. With France overrun by the enemy the book had become so poignant that he could not bear to open it.

The following year (1941) he undertook a strenuous lecture tour in the U.S.A., under the auspices of the Institute of International Education, strongly backed by the Ministry of Information, then in charge of Duff-Cooper. America was not yet in the war, but as events at Pearl Harbour occurred four months after his arrival, Charles was there to see the curtain go up.

Back in England in 1942 he returned to Naval Intelligence, to an independent instead of a routine task. At the same time *The Times*

---

[1] A decision made against the wishes of his family. In 1942 Roger, on his own initiative, returned to school in England. Shirley enrolled in America as a British Government Volunteer and with her mother came home in 1943 to serve in a London government office.

[2] *The Burning Glass.*

asked him to contribute a weekly article, entitled 'Menander's Mirror', to the *Times Literary Supplement*. These essays, occupying the chief place in the paper, dealt with life and literature and their changing values. They were written with the urbane yet incisive pen of the true essayist.

'A small, happy adventure' befell Charles at about this time, when, to a gathering of exiled Frenchmen in London, an ode written by him was read aloud by Robert Speaight. The rest of the programme, to his pleasure, was contributed by Shakespeare, Corneille and Molière. As he wrote to Hilda, 'It is something in this horrid world to be asked to write an Ode!'

> *Thou art the wisdom, O France, within all knowledge,*
> *The salt of all delight.*

Never was Charles more convinced that France was an Idea necessary to Civilization. Meeting General de Gaulle in London in 1943, he wrote: 'I believe that we and the Americans are greatly underestimating a firm, clear-headed and courageous man.'

Among Frenchmen of the Resistance the name of Charles Morgan was potent. Articles from his pen appeared in *La France Libre* and were afterwards secretly circulated through France.

The end of the tunnel was reached on 25 August 1944 with the liberation of Paris. In the second week of September he, with three others, flew to Paris in a Dakota, to a city given over not to wild rejoicing, but to 'passionate relief'. It is difficult to read his account of those days without emotion; days which were as 'the shiver of renaissance in the air'.

> Memory of those re-encounters will never fade while I live: how eyes widened and held their gaze like the eyes of children; how hand clung to hand, feeling with incredulous avidity the living flesh and bones; how even the sun, and wine in the glass, were as wine and sun had never been before. . . . I for my friends, my friends for me, were all in that hour young again and newly risen from the grave.[1]

There were the Lalous in the rue de Seine, Louis Bonnerot at Vanves, the river and the Île St. Louis and all the loved background of *The Voyage*, even if in their hotel in Montparnasse the travellers went to bed 'by the light of a single candle brought from England'. Englishmen, above all others in those days, were loved and honoured in

---

[1] Introduction to *The River Line*: A Play.

France. 'It was no longer necessary to seek out personal friends to have friendship in Paris. To be English was enough.'[1]

To be Charles Morgan was a great deal more. Perhaps the crowning moment was his recognition by a student in the Boulevard St. Germain ('Vous êtes bien Charles Morgan!'), unrivalled even by the party of distinguished men and women hastily summoned to meet him. They included the poet Paul Valéry. When the two men had shaken hands and sat down together, 'what Paul Valéry had it in his mind to talk about was George Meredith'. Civilization still endured!

In little more than a month Charles came again to Paris for the re-opening of the *Comédie française* when his *Ode to France* was read to the assembled company. He described it to an old friend who herself had been born in Paris in the siege of 1870, Mrs. Belloc Lowndes (sister of Hilaire Belloc).

> It was very exciting — the most exciting day of my life. I care desperately for French honour. The programme consisted of poems of the Resistance — Claudel, Eluard, Vercors, etc. The National Guard in helmets and plumes. De Gaulle in the stage box . . . My ode came last . . . When I bowed to the audience I suddenly heard a noise like the wings of angels and then I saw that the whole audience of the *Comédie française* had risen . . . An Englishman can't ask much more of life.

Next day Charles was called on to grace a lecture on his works at the Sorbonne with 'the young almost crawling up the walls'. Meanwhile, while Paris celebrated, the fighting still went on in Belgium and Holland and Charles went up to the forward areas to report on the war for the American public, with an article in the *Atlantic Monthly*.[2] His guide and companion was Colonel Robert Henriques, who found him 'a superb campaigner'. Together they visited forward observation-posts under shellfire; by night Charles slept happily on a stretcher, or on the floor.

For him this experience was a linking up with the First World War and his own brief campaign between Antwerp and Lierre. To be there at all was 'to understand the feel of being an English soldier in this, the thirty-first year of what seems to us of the first generation virtually a continuous war'.

[1] From an article by C. M. in *The Times*, 4 October 1944.
[2] January 1945.

The official end of fighting in Europe came on 9 May 1945. Two months later a General Election took place in England when Winston Churchill's Government was defeated. Charles Morgan took the news hard. 'England has clearly done what she did not intend to do,' he wrote to René Lalou. 'Everywhere today there is shocked and ashamed astonishment and no rejoicing. I think we have ruined ourselves, ruined Europe, and in effect, lost the war.'

About this time he contemplated a new short novel — 'a very moral story', and was pleased when in February 1947, the year of its publication, St. Andrews University conferred upon him an honorary degree. It was an LL.D. 'No damned Litt. about it,' he wrote to Orlo Williams. 'They must have heard that my new novel is to be called *The Judge's Story*!'

Morgan was now writing the main book review regularly for the *Sunday Times* — articles which brought a 'gigantic correspondence' in their wake, and gave him fresh opportunities for choosing his favourite themes. In a long notice of *Henry Vaughan: A Life and Interpretation* by F. E. Hutchinson,[1] he stated: 'We miss much of Vaughan if we read him with the polite accent of twentieth-century England.' On this occasion, as once before,[2] when he confided to the Sorbonne students that he was *de sang Celte*, he nailed his colours to the mast.

For my own part, though Welsh by blood, I am English by up-bringing . . . But I know that Vaughan's conception of the whole universe being indissolubly interconnected and of the perpetual 'commerce' between earth and heaven is familiar to the Welsh mind.

He went even farther when, writing to a Welsh acquaintance, he wondered 'how many purely English people there are who have the least notion of what Vaughan was talking about'.[3]

To feel a foreigner — as Charles did occasionally — was to suffer a sense of loss, even if there were the compensating joy of being understood by the French. In a letter to Lalou (22 February 1936) he drew up a list of those aspects which he found alienating in the English character, such as their incapacity to find *pleasure* in art, and 'their

[1] O.U.P., 1947.
[2] Lecture on Creative Imagination, November 1936. Published in *Reflections in a Mirror*, Second Series (Macmillan, 1946).
[3] In a letter to my mother, Eveline Lewis.

extraordinary habit of "hoping for the best"'. (No-one could accuse him of that tendency.)

The Judge's Story was published in the later summer of 1947. It is a book that reflects its author's innate puritanism and is concerned, as much as any medieval morality play, with the conflict between good and evil. By the end of the story Judge Gascony, stripped of possessions, is left secure in the fortress of his mind, able to write his scholar's book. He is uncontaminated.

The opposing character, Severidge, is a study of evil. Like Blachère in *The Voyage*, the only one of Barbet's prisoners to remain *outside* his sympathy, Severidge is a rebel, separating himself from the human community. He will 'always try to force or beguile or tempt the others to be false to their inner truth'.

A great deal of Charles Morgan's fear of mass thought and the assault on the individual mind lies in this book. Severidge remains a disquieting study. His sense of isolation has dogged him from boyhood, 'as if he were invisible and life were going on in his absence. He wished to be seen, spoken to and touched.' In the character of Severidge, so carefully drawn, Charles seems almost to describe a self-imprisonment, a hunger of his own spirit.

The year 1948 brought three visits to the Continent. Early in May he returned to Holland after an absence of more than thirty years. The occasion was the Congress of Europe, held at The Hague under the presidency of Winston Churchill — its object to voice the feelings of the free countries, its ultimate aim to work for a full European federation. Churchill, in his oration, spoke eloquently of 'Christendom', and there were speeches from John Masefield, Bertrand Russell and Harold Macmillan. Charles was one of the delegates, but in the words of his Dutch host 'he did not take his duties very seriously'. Rather than accept official hospitality, he chose to stay with Hugo van Manen, an enthusiastic reader of his novels, who had begun a Dutch translation of *Sparkenbroke*.

When the congress was over van Manen drove his guest across the breadth of Holland to Rosendaal. Unlike so many journeys in search of the past, this one did not disappoint. Two of the Pallandt family entertained them at the castle. The dower-house and the cottage that had sheltered the three Englishmen were still there. On the way back Hugo van Manen, carried away by the emotion of the whole episode, drove his car into a ditch near the Fort of Wierickerschans. The car was extricated, the fortress revisited and the day ended with an excellent dinner at Leyden and Charles at his best as a *raconteur*.

Five years later he returned to Holland for the international P.E.N. meeting at Amsterdam under his presidency. The Pallandt circle, as he knew it, was broken, and he never went back to Rosendaal; there would have been 'too many lovely ghosts'.

The second visit abroad in the summer of 1948 was a lecture tour of French universities — Paris, Caen, Bordeaux, Toulouse and Montpellier — described by the *Mercure de France* as a 'triumphal journey'. Civic receptions, speeches and *vins d'honneur* proved more exhausting than the lectures. In Paris the book shops were full of his books ('*Le Juge Gascony*, just out, is selling like mad') and everywhere there were packed and overflowing audiences. Caen University proposed an honorary degree; Toulouse offered a doctorate (*honoris causa*), and 'the Mayor of Carcassonne', wrote Charles, 'has given me an antique lamp . . . It is really like a very odd dream!'

As always, he was happy in France. There were the Ingres pictures to see at Montauban, and Toulouse-Lautrec at Albi. Best of all, there were Jacques and Germaine Delamain at Jarnac. The three of them had not met since 1939, before the war, and to his delight the Delamains appeared unchanged. 'They are wonderful human beings', he told Hilda. To Germaine he wrote:

> I could not have been happier than I was in your house. It is full of happy memories for me, and of glorious expectations. For many years, Jacques — with his *lunettes en bandoulière* — was for me a symbol of peace, and to have seen you also for the first time since the darkness lifted was a strange joy and satisfaction — a fulfilment of prophecy.

The third continental journey of 1948 was taken in order to receive his honorary degree from Caen University (in company with the Speaker of the House of Commons) and to attend another ceremony in Paris — a promotion in the Legion of Honour, performed at the Bibliothèque Nationale.

Throughout the year Charles had been working on *The River Line*, his story of Occupied France and a small group of officers — English with one American — in the act of escaping from the enemy by a secret network of communication. His first thought had been in terms of the theatre, but for a time 'the structure of the play eluded him', and it was as a novel that *The River Line* appeared in 1949. It is a story full of movement, even violence, yet the action takes place in retrospect, in the mind of the American. 'Old Henry James never set himself a harder task,' Charles told Bonnerot. When, reverting to his first intention, he turned the book into a play, he prefaced it with an essay 'On Transcending the Age of Violence'. It ends with Mazzini's words of 1849: 'We must act like men who have the enemy at their gates, and at the same time like men who are working for eternity.'

In Charles Morgan's mind there was no doubt that the enemy at the gates were 'the great hordes who have rejected, or have never learned, the traditions of Rome and of Christ, of Athens and of the Renaissance'. His central character, Heron, is an English soldier wrongly suspected of treachery and killed by his companions and by the Frenchwoman who shelters them. Heron 'works for eternity'; or, as his creator puts it, 'he travels light with no baggage that violence could take away'. More than that, he is able to absolve the guilt of the others by his own acceptance of life and death. He suffers 'loss without losing'. The final scene in both novel and play has an element of poetry that transcends the ordinary means of communication. For a few moments Valerie, the dead man's sister, *is* in truth her brother.

This presented a certain difficulty when a French production was being considered. 'The one thing that must not be attempted is to *rationalise* the third Act,' Charles wrote to Lalou (September 1952). But the difficulties were never resolved. It was not finally the 'element of poetry' which prevented Jean Mercure from producing the play in Paris. On the contrary, he was deeply impressed by the first and last acts. The obstacle for a French audience lay in the harsh, too close realities of their own Resistance, which they felt to be over-romanticized.

The play was a success in London, and ran for a time, in its French version, in both Brussels and Lausanne.

The River Line was Charles Morgan's last work with a (partly) French setting. In the preface to the play there is a mention of Jacques Delamain as a French soldier of the earlier war who had observed 'during the intervals in the bombardment of his trench that swallows were late that spring'.

Delamain died in the Charente in February 1953 while *The River Line* was running in London. In a letter to Stephen Pasmore (26 February) there is a last salute to his friend.

D

The French soldier of whom I spoke ... was Jacques Delamain, who wrote *Why Birds Sing*, and was an almost saintly bird-watcher. He went very far into the interior of things.

At the conclusion of the French visit in November 1948 Charles was 'not ill but completely exhausted'. There had been too many public engagements. Wanting 'to be writers again', he and Hilda found a retreat in Pembrokeshire, between the Preseli hills and the rugged sea coast. In a house named Felindre, sheltered by banks and trees from the Atlantic gales, the Morgans spent two winters and two springs. 'We have a room each with an open fire and a good lamp,' he told Lalou. Characteristically, Charles managed his lamp perfectly, lighting it each evening, and, according to their hostess, 'never once did he blacken the glass!'

The first letter of 1949, to Stewart Hunter in Scotland, mentions a 'vast work of which the provisional title is "Darkness and Daylight"'. Planned on the grand scale, it had been set aside for other tasks. Now, at the age of fifty-five, he returned to it, wanting 'to say what I have to say in that book before I die'. The title was borrowed from Henry Vaughan:

> *Darkness and Daylight, Life and Death,*
> *Are but mere leaves moved by Thy Breath.*

The theme, the divided loyalties of a modern scientist, dealt with a problem fast becoming an obsession with the writer. His sombre vision foresaw the void and nothingness into which the discoveries of science, outstripping man's moral nature, would lead the human race.

There were times when he looked beyond even this ultimate catastrophe, as shown in his letter to Father Hennessy (5 June 1951), seeing the fear of annihilation an 'empty fear', and quoting Emily Brontë's lines:

> *Though earth and men were gone,*
> *And Suns and Universes cease to be,*
> *And Thou were left alone,*
> *Every existence would exist in Thee.*

But the dilemmas facing his characters in the unfinished novel produced in Charles an almost unbearable anguish of spirit. This mood marred the first weeks of the stay at Felindre. Then, at Hilda's suggestion, he laid it all aside and wrote a new short novel, an evocation of young love in the setting of his own childhood. This was *A Breeze of Morning*, finished in the early summer of 1950 and contrived in the timeless days and healing airs of the Pembrokeshire countryside.

In a letter to his fellow-writer E. M. Almedingen, Charles wrote: 'I am sure that all my best work has been "outside and beyond the intellect" . . .' The schoolboy narrator in *A Breeze of Morning*, while wrestling with his Latin elegiacs, has 'a sense of being dictated to by a voice of which the precise accents could not just be caught by effort and attention'. In the same way Charles, pausing in the toils of his immense book, received something from outside himself, and wrote instead a tale of innocence and grace. More than twenty years divide this book from *Portrait in a Mirror*. In both the influence of Turgenev is apparent. He was a listener, not an imitator, but Turgenev's masterpieces, *Torrents of Spring* and *First Love*, and Morgan's two novels — so far apart in time — all four belong to 'youth itself, the feel of being young and alive; and love'.[1]

An interruption of some importance occurred in the last week of October 1949 when Charles Morgan was elected a member of the Institut de France. As he explained in a letter:[2]

> There can be no foreign members of the Académie Française, so they elected me to the Académie des Sciences Morales et Politiques, which is the nearest possible and makes me a member of the Institut. No other English novelist has ever been elected to the Institut except Kipling. So it means a great deal to me.

In the words of the President of the French Academy, 'Notre choix s'est porté vers un grand écrivain philosophe, et vers un ami éprouvé de la France.'

It was an honour that brought particular pleasures, including the necessity for an elaborate, green, hand-embroidered uniform (made to measure in Paris by Lanvin) with cocked hat and sword. The 'grand écrivain philosophe' was not above taking an amused but real delight in these sartorial splendours. The cost of the sword, with its finely wrought hilt, was contributed by his many French friends, and it was from the hands of the Academician, Georges Duhamel, that he received it. From the Lalous' home in the rue de Seine, within sight of the

[1] 'Turgenev's *First Love*', in *The Writer and his World*, p. 183.
[2] To Stewart Hunter.

famous 'Coupole' of the Institut, Charles set out for the great occasion. To René Lalou afterwards he wrote:

> I value your friendship even more than the prizes it has brought me, and what I thank you for now is not so much the last few weeks as the long friendly years.

He could smile at himself too by quoting, in the same letter, Gilbert's rollicking verses:

> *When I first put this uniform on*
> *I said as I looked in the glass . . .*

The title *Liberties of the Mind* was chosen for his next book of essays (1951).

'The problem of the liberty of thought', he wrote in his long introduction, 'is in my own view spiritual.'

> Either there is an immortal part of us or there is not. If there is not, then all argument above the level of comfort and expediency is vain, and we are to think of our lives as we should of a month's stay in a boarding house. . . . We should not be concerned with the continuity or growth of our own or our neighbours' selves. If, on the contrary, there is an immortal part of us, called the spirit, whose lodging-place is in our minds, it is our primary concern that our minds be not corrupted or disabled.

He foresaw the integrity of the human personality threatened on all sides by 'barren and superficial materialism' and such dangers as Possessive Control. Most of all he feared submission to the powers of evil, which seek to destroy 'the validity of the human mind, its right to distinguish between good and evil'.

Never did Charles write more cogently or more passionately than in these essays, warning our age, and especially our scientists, against 'the form of suicide that the Litany prays against — a hardening of heart, a Contempt of the Word'.

To read his message with an attentive ear is to catch once more an echo of Henry Vaughan's poetry:

> *Resume Thy spirit from this world of thrall*
> *Into true liberty.*

Like Vaughan, who lived through the stresses of the Civil War, Charles felt the 'need of spiritual peace enforced by public calamity'.

The remarkable thing is that while he himself was storm-tossed, he could provide others with a life-line. About him after his death Christopher Arnold-Forster wrote: 'He, almost alone, gave me such faith as I have in the purposefulness of existence and its continuity.' Mutual understanding and sympathy helped there. It is extraordinary to find the impression made on a spectacularly different character, such as James Agate, a man so dismayed by the thought of death that he hated passing an undertaker's shop, and could be put off his day's work by the passage of a funeral outside his window.

Yet to Charles Morgan he wrote:

> I am very grateful for your letter[1] which is the first instance I have met of what I should like to call rational mysticism. . . . You have enabled me for the first time in my life to conceive, or rather go a millionth part of the way towards a conception that the state of death may not be the same thing as nothingness.[2]

As always, he was a shrewd observer of affairs, and when in the summer of 1952 the *Sunday Times* sent him on a mission of enquiry to South Africa, he wrote in the first of three articles that

> Where the races are concerned, what is needed is good will, patience, courage, a cool head — above all Time. Time is as precious to South Africa as rain, and, in the desert of White anger, it is being allowed to seep away.

The following year saw the production of his third play, *The Burning Glass*, which ran in London for four months and posed the question still uppermost in its author's mind: How can man be safeguarded from his own inventions? In the play Christopher Terriford, a peaceable and unambitious scientist, stumbles on a new immense source of power, which can be used for destructive purposes. Charles prefaced the printed edition with an essay 'On Power over Nature' in which he wrote: 'To doubt that there is a way out is to acquiesce in chaos and to doubt God's mercy.'

In 1953 he was elected International President of P.E.N., as successor to Benedetto Croce, and for three years shouldered its exacting duties. The record of such high offices, and all the meetings and conferences they entail, can make very dull reading. Seen in retrospect,

---

[1] No. 65, 14 April 1935.
[2] *Ego 2, Autobiography of James Agate.*

Charles Morgan's presidency was unusual; his speeches vibrated with intensity of thought and feeling. At the opening of the Amsterdam Congress he took for his theme the phrase *A June Night and no War*, and drew from it an extraordinary sense of the value of peace. That thought should be free; that literature should be without frontiers — these things had been prized by him all his working life. 'We labour', he said, 'in order that there may be no more writers in exile.'

It was a time of international tension and some disagreement. Firmly and fearlessly Charles upheld the freedom of the writers. He was not at heart an ardent reformer, but, like Turgenev, his master in many ways, he was concerned in 'the strange variability of the human' and moved by 'a fusing of individual spirit with individual spirit'.[1]

His term of office ended with the London Conference of 1956 when he was host to a formidable multi-lingual audience. 'There was a kind of grace in all he did,' writes Veronica Wedgwood, President of the English P.E.N., 'and it was the grace of courtesy . . . He did not want to be a distant figure-head; he wanted to be an active, hard-working President.' All that this entailed took its toll of both strength and health.

The last of the novels, *Challenge to Venus*, was published in the following year (1957). In spite of its carefully drawn portraits and the gilded light of its north Italian background, the book is a disappointment. It is a tale of futile passion between an Italian princess and a middle-class Englishman, with a flat ending. Where has gone the 'wine with the sun and the earth in it'? Martin Lyghe, the chief character, is troubled by the solitariness into which his 'certainties' can lead him. 'The rapture of being certain had held within it the terror of a complete break with common experience.'

Why *terror*? One asks the question seeing Charles like a man who holds a shell to his ear, entranced by the sound of a distant sea. Sometimes he wishes not to listen; to hear instead 'a cart go jolting down the street'. But because he is under a spell he must needs attend to those far-off tidings. Martin Lyghe, in this last novel, is the opposite of Barbet in *The Voyage*, happiest of all his people — a character with whom the author himself seems in love. We see Barbet as a man in harmony with all living things, part of a natural and miraculous world, which he recognizes with 'a passionate acceptance of unity'. For him nothing is 'separable, inconstant, mortal'.

[1] 'Turgenev's *First Love*', in *The Writer and his World*.

November 1956 brought the death of Germaine Delamain at her home in the Charente, while she was at work on the translation of *Challenge to Venus*. It was the end of an association of the utmost importance to Charles, for she had been the sole interpreter to his French public, from *Portrait in a Mirror* onwards.

Letters of this period show that he was increasingly troubled by a difficulty in breathing and by the curse of writer's cramp. 'Rejoice with me. I think I have my writing back,' he tells Hilda when he found a new way of holding his pen. But it was slow. He estimated that 'On the present principle I could write *War and Peace* in about twenty years!'

Early in 1957 the Morgans sailed for the West Indies. This was his last voyage and it gave him sun, swimming and the peaceful monotony he loved. While in Tobago he wrote a one-act play, *The Confession*, for broadcasting. Other work hung fire. 'Darkness and Daylight', the huge novel, had been abandoned; a play, begun in 1956, was unfinished, its theme of non-violence in a violent world still unresolved. The problem had been occupying a part of his mind from 1918 onwards. Two wars and the threat of another had not convinced him of the rightness of Tolstoy's answer, but he was growing less sure of its total rejection.

He still retained an 'unabashed loftiness' of standard in his writing, but standards were changing. 'Urbanity and good humour and proportion appear to have vanished from criticism,' he complained to E. M. Almedingen. In spite of the immense sales of his books, he was becoming isolated; misprized by the younger writers and intellectuals of his own country.

In the last year of his life Charles gave the impression of living between two worlds. His essay on Emily Brontë[1] — written, as it were, from the inside — gives a clue to this duality. 'Emily had two lives,' he explained. To the duties of existence at Haworth parsonage she clung, 'as visionary and contemplative men cling always to the discipline that they have cultivated as an enablement of their vision'. (The last phrase aptly describes Charles Morgan.) Her other real life was 'set apart from all these things and was profoundly secret'. Being an artist, she communicated it in her writing, but was reluctant to confess it to the world.

He believed that Emily Brontë had undergone a 'complete mystical experience' in early youth, and that having once escaped into absolute

---

[1] In *Reflections in a Mirror*, First Series.

freedom she pined for i t and was 'tired of being enclosed'. The Welsh word *hiraeth* — inadequately translated as 'longing' — comes to mind (not unsuitably, for Emily Brontë was by race both Irish and Cornish). This, too, is the theme of *Sparkenbroke*, in some ways the most autobiographical of the novels.

Of death and Emily Brontë, he wrote: 'She did not know whether to dread death as a cessation or to desire it as an opportunity . . . she was not certain that, in going from this world, she might take her ecstasy with her.'

'He minded spiritual things; minded them very deeply,' said St. John Ervine, speaking of Charles. So much of his critical writing — necessarily ephemeral yet handling eternal questions — lies drowned in the files of *The Times* newspaper. The dredging up of a notice on *Peer Gynt*[1] brings to light a notable analysis of Peer's character:

> *Peer Gynt* is a dramatic essay first on the spiritual perils of self-dramatization; second, on the agony of the man who, inwardly desiring it above all else, cannot accomplish the supreme imaginative act of self-loss. This is the significance of Solveig, who is for Peer the death of self from which renewal springs.

Renewal! It was the theme above all others for Charles Morgan. When in *The Fountain* Lewis Alison goes out to the ramparts on his last day in the Fort, he sees the cottage gardens beyond the moat flecked with snowdrops and the rooks pairing in the elm-trees. The miracles of a mild February day are around him.

> . . . and I . . . he said, I am frosted in knowledge and cannot renew myself. I listen but hear no voice. I am like a tree in which the sap does not rise. And he began to ask himself . . . by what discipline he might attain to that stillness which should enable him to hear and to that brilliance of perception which should enable him to see.

Charles Morgan died on 6 February 1958, a few days after he reached the age of sixty-four. It is possible to feel that, in a sense, the tree was sapless, and that as he wrote of Turgenev's last years, 'the life-giving tensions were released, the light had gone out'. But his essay[2] does not end there. He goes on to speak of Turgenev's vision — of innocence within guilt, of youth within age, of eternity in the instant.'

[1] Produced at the Old Vic, September 1935. Translation by R. Ellis Roberts, with William Devlin as Peer. Florence Kahn (Mrs. Max Beerbohm) played Ase.
[2] 'Ivan Turgenev', in *Reflections in a Mirror*, First Series.

In his last letter to a Dutch friend, Charles wrote that he was 'contemplating new work'. Like his old Frenchwoman in *The Voyage*, who was the mother of Barbet, he 'neither clung to life nor clamoured for death', their continuity being clear to him. And with her he might have said, 'When you grow old, Thérèse, do not say good-bye to the nightingale. It is not necessary. Nothing vanishes.'

1. TO MILDRED MORGAN.   *Written while he was work-ing on the first draft of* The Gunroom, *during his captivity in Holland.*

Wierickerschans, Holland
16 November 1915

YOUR letter and Marcie's were absolute masterpieces of just the kind of detail I want and some of your comments — e.g. those upon danc-ing — were full of joy. No, I don't think you need have any fear that the portraits I draw will be unpleasantly personal. All my people will be very largely 'composite'. For instance, one girl may be two-thirds Mildred, one-third Marcie and flavoured with imagination. As a matter of fact I haven't attempted any such mixture as that, but it is illustrative of a system. Also, when the tale is finished I will submit it to those in any way concerned and, if they object to anything as too indicative of its origin, I will cut and compromise. The tale, I may say, is chiefly concerned with H.M.S. and the earlier chapters only deal with less general subjects. I think I have more to fear than anyone else, for if, in writing of the Service, I make my principal go to Osborne and Dart: and the Cruiser and, indeed, to the same kind of ships and the same stations as I did, then people are sure to turn round and say: 'But this is surely a glorified and debased portrait of yourself.' People, however, will take a lot of convincing. And I'm not at all sure that so far as I am concerned it matters much what they think on this point, but I promise you quite definitely that I won't attempt to publish without letting you and Marcie read the MS. and without yielding to any prejudices you may have where you personally are concerned.

2. TO CHARLES MORGAN, senior.   *(The reference in the second sentence is to Mme Elout van Soeterwoude, née Helen van Pallandt. See introductory Memoir, p. 9.)*

Rosendaal, Holland
6 April 1916

AS regards general topics, I was very pleased to get the *Westminster Gazette* which you sent me with my poem marked. It was the first intimation I received of its having been accepted, although Madame

Elout, who takes in the *Westminster Gazette*, came running up shortly afterwards with her copy. I am especially pleased about getting this in as quite recently the *Westminster Gazette* published an announcement saying that since the war they had been 'deluged' with poems, many of them from the trenches, and that they had now so great an accumulation that they begged contributors to cease pressing for publication for a time at least. . . .

At present I am pegging away at my novel, writing very slowly and with the greatest possible care. I feel that there is no hurry about this as I have no intention of publishing until the war is over, so I am taking my time and writing as well as I possibly can. I believe the early chapters are good, and the subject — an analysis of Osborne, Dartmouth and all Naval training and a parallel between that and the ordinary inefficient methods of educating boys — should be one of very general interest. In the meantime I am anxious to get some short stories in the best magazines, but I find it very difficult to get a plot 'healthy' enough to suit the really big and dignified people like *Blackwood's* and the *Cornhill* and the *Westminster Gazette*. . . .

We went to call on the Baroness Pallandt at the Castle after her return from Switzerland. She was very nice to us and had actually brought each of us a 5 Pfennig piece from Germany. These are rather interesting nowadays as they are all made of iron. Also she brought a piece of German bread which I enclose and a menu (*Fettlos* = without fat, i.e. no fat is used throughout the meal) of a big German hotel which I will enclose if I can find it. I expect the latter are very rare in England and might amuse the authorities (whoever *they* are) if you cared to send it them. Likewise an analysis of the bread might disclose some interesting facts about the food question in Germany.

I wonder if anyone who has spoken to you of the *Westminster* poem has noticed that it was really an experiment in metre. Everybody has always said that it is impossible to imitate the Latin hexameter with any success and I quite agree with them. I was thinking about this when I got the notion of trying a part imitation of the Latin. The result is that the first part of all my lines is the first part of an hexameter, though the second part is my own effort to avoid the appalling effect produced by a complete imitation of the hexameter. It was an amusing experiment and came off successfully.

The funny thing is that nothing I submit to editors can be type-written out here, and so everything has to be written in my own

special variety of copper-plate *like this.*

3. TO MRS. BLANCHE ALETHEA CRACKANTHORPE,
a friend of Meredith, Hardy and Henry James.   Her son Hubert Crackanthorpe was one of the founders of The Yellow Book. (God, The Invisible King, *by H. G. Wells, was published in 1917.*)

Rosendaal, Holland
27 May 1917

I AM eager to learn what you thought of *God, the Invisible King.* I have read it very carefully. For a long time after I had finished it I could not discover why, for all its rightness, it seemed yet to be wrong, to be lacking in something that was essential. And now I see what is lacking. Mr. Wells takes Jehovah and sweeps him away; he sweeps away too the conception of the Trinity together with many other ecclesiastical formulae which did not spring from Christ; so far, so good. Then he looks round for a new God and finds one whose essential attributes are as follows: God is Courage. God is a Person. God is Youth. (Chap. III.) God is a Friend who stands by one's side. God is a Fighter.

All this I believe, but the God whom Wells endows with these properties is not my God. Why does he confuse the issue with that piece of 'fine writing' on page 77 — with that picture of his God which is so like an Academy picture? Why does he declare for a new conception of God? Christ is his God though he does not know it. Christ possesses all the attributes possessed by Wells's God. Christ is Courage, Christ is a Person, is Youth, is a Friend, is a Fighter. He struggled and suffered as men struggle and suffer. He is a clear, finite conception. When He shed His 'precious blood' — and I hold to those words despite Wells's scoff — His Spirit entered into us all and remains with us all, just as our spirits when we die are merged, as Wells says, in His Spirit. Why this bitterness, why this modernity, this air of having invented something? Strip Christianity of ecclesiasticism, as Wells has rightly done, and you come down to essentials. And the essential is not some invention called a modern God. The essential is Christ. Why not give Him His name?

4. TO MRS. ROBERT MENNELL.   *Written after his return to England. (Lilias and Robert Mennell, and also Rosa and Stephen Hobhouse, were active as Quakers and Pacifists during the First World War. The District Court Martial referred to was one that sentenced Robert Mennell to a further term of imprisonment.)*

Woodhurst, Kenley, Surrey
15 November 1917

I HAVE just heard an amazing story from a friend of mine who is an influential supporter of the Extreme Left and who is on the Executive of the Women's International. She tells me that Mrs. Stephen Hobhouse has been arrested and brought into court on a charge of distributing seditious literature, and that the literature in question was a pamphlet on which was printed the Sermon on the Mount. My informant at first said Mrs. Hobhouse was committed on this charge, but, on my pressing her, said she was not sure of this, but that certainly the arrest was made. Marcie tells me that you know Mrs. Stephen Hobhouse, so I write to you for confirmation or denial. So much seems to hang upon this point. It is symbolic of so much that I have discovered since I returned to England. If our existing system of government has indeed brought about the arrest or imprisonment of a citizen on a charge of selling the Sermon on the Mount; if this was done knowingly and in cold blood and was not the result of an error by some subordinate; then that fact, coupled with many others that have come to my knowledge, makes me see quite clearly that the existing system must go. If we can break it by constitutional means so much the better. By tradition and upbringing I am a Tory: I care enormously for peace: I hate the idea of adding the suffering of revolution to the suffering of war. But, if things are as they seem to be, and if no constitutional and peaceful means can rid us of the yoke, then — cost what it may — we must save our children's children.

I have been out of England for sixteen months. I have returned to an island which undoubtedly bears the name of England. Certainly it is not now what once I thought it to be: perhaps it never was. And are all those fine people, with such an infinite capacity for beauty, to suffer for this corpse of England that remains? Is all we loved to be washed out in order that — in order that — what *are* we fighting for? Not for freedom surely, not for peace. All that has been forgotten long enough ago. Now it's revenge, and a little money, and a little territory, and a little spitting into the face of Christ. If men hated Christ, I could bear that. If they said he was wrong, I could bear that. But now to Englishmen Christ is neither hateful nor wrong — he is merely a poseur. . . .

Once I thought that with patience we might break up the public school system and educate men out of their stiff collars. But there comes a time when education is useless. You can't train a mad dog. You can only kill him so that he may not bite your children.

It is very difficult for me to discover how bad things are. But everywhere I go I hear of honest, sincere men — my father among them — talking of crushing the Germans and keeping their Colonies. It seems we are to keep their Colonies because our Colonies insist upon it. Which is the first fruits of Imperialism, I suppose. Blake says: to 'Hold Infinity in the palm of your hand, And eternity in an hour.' And he says again:

> *If the Sun and Moon should doubt,*
> *They'd immediately go out.*

The difference between the spiritual and political methods is this: The follower of the political method has the pleasure of being in a recognised minority. The follower of the spiritual method is in a minority without cohesion, a minority whose very existence few would ever realise. But it is by the hands of these few that Jerusalem will be builded. I have never yet found a man who has courage to be of their number. I have never heard of one except Christ. And I look to a second Incarnation. I can see no other way. St. Paul did so much harm.

Marcie cannot come to the District Court Martial and I will not come in uniform — which I am bound to wear. Not because I don't feel with Mr. Mennell, and not, believe me, because I am afraid of what others will say and think. But I feel this . . . I do at present hold a commission under the law of the State and cannot consistently identify myself with those who resist it, unless I am prepared to appeal to the right of man to revolt. And now I am anti-revolutionary and shall be until I have clear evidence of ill-intent among our governors and clearer promise of betterment by revolution.

5. TO MRS. ROBERT MENNELL.   (*The pamphlets distributed by Mrs. Stephen Hobhouse had indeed included the Beatitudes, and other more controversial matter as well.*)

Kenley
22 November 1917

MANY thanks for your two letters and for the trouble you have taken about the Hobhouse case. I am afraid I cannot agree with Mrs. Stephen Hobhouse that the case was substantially as I had heard. She appears to have distributed many pamphlets, some of which may have contained an advocacy by implication of an immediate conclusion to this war, no matter on what terms. If this was so, I cannot think it illogical in a war government to take action against their distribution among the troops — and for this reason. The Government believes that this war is right and necessary, just as the distributors of the pamphlets believe it to be wrong and unnecessary. The action of each party, with respect to the specific issue of *this* war, is reasonably based upon its opinions on the specific issue. The dispute is properly to be decided, not by the treatment of a particular case, but by a consideration of general principles. For this reason I think that, while a government would be wrong to suppress an advocacy of principle — e.g. a pamphlet containing the Sermon on the Mount and nothing but the Sermon — a government is none the less justified in suppressing a pamphlet which treats of the particular instance of this war and advocates action which — by existing law — is treasonable.

There appear to me to be two logical courses open to a member of a Pacifist group. (1) He must say: 'Things have gone too far. The mesh of the past and present, standing between the world and Christ, is too complicated and too strong to be cut by political weapons. Therefore I will stand aside. I will not attempt to compete politically, any more than Christ attempted to compete politically. I do not look to my actions to bear early fruit. If my principles prevail, they prevail because I have given an example, not because I have persuaded. Christ would not

The Cadet, 1911

Rosendaal Castle

Wierickerschans Fort

preach in Tyre and Sidon . . .' And that attitude leaves it to him to
live rightly; to render unto Caesar what he believes to be Caesar's and
unto God what he believes to be God's. And it debars him from any
form of political agitation. It leaves in his hand no sword, but that of
the spirit.

(2) The alternative: He may say: 'I believe that the mesh can be cut
by political weapons if rightly handled.' If he says this, if he enters into
competition with politicians, if he decides to use political weapons,
then he must not complain if he is met with a political shield. And, if
we regard war politically as an existing fact, we must admit that the
exceptional crisis justifies exceptional action. If it is to wage war, a
government may reasonably suppress an action which impedes it in
the waging of war. It is open to attack, not because it suppresses a
pamphlet, but because it is waging war. And, going nearer to the
source, the pacifist must attack — not the individual government —
but the conditions which force it to act as it does, i.e. a matter of general
principle.

The first method — the spiritual method of complete withdrawal
from politics — seems the more consistent. I doubt whether any man
is brave enough to follow it. It amounts to this: that a man lives like
Christ *without saying so*. It means no advertisement, no defined opposition. Only obscurity. Such a life, lived today, will inevitably appear
fruitless. It is only possible to one who can see clearly that the
sword of the spirit — though no man fear it — is indeed the only
sword.

Then we are to dig up indemnities and penalties (if we can) — in
short we are to amass all the fuel of future wars. And we are to break
German Imperialism — but not our own. And we are to break German
Imperialism, and to regret the breaking of Russian Imperialism.

I have heard — I myself have heard — people deploring the Russian
Revolution — the same people who condemn German bureaucracy —
the same people who support Carson and Milner.

The muddle is appalling. And men think with such terrible bitterness. No one cares for beauty any more. All their speech is of food;
all their dreams of killing.

I gave my father *Black 'ell* to read last night, but have not yet heard
his comment. In any case he won't take it seriously — 'the vapourings
of some crank'— you know.

Of course, admitting on principle the right of a people to 'revolute'

E

(revolt is too small a word) I believe too that fighting is sometimes inevitable and right. First let us publish peace terms — real terms of *peace* — and then fight until the German government allows their people to accept them or *goes*. First, I say, let us publish *peace* terms. But this Government will never publish them. We have to find a Government that will and we have to rid ourselves of this Government that won't. Is there any way but revolution? Revolution will mean that we shall not be able to fight — even for true peace; so that, if we have a revolution, everything depends upon whether the Germans can break their Government too. If they fail and we succeed, or if we fail and they succeed, the result will be a ghastly bureaucratic triumph for one side or the other. It is an enormous risk to take.

Do you know how many of the left are definitely revolutionary? And do you know if Mrs. Hobhouse was really taken for distributing the Sermon on the Mount? I am sorry to worry you like this, but it does seem to matter tremendously. Do you think you could get full, particulars of the Hobhouse incident? I should be very, very grateful.[1]

6. TO MRS. ROBERT MENNELL, *after the Armistice.*

Kenley

12 November 1918

MAY I tell you quite simply how glad I am that now, when everyone is celebrating the armed victory, you and your husband and the people who stood in with you have won through to your own victory without arms. To me the news yesterday brought relief, not gladness — a dull relief without fire or passion. I feel that we have gained a pause — for which thank Heaven; not that we have advanced or achieved or accomplished. If I had taken the other side — your side — I should have been glad today with an amazing quiet fierce gladness; nor should I be oppressed by this intolerable sense of the unreality of victory. What-

[1] In May 1916 Mrs. Stephen Hobhouse and Mrs. Clara Cole walked from village to village distributing leaflets, of which one — issued by the Fellowship of Reconciliation — included the Beatitudes. At Kettering they were arrested, brought before the magistrates and sent for trial. Mrs. Hobhouse took her stand on the Gospels, and Moffat's translation of the 'Kingdom of Heaven' as the 'Realm of Heaven'. 'It helped me', she writes, 'for as we were charged under the Defence of the Realm Act, it led me to show that we too had a Realm to defend.' The two ladies were sentenced to a fine of £50 each, or three months' imprisonment. As they refused to pay the fine they were committed to Northampton Gaol.

ever advance the world has made, it has made along that path of which the Sermon on the Mount was the beginning, the adoption by all men of 'your people's' attitude the logical conclusion. My sense of the moment tells me you were wrong — and even now I think I would volunteer again; but my sense of Eternity tells me that you were right.

In a book called *The Fortune* by Douglas Goldring there is this passage about an officer who died fighting the Dublin rebels: 'The tragedy about him was, not that he was on the wrong side, but that he knew it.'

I hope the Government releases the C.O.s *at once.* It is so important that there should be no bickering about it. Doesn't England see that the C.O.s are in prison for expressing in one way just what we who volunteered set out to express in another — the end of tyranny, the freedom of the spirit?

7. TO HUGH WALPOLE.   *A young writer's first encounter* with the problems of publication.

Kenley
27 September 1919

STATEMENTS on your authority have recently appeared in the Press to the effect that publishers are unwilling to consider first novels. That is, of course, their tendency; but it would, I think, be less discouraging to the younger men who are trying to do serious work if they knew that there are publishers of the first rank who insist neither upon established reputation in the author nor upon an obviously commercial appeal in his book. My own experience is fortunately very different from that which the Press statements would lead one to expect. I cannot make any public reply without advertising my own book; and for this reason you will, perhaps, forgive my writing to you personally to explain that your general rule is open to exceptions.

During the war I was a prisoner in Holland with the Naval Brigades. There I wrote a novel which I tore up because I did not think it was good enough. I wrote it again, and in November 1917, when I came to England on parole, brought it with me, nearly completed in manuscript. The ship in which I crossed the North Sea was sunk by an enemy mine within an hour of England, and, though I was picked up by a destroyer, all I possessed — including my manuscript of which I had no copy — went to the bottom. After I had been a few months in England, I began to write my novel a third time. It was difficult to begin again, and I felt it would be easier to go through with my task if I had some kind of assurance that, when it was finished, it would at least be considered. I have no influence with publishers or literary men, so I wrote, quite by chance, to A. & C. Black Ltd., who happened to be the publishers of *The Writers' and Artists' Year Book*, which I had beside me. I told them what had happened; I said that I was writing a novel called *The Gunroom* dealing with the lives and education of junior officers in the Navy from a new, and I was afraid an unpopular, standpoint; and I asked that, if a firm of their standing could not in any case consider the work of a new author while the price of production remained so high, they would frankly say so. They asked to see what I had done, and I sent them two chapters. Within a few days they replied that their reader's opinion was such that they strongly recommended me to finish the book, and they asked me to call. I saw their reader, who said that, if the book maintained the standard of the first two chapters, Black's would publish it. In February 1919 I sent in the finished book, and at once received an offer for it on a royalty basis, the publishers to take all risks. This offer, in response to my requests, was afterwards increased, and the final agreement, in the opinion of men experienced in these matters, is extraordinarily favourable to me. *The Gunroom* will, I think, appear in the early days of next month, through Black's in England and the Macmillan Company in America.

I have nothing whatever to complain of with regard to my publishers. Their enterprise is, I think, the more remarkable because, first, they are a conservative firm established more than a hundred years; second, I have written nothing before except a few articles or poems in the *Fortnightly*, the *Westminster* and other newspapers and reviews, and am therefore altogether unknown; third, this is the only novel Black's have accepted for many years, so that they have even struck out on a new line of policy on the strength of a first book which sets out to be, not primarily a best-seller, but a serious work.

I am sorry I have written at such length. I am very grateful to you for having drawn attention to a condition of affairs which certainly does bear heavily on new writers; but I thought you might care to know that it is possible to get a hearing, and that without the help of agents or personal introductions or anything of the kind.

8. TO HILDA VAUGHAN, *who later became Charles's wife.*
(*The manuscript referred to is an early draft of her novel* The Invader.)

Eze, Alpes Maritimes, France
13 April 1922

I'VE read 'The Invasion' amid this sunshine. I've read it slowly,
putting it aside for longish intervals, re-reading it, wondering slowly
where something has seemed wrong exactly what has been wrong —
anyhow, trying to be desperately impersonal about it. I finished it this
afternoon on the shore, in a river of sun that threw blue shadows
across the page. And now, after tea, I want to fight it out with you by
question and answer, to hear you slash my criticisms and so balance
and correct them, to get down to the truth as one can't in a letter. . . .

First — and this is the joy of the thing — you've got what is the
rarest of gifts nowadays, the gift of narrative. Hardy's the supreme
living master of it; that's why he stands so far apart. Every chapter of
his is an integral part of the narrative; you can't omit one chapter
without breaking the thread and making the rest unintelligible; he's
always 'getting on with the story'. . . . The great thing is that you
have a tale to tell and you tell it straight. It's a gift to rejoice in — first
because it makes for good art and strength and simplicity, secondly
because it's rare, thirdly because it's what people want in the books
they read. . . .

Thanks so much for letting me see the MS. It's really exciting. 'You',
in the plural, have got to be a great writer. And that means the courage
to cross out and cross out and re-write and re-write; and be damned to
everything but the absolute best and finest that's in you. The world's
in a miserable mess. I'm not at all sure that artists can't do more to
save it than anyone else. Art is one of the two things in the world that
can't be bought.

9. TO HILDA VAUGHAN. *Written from a flat which Charles shared with Gordon Alchin on their first coming down from Oxford. (Charles was then writing a weekly 'Wednesday article' on drama for* The Times, *in the absence of A. B. Walkley.)*

26 Queensborough Terrace, W.2
4 August 1922

YOU know, when I wrote of the advice I imagined you gave me about the first Wednesday article, I felt it was the advice I wanted you to give just then; and you mustn't wonder whether you're always going to give me the right and sane advice. What you're going to do, and what I'm going to try to do for you, is — altogether apart from definite and absolutely frank criticism — relight for me sometimes, by the flash and inspiration and perhaps the faith of you, a spark that's liable to be dulled when habit and efficiency make things easy. A thousand-word article can be brilliant or merely competent; and against mere competence in each other you and I have got to fight for each other's sake. I'm in danger, because I write so much and have, by the grace of Heaven, an assured market for much of it. But I want to write always — even unsigned stuff — as if my eternal reputation depended on it. Sometimes, it may be, one is tired and it's physically impossible to touch the absolute top line. But, however tired you are, there's no reason for not writing at the top line for the time being. It's not a question of doing one's best. It means that you must always do a little more, in the long run, than seemed your best when you sat down to write. And the thing about you, Hilda, is that you make me ashamed to accept the easy way. You stretch me always a little beyond my best. Now and then, something may snap and what I called 'arrant nonsense' be the result. But not often. If it does, tell me. I may be very angrily in disagreement, but next morning I shall see that you are right. The artist in me, you must strain mercilessly: there's no breaking or killing it except by self-indulgence, and you must drive it with all your whips, as I shall drive the artist in you. But to the man in me, dearest, give the peace you can give.

You know, it's only shallow thought which makes some women say that it's an insult to their individuality to ask them to belong to the man who loves them. It's even shallower thinking, when they say that they don't want the man to belong to them. The phrase 'free

love' seems to me to be a contradiction in terms. I want you to belong
to me absolutely, because I worship you — and I mean *worship*. It's
not belonging in the sense in which a chattel belongs, but in the
sense in which God belongs — the one thing in a shifting world
which is indestructible, the one thing sure, the one thing above and
beyond all fear for its loyalty. That's what I meant when I spoke of
jealousy. The conventional idea is that if I became jealous of you, I should
want you more, and the awakening of jealousy is on the stage a recognised
way of re-awakening desire. That may be. Perhaps if I were jealous, I
should want you more physically; I don't know. But I do know that if
once I doubted you, something in my worship for you would snap.
One doesn't fight for one's God. When one doubts him, he ceases in
that instant to be a god. Am I wrong to think of you like that? I've
never thought of anyone in quite those terms before. It's simply that
a knowledge in me says: 'You love Hilda. You can trust her, without
thought, without watching or calculation, with the whole vast inheri-
tance of the spirit. If you can become a great man, then there's more
to trust her with and that's why it's worth struggling to be great.'
It's the fact that my innermost heart says that of you which gives meaning to the peace you bring. It's not quite an earthly peace. I can't
argue about it or define it. It's the peace which passeth all understanding.

10. TO HILDA VAUGHAN.   (*For several years Charles
contributed a monthly article on the London theatre to the* West Sussex
Gazette, *of which Roger Barrett was Assistant Editor. When he left
England to work on a Hong Kong newspaper, Charles wrote:* '*I shall
write the* W. S. G. *article, but it's like writing to a stone wall. You
were my audience, though I didn't know it.*')

Queensborough Terrace
8 August 1922

THIS morning I wrote five of these pages for the *West Sussex
Gazette*; then three or four letters; then down to *The Times* to return
the George Moore book which they want for review in the *Literary
Supplement*. I walked most of the way back, for the sun was shining at
last. Having neglected lunch, I had an amazing tea of Devonshire

cream, and, coming home, sat down to the Wednesday article. It became so exciting that I knew nothing until I discovered it was half past nine, so I went out rapidly and fed, came back and finished the article, posted it, and here I am — 11.30 p.m. This, I'm afraid, hasn't a chance for the midnight post, for I've sworn not to write to you tomorrow — the evening being my dinner at the Evans's and all day being, so far as I know, free. Think of it — no theatre; no leader; no Wednesday article until next Tuesday; and someone to talk to in the evening. So it's all day for the novel[1] and I'm very excited about it. I'm still not sure of two chapters, but the ones I am sure of have become trebly sure in my mind and have grown and flowered somehow, so that I have only to set them down. And the rest will come, though I don't see it clearly now, when once I get pen to paper.

No: bless you, I'm not being overworked. It's merely that I talk of it all rather selfishly to you because I love to tell you even of its details. And it looks very formidable all set out in order. For instance, if I tell you that today, when I've written this letter, I shall have written about 4,000 words it sounds a lot, but it's all happy work of the kind I used to imagine myself doing when I was in the Navy. Think of it: I might be there still, or a stockbroker going to his office every day instead of sitting among my own books at my own table and writing my own mind. Besides, there's early bed tonight, and Powys Evans tomorrow, and one Chris Hussey who has asked me to dine on Thursday, and there's you in the world. And I feel like a child when the sun's out. . . .

Good night, dearest, and don't worry about my work. I've got it inside me that in the world of books we shall both win through in the end, though we may be desperately poor in the process, because it seems that, like other mortals, quantity with me doesn't make for quality, and, for a time at any rate, I should be almost sorry if you earned much — not, I hope, because it would worry me if you out-stripped me in that matter or any other, but because with you, if you're going to write what's in you, anything like 'popularity' ought not to come too quickly. I fear for you, more than for myself, the adula-tion of fools, because you start with a greater goodwill towards man-kind. I'm not afraid of the circulating library lady — you won't take any notice of her. But I know you'll meet people, who are artists in their own way, who'll like all the wrong things in your work and express their opinions with airy emphasis. And though you'll probably

---

[1] *My Name is Legion.*

know they are wrong, their damned enthusiasm will leave its mark. Your line is to write like a rock — with a rock's austerity; your passion, the passion of naked hills; your colour, the colour of a beacon on the skyline; your music, the songs men sing in the open air.

11. TO HILDA VAUGHAN.   *On a story she was contemplating.*

Queensborough Terrace
15 August 1922

THAT story which J. H. told you is a wonderful story. But I don't see what your trouble is about not knowing the underworld of London. I believe that, even if you did know it, you ought to omit it from that story. The point is that one wants to see the harlot, not as a thousand novelists have shewn her, but through the eyes which are accustomed to the Welsh hills. In short, what you want is not the fact but the result of her London life. If you twisted suddenly into night-clubs, you would interrupt the book's music. Leave them out; suggest them only. Above all get into the girl's mind *when she is returned to Wales*. Once I tried a narrative poem on that theme — the country girl returned from that life to the country place — the harlot's holiday. But I couldn't work it out. There were fragments, but no more. — Honestly, I don't see that you need dip into the night-clubs. What's more, they are in any case only the surface of the thing. If you — with a woman's mind — could write of the life in an established *maison publique* and write of it without sentimentalizing its tragedy — well, then you'd have written the book which can, perhaps, never be written, for I doubt whether any man has enough imaginative stretch to reach the full limits of the woman's tragedy in those circumstances. But apart from that — which you most certainly can't attempt without unattainable experience — I see nothing against your writing the story. Hardy could write it of Wessex folk with scarce a scene laid in London itself. It is one of those astonishing simple stories, with all the nerves of tragedy in interplay, which happens so rarely.

But beware of the boy's affection for his young aunt. That doesn't ring true to me. It sounds like an artificial complication. The elder sister is the centre of your story. Keep to her. Let everything come through her. Only with her as fulcrum can the story balance, and with her it balances perfectly. The sisters disappearing from the country one by one. Always the old people's feeling: 'They'll be safe with her.' Her knowledge of it. The eyes, half-pitying, — yes, but mocking too — with which she regards their innocence. The curious mixture of softness and callousness in her; which makes her fight and fight when one of them falls ill or is cruelly treated, and yet makes it possible for her to hand over the life once saved to the man with whom she can make a good bargain. I wonder if even you have realized how vast a story it is. Ah! if we could collaborate on that! And yet I believe that even we should be afraid of our own knowledge. — I wonder if it ought to be done as the girl's diary — first the crude jottings of a child, then more, then more and more. My God! How it all grows in my mind as I write.

If it were mine, I should make of it a horror beyond endurance — and I'm not sure it ought not to be written. We're such a damnably Christian country that we're all afraid of the scourge with which Christ purged the Temple. I am firmly convinced that prostitution is an inevitable evil. No book and no law and no public opinion can extirpate it. It seems a hopeless thing to say. One likes to believe that there's a way out of everything. But from that I'm sure there's no way out. But people ought to know. It's wrong that they should pass these girls in the street with no power to imagine their lives. Their lives aren't all misery. If they are naturally Bohemians they get to a 'Who cares?' attitude, and there's pleasure in it. But there is misery unspeakable — the sudden looking forward; the hopeless realization that they can never again be quite women in the fine, proud sense; that they have touched the vile thing which, from a woman, can never be wholly washed away. You must write that book, but not yet.

12. TO HILDA VAUGHAN.

The Wheatsheaf, Arundel, Sussex
19 August 1922

YOU, without having 'literary competence' yet, have within you a capacity for greatness — somehow the sweep and poise and balance, unexpressed in your writing as yet but expressed in every movement of your body and mind, which is drawn deep from the blood and breed of you. . . . It is to the mind what a straight carriage and a breadth of hip and shoulder is to the body. I myself haven't got it and don't pretend to it. My own power is to see and make permanent the soul's innermost flashes and, in physical description, the chance attitude, so swiftly passing, which gives to a scene the air and colour that dwells in the watcher's mind without his being able to ascribe a reason to it. But you have the 'narrative gait', the processional rhythm of a story — in the tradition of the great English storytellers, unhurried, without what, perhaps, I get sometimes — an almost inspired leap upon an effect, but having no need of it — just as the instinctive aristocrat of manners has no need of the intricacies of behaviour.

13. TO HILDA VAUGHAN.   *About her novel* The Battle
    to the Weak.

Queensborough Terrace
22 August 1922

I WONDER what is the trouble with your novel. I hate to think of your being stuck, because I know how distressing it is; and particularly I hate it now because, having been rather more than stuck with my own novel for a year, I've at last got into the swing of it again — and to do creative work once more is with me to become young again and to feel that I'm not useless; and that makes me happy and I want you to be happy in the same way at the same time. But, my dear, if the story *won't* go it won't, and it's useless to force it. Probably what you need is to read what you've done to someone who is good at plots. Roger Barrett is a god-send to me in that respect; but I myself am a poor plot-weaver and should probably not be of much use to you. I'm looking to you in the future to batter my plots for me; and I may be able to help you with the way of telling, and the turn of phrase, and the 'worth-whileness' of the story. . . .

Sometimes I wish you were here so that I could read the novel to you as it is done. In fact I nearly sent you sixteen pages from Arundel, but I restrained myself because it is in fact much better that you should have it not in snippets.

Gordon and I watched cricket at the Oval for an hour this morning, but it was too tedious for either of us, so we wasted no more time there. I thought of your warning that you weren't to be taken to cricket-matches. It's a grief, because I confess to an occasional pleasure in that particular form of laziness; but it's an irrational pleasure unless the surroundings are unusually delightful and I'm not surprised that you don't share it. The Welsh and Scots never do. With them the ball is always rolling over the edge, down the nearest precipice, which naturally makes it an exhausting game to play and a dull one to watch. And of course if one happens to be both Welsh and Scottish, cricket enthusiasm is an improbable quality. . . .

You know it's a quiet, happy, peaceful thing to have you to write to. One talks on and on and then one says: 'Now you curl yourself up in that chair and read while I finish this article I ought to be writing now, and then, with a free mind, we'll go to the play together.'

I'm sorry to say that a lady who has been singing the Bonnie Banks of Loch Lomond for an hour has just died. Anyhow she has stopped.

14. TO HILDA VAUGHAN.   *With some explanation of the literary method used in* My Name is Legion.

Queensborough Terrace
24 August 1922

YOU see, all my life I've been a queer mixture of pride and humility. I've known, deep in my own heart, that I've got it in me to do 'great work'; and I've known, too, that 'great work' and even what we call the artist's immortality are no more than fragments of dust which the great tempests of the past and future sweep up and blow away. There's something insubstantial in all the mind deliberately creates. The plays of Shakespeare won't matter on Judgement Day. Great work depends for its permanence on mankind's remembrance; it has no real existence apart from its audience and the audience of all the world spins on a planet and vanishes into space. But if I could make you happy; if, when we are married, I could make your soul and body thrill with a knowledge of completeness and peace; then I should have created something which is given instantly to a real immortality, having nothing to do with mankind and so unperishing.

As for the 'great work' I spoke of at the top of the page — it seems

a boasting phrase if I leave it so. I remember your asking me once
what it was which in all the books I was to write I wanted to say — and
I remember I was without words with which to tell you. It's little less
than this — that I want to write of the modern world, of the intimacies
and passions of men and women as they are seen through the eyes of
God — and so, in writing, win my way into the heart of what we call
God. That's why the people in Flare [characters in *My Name is Legion*]
act 'unnaturally'. I told you once that I was trying to express their sub-
conscious minds in the terms of visible action. In a way that's true, but
not all the truth. They are 'unnatural' because, to us, 'natural' is the
word with which we describe the reactions of reason, of intellect, of
physical desire. But beneath reason there is spirit, beneath intellect there
is spirit, beneath desire there is spirit; and what God regards as natural
is the reactions of the spirit. He passes over, or passes through, reason
and intellect and desire. He sees *through* them; and the world he sees is
as 'unnatural' to us as the material world would be if all matter —
walls, and clothes and hills and pavements — became suddenly transparent. What we observe, what ordinarily we write about, is for him
transparent. He sees the spirit naked. And it's of the world, viewed
thus, that I'm trying to write.

I may never be able to make it clear. I've never even been able to
state it until this minute to you. I'm trying to do something im-
measurably greater than literature — or at any rate the novel — has
ever before attempted. It may be an impossible task, and from time to
time I shall put it aside and write more within reach. And those books,
which I may hope will still be fine books, may succeed. The rest may
prove a futile attempt to adapt the literary medium to something which
is beyond it. But now at least you'll have somewhere at the back of your
mind some idea of what I'm getting at. And if, at the end, there's failure
before the world, you won't think it a little failure. But if that happens
don't try to explain to them. They wouldn't understand if I haven't
by then made them understand. They'd only laugh at the fool who
tilted, not at windmills, but at high heaven. But I should like you to
know, because I love you, and in your love I have an immortality that
the world's laughter and the little scorn of the efficients can't hurt or
touch.

I believe that now, almost without meaning to, I've set down my
main idea in a form more clear than any in which I have yet seen it. It
may drift away and become cloudy again. Will you keep this letter so

that some day I can read it to you and to myself, and so remember what my job really is. . . .

Now it's deep into August 25th and I must go to bed if I'm to write tomorrow. And you won't think wrong of me? You won't think I'm proud. I'm not. I'm appalled by my own littleness before the work I have to do, and before the love for you which the man in me can only clumsily half express.

15. TO HILDA VAUGHAN.

London
6 September 1922

I WORKED at the fatal chapter all yesterday until after midnight. I've never had such a time. There are about six pages of trouble. I've pulled them to pieces, written and altered and rewritten and started all over again — writing with immense care and judging the effect of each word and the position of each phrase. I've even gone to the length, when it was baffling me to get the meaning I wanted into a sentence, of writing a kind of short essay on it, and then, having got my own meaning clearly worked out, trying to fit it into the troublesome sentence. It's like drawing a 'study' of a finger-nail in the course of painting a portrait.

16. TO HILDA VAUGHAN.

Arundel
22 September 1922

I'VE waited until the noon post, expecting a letter from you and, having watched a sunshiny postman loiter and gossip at door after door, have been ultimately rewarded.

I don't know what to say about scenery. My own rule, if you can call it a rule, is: write of scenery with a free hand so long as in your own mind the *personal* are still clearly dominant and, again in your own mind, your scenery remains an accompaniment and subordinate to the action. But the moment you find that you're writing scenery for scenery's sake — stop: for it's going to be dull as an empty stage.

Chapter One of *The Return* [*of the Native*] is an extreme case. I think I'd even go so far as to say that if I'd written it I should have cut it — not without a sense of loss, but with a greater sense of gain to the narrative. But it has this justification that it doesn't interrupt the narrative *because it is at the beginning.* It is the orchestra to the play. But then I confess that on this kind of thing there's no advising. Go your own way. Follow your own instinct. If *you* feel the scenery essential, probably your reason will feel likewise. I'm in a different position, because I don't describe scenery I've seen — only scenery I've imagined, and it has no existence for me as a separate entity, but only as a setting to which my creatures' minds react. You have the virtue of much simpler treatment. You draw upon an observation of familiar things which others have, consciously or subconsciously, shared with you. My only source is imagination; yours is imagination applied to things seen. You're in the great tradition; I'm struggling with an individual newness — which is an agonizing process! I've made progress this morning — a good deal — but I'm always hearing my reader say: 'Where the devil are you getting to?' and wondering whether to go on or pause and explain.

17. TO HILDA VAUGHAN.   *Written from rooms in the Temple occupied by Gordon Alchin and Charles.*

1 Brick Court, Temple, E.C.4
[undated: late in 1922]

YOU know, strange things are happening to me, I think. Long ago, I used to be able to know beforehand when I was going to be able to write — an odd feeling of something gathering, of wanting to say something — the substance of it not yet known. I always used to know. For a long time I've never felt like that. I'd begun to think I'd never feel like that again. My mind was for ever agitated and broken by a thousand things. Now there's a sense of things unifying — flowing together; and a knowledge that all I want is time and quietness and that the thing's coming again, because I'm all happy and the devils have gone home. O it's selfish and vain of me to write of what's going on inside myself, but it's good to come to life — so good; and someone I must tell — and who but you, who are the cause.

18. TO HILDA VAUGHAN.

Brick Court
8 December 1922

YOU blessed one, I know how wretched it is when old work seems dull, but I know, too, that I myself began to develop a fear of dullness in my own writing — an excessive fear that had to be checked (you checked it!) because it's unsettling and makes for bad work. I don't think you, above all, need fear it. Your action always moves forward with simplicity and steadiness; you haven't got my fatal tendency to fall in love with a point of light on the tag of someone's shoe-lace and to write a couple of thousand words about it. As for your doing work in part for my sake — it makes me curiously proud and eager; but, as for your being nervous of my criticism — feeling, as you say, that I should be dissatisfied with sound, competent work — well, there's this to say: I want to feel, and I want you to feel, that we belong to each other as artists, just as we belong to each other as human beings.

If ever you, as most people apparently are, were a little afraid of me when first you knew me, didn't that all change very soon? Weren't you wrong or wasn't I wrong? So it is with the artist in me. The artist and the man are much the same in me, I think: rather a forbidding pride, deep-down an instinctive self-confidence, sometimes flashes of it on the surface that sound like conceit, and sometimes a contrary misgiving born, I think, not of a lessened view of my own powers but a suddenly enlarged view of the greatness of the spiritual world through which the power of an artist goes like a solitary pilgrim across an unmapped continent. It's the thought of that which kills conceit without destroying pride; for to lose pride is to become smaller, but to lose conceit is to see the world bigger. And it seems as strange to me that you should imagine my judgement could hurt you as if you shrank from me in expectation of a blow. You say I am gentle — it is only that our love has shown me a world stronger than strength, a world that can hurt so desperately that there is no sane course in it but the way of gentleness. I feel of you, as a woman, that only in our love for each other and our gentleness and our infinitely patient vision have we any weapons against evil. And in the artist's impersonal world I feel of you as an artist much the same thing. My faith in myself lives or dies in your faith in me. I accept your faith, as I accept your love, as an

Hilda Morgan
From a painting by Christopher Fremantle

Left: With his son Roger

The Dramatic Critic, at *The Times* office

With Hilary Saunders at Nîmes

absolute thing, believing that though I falter and though you will tell me straight enough when I am wrong, that won't shake your faith.

And you, please, must think of me in the same way. Our work is one from now onward. If I criticize your work, I'm criticizing something that is a part of me. The faith in you won't change. I know you have it in you to write splendidly; I know I have it in myself to do likewise. Either of us may or may not succeed, but that doesn't alter the fact. If some work of yours doesn't seem to me 'to come off', I shall feel about it not: 'She's not an artist', but 'Well, *we* haven't done our best work here.' I shall, quietly, regard your successes as my own; so you must let me feel about your failures, too, as I shall feel about my own failures. If I fail I shall think: 'Anyhow, thank God, *she knows* that I'm an artist.' And you must think: '*He knows.*' He does. You see, we've got to be indomitable. We can both prove ourselves great artists if we hold on — it may be through years of stumbling. If you get there first or I do — what does it matter? But, by now, your novel will be in swing again and the despairful mood passed. But if it comes again and you feel suddenly lost in a crowd — well, bless you, there's one hand near you through all the crowds. Don't doubt it. You'll find that, in its despairful moments, it will twine round your fingers often enough — simply feeling at the touch of you: 'Here's someone whose faith is sure and gentle.' Believe that of me too.

19. TO HILDA VAUGHAN.

Brick Court
12 December 1922

THERE'S the scheme for my next novel. I've been thinking about it vaguely a good deal since you first wrote of it, and always with an increasing conviction that it is (1) very difficult (2) very right. Much of the difficulty is cleared up by your letter. You're a very amazing person to be able to think things out ahead like that. I wish I could. The thing that strikes me is that, in a way, you've arrived independently at the idea that I had in my mind when I first called this present novel 'Ballet'. That was the idea of the vivid instant rather than the consecutive story. It's an idea which, in the present novel, has been in part

F

carried out, but mostly abandoned — hence the fact that *My Name is Legion* has such an oddly 'mixed' appearance. But it was abandoned, I may say, because I found I couldn't quite keep it up — the reason being, I think, that I wasn't writing in the first person singular. If I do that, as we both agree I should, that part of the problem should be much easier. The first-person method has, however, immense difficulties peculiar to itself — a temptation to perpetual digression and a loss of the objective point of view in external events. The result is liable to be dullness — Oh fatal word! — but there's something in it this time.

I feel that you're tremendously right; that it is a very big idea, peculiarly suited to my particular variety of literary madness; but I don't forget that everything depends upon attack from *exactly the right angle*. If one begins a hair's breadth wrong, or wavers afterwards, one will be lost in chaos. It's like running across a rim of land with a precipice on either side. And, like running in such circumstances, it's easiest done at high speed. I mean that it ought to be a book, written at white heat in a single mood — with no interruption, no break — short, swift, passionate, clear. It must be a kind of Dostoevsky book — suddenly, by a miracle, shaken into a pattern of surprising beauty — with a certain formality or at any rate a formal rhythm like an ode.

20. TO HILDA VAUGHAN.

Brick Court
25 January 1923

YOU know, bless you, the writing of novels makes for the writing of bad letters, but just for a few days you'll forgive that. I'm properly wound up at last and, instead of writing the book at long, long intervals, I go on thinking of it all the time and come back to it after an interval, not enjoying it I admit, but hungry to get it done. I've got scene after scene in my mind now — packed with tiny detail — and the paper is simply waiting for it all.

The *heat* of writing is an odd thing. To leaders and journalism generally I come dead cold — the brain does its best that's all. But a story teems with imaginings. It always seems alive. When I write that someone walks down stairs I feel the nap of the carpet and the cold of the banisters. Sometimes such a detail goes to paper. More often it doesn't. But I see and feel it all even over the dullest-sounding sentence. It's that which makes writing so intense a joy or so intense a horror. One's own emotions are enough — but to live ten lives all at the same time from the *inside* of each — well, it leaves me limp and a bad letter-writer!

21. TO HILDA VAUGHAN.   (*Charles was now writing leaders for* The Times. *The speech mentioned was the Earl Grey Memorial Lecture, given by Viscount Grey of Fallodon.*)

Brick Court
6 February 1923

I'VE been wasting more time over a leader yesterday and today. Lord Grey delivered a speech on Democracy and Public Opinion. He spoke of public opinion as 'the supreme statesman', which struck me as a good phrase. So with great lightness of heart I began yesterday afternoon to write a leader called 'The Supreme Statesman'. The damnable thing was that I got interested in it. I found myself trying to put into a leader my memory of large volumes of Dicey and Lecky and ideas of my own. Anyhow it became both a jigsaw puzzle and a philosophy and I thought it good so far as it went. . . . So it has gone in. But, because it is vaguely political, I suppose it won't be published. However, if it is you might read it and see whether I've made my point clear. The main point is not at all profound or remarkable — simply that there is need to consider first of all what is the essential problem of our age before we go about trying to solve a thousand little problems piecemeal. What is the future of the representative system, for instance? Are we to struggle to improve it or are we to try to find a substitute for it? And so on. But the leader is fairly pregnant with suggestion — conveyed chiefly by elaborate historical parallels — and it's just possible this may have obscured the main thesis. Anyhow, if it comes out, tell me what you think. I wonder if anyone on *The Times* will ever guess the incredible amount of work represented by one of those half-columns of mine. It's like engraving a jewel and this time I was deep in books before I'd finished. Probably it's a waste of time. Leaders are written 'for the day'. I suppose the best leader is the one which is, with certain other qualifications, most clearly 'written for the day'. Yet I don't

know. I'm inclined to think that why imaginative writers have sometimes found that journalism has ruined them is that they've allowed
themselves to write easily — although they knew, as I know, that they
couldn't write good stuff without intense labour. Of course some
people can; some people are by nature easy writers; but the point is
that, if your imaginative writing is difficult, you probably do yourself
harm by allowing your journalism to be easy. It means writing without
really thinking and that becomes a habit. The reason that my imaginative writing is difficult is that, unlike some fortunate and good writers
who see one thing clearly and unlike bad but fluent writers who in fact
see nothing at all, I see a thousand details at the same time. If I'm describing a face, I suddenly see the back of the head and if I'm describing
what a girl is thinking while she's enjoying doing some wickedness, I
suddenly wonder what she'll think in retrospect of the same thing in
the hour of death. And, seeing so many things, there's the hell of
choosing and rejecting and preventing a multiplicity of ideas from
producing obscurity. (I don't know why I said 'hell' for it's amazingly
exciting and pleasant.) Of course I fail again and again. But when I'm
obscure it's always because I've seen too much, not because I've seen
too little.

I'm afraid all this hasn't much interest or anything much to do with
the leader. I've been more or less thinking aloud, I suppose, and am
a little shocked by the pages I've covered. But it's a kind of vanity in
me — that I like talking about even the absurdest secret methods of my
work to you. I like to feel that, if ever I do write a book worth writing
and give it to you, you'll know just what's gone to the making of it.
It's like the small boy who wants to tell how his engine works. I reflect
that the small boy can be a bore.

22. TO HILDA VAUGHAN.

Shakespeare Hotel
Stratford-on-Avon
14 May 1923

DEAR one, do you know that this is the *third* letter I've written to
you today. As a matter of fact it's not 'today' any longer, for, since the
play, which was *A Midsummer Night's Dream*, I've been sitting over

the fire downstairs talking to Bridges-Adams — whose talk I always find irresistible. And now, here's a bedroom fire, and a dead quiet around me and all the old, magic peace of you with me. And I think of the long hours that are to come when there's going to be no sound near me but the flicker of flame and the scratch of a 'going' pen that's the best of all sounds; and then the knowledge that, one wall away, your pen too is moving and that the men and women you create are living for you as they will be living for me. . . .

Oh and yes, we'll *make* each other work. We'll keep to our time-table once fixed. 8.0 a.m. *up* — I agree. All the morning closed doors and no one to lunch — I agree. But I shall have to be allowed to work at night sometimes. And there's one practical hitch in your plan. It would, I agree, be much better if you could postpone the household dealings until after lunch — but I believe you'll find they'll have to be done earlier than that, firstly because such tradesmen as call do so in the morning and will have to have orders and secondly because some kind of evening meal will have to be provided and the afternoon will be too late to arrange it. However, we can enormously simplify things by having a standing order for many meals. I'm perfectly happy eating the same meals precisely for six weeks on end. Then we could issue a new set of orders for the next six weeks. Anyhow, that's for you to do in your easiest way. And if, one evening, you say there isn't any dinner but there *is* bread and jam, why that's all I want. If I felt that I was eating an elaborate meal that had taken your mind away and made you worried, I should turn against all my favourite dishes — if I have any! That bit of routine will adjust itself — not, thank God, because I shall be 'forbearing' but because, so long as you're happy and we're not too hungry to work, I honestly shan't care or notice.

But if you neglect your own work, I shall descend upon you as I hope you'll descend upon me. I mean, if you write scrappily and let *even pleasant people* interfere with your writing, I shall become a task-master. For I believe in your work and its power to be really great if only you'll shun cranks as you shun the plague. Don't let them creep into your writing. Nearly every twentieth-century crank has been anticipated and has had the truth sifted out of it by the Greeks 2,500 years ago. That's nothing against rediscovery and re-experiment. But, when a thing sounds on the surface like an attractive crank, the way to deal with it is I'm sure to say of it — in *this* order — 'That's a lie. Is it a lie, though? How shall I know if it's a lie? What are the historical parallels? Who has had this idea before? Was it fruitful or sterile? If fruitful, was it fruitful of evil or good? Against what experience was it tested? If the experience was a permanent part of human nature and the idea was broken by it, then the idea was bad. If the experience of the past was not permanent, in what respects does it differ from the experience against which the idea must be tested today?' — And so on. I believe one must apply a scientific method to the analysis of ideas. I go on the basis that, if on the surface they appear to be subversive, then they are bad until logically proved otherwise. If one goes on any other basis, experiment becomes a selfish vanity. One allows one's ignorance to hurt others. Personally, for example, though I know that the present economic system is in many ways bad, I shall defend its essentials until I am convinced of a constructive alternative — which no one, in my opinion, has succeeded in discovering. Hence, politically I'm a conservative because I can see no profitable economic or political revolution. But spiritually and individually I'm revolutionary because I do believe that there is a constructive spiritual alternative. It means that individually men must be born again. And that is a long process — so long that I am sickened by the impatience of economic reformers. They can alleviate distresses; but they can't change the world.

23. TO MRS. BELLOC LOWNDES.   *Written from the first home of Charles and Hilda after their marriage in 1923. (The book mentioned is* My Name is Legion.)

3 More's Garden, Chelsea
1 April 1924

I DELAYED writing to thank you for your long and kind letter, because I hoped from day to day to have Heinemann's verdict. This was longer postponed than I had expected and it was not until this morning that I was summoned to see Mr. Evans.

A curious interview which leaves me in a difficult position. He took the book away to read himself before sending it to the reader. He read the first third of it in a train, 'was more moved by it than by any MS. he had had to read' and 'very nearly sent a telegram to his partner to say that they had found the greatest novel of the last twenty-five years'.

For this reason, whatever view I might take of what he had yet to say, he would publish the book, but —

The 'buts' were many. In the last two-thirds of the book, although there were many passages of 'marvellous force and brilliance', he felt that 'the tremendous tension of the *story* (as opposed to the theme) lapsed'. His interest had weakened or, if not his interest exactly, his excitement. The outline became blurred through constructional faults. He sent it independently to two readers who more or less endorsed his opinion. He is seeing Storm Jameson[1] tomorrow — her enthusiasm having been in general terms — to find out her view of this matter of construction, and he is seeing Edmund Gosse on Friday to try to persuade him to give an opinion on the MS. In the meanwhile I am to think it out for myself and, if I can, obtain other critical opinions.

I said that even if I assumed that he was right, I very much doubted whether any work that I could *now* put into it would do any good, but I would think it all out carefully. He then said something to this effect. 'The suggestion I make is made in your own interest. The early stages of a reputation are vastly important and I believe that, if the construction of the second two-thirds could be strengthened, this book would at once put you in the first rank, but I am afraid that, if it goes out as it is, the reviewers will feel the slump of interest which I felt and will write half-hearted reviews. I may be wrong. It is for you to decide. I won't conceal from you that in our opinion, although this example of your work is imperfect, we believe it is the writing of what I may even call genius. Therefore I won't force your hand or bring any pressure to bear. If at any time up to the last week in August you say to me 'go ahead', I will publish the book as it stands this autumn and do my utmost for it. Therefore, decide simply in your own interest. My advice is to put the book away for several months; get on with new work; then come back to it and in August make your decision.'

So that's how it stands. My own feeling is that, at any rate for a year or so, I can do nothing useful to the book. My choice lies between (1) publishing it now as it is and risking the half-hearted reviewers and (2) writing another book as my first and, perhaps years hence, publishing this in its present or in another form. My instinct is to publish

[1] Margaret Storm Jameson, novelist, then reading for Alfred Knopf, the American publisher. She writes, 'I referred *My Name is Legion* to him, though knowing it would not sell, but sure as sure that here was a writer ... Charles Evans sent me the typescript (for Knopf) telling me it was something I must read.'

now, but I know that, in this matter, I've lost my own power of judgment. I simply don't know whether Evans is right or wrong.

I feel very guilty in troubling you with so long a story of my own concerns, but I thought you might care to know what had happened. If Gosse gives an opinion, that will weigh much with me. Apart from that, my decision is all in the air.

24. TO ROGER BARRETT.   (*Squire was Editor of the*
London Mercury, *1919–34*), poet, writer and critic.

More's Garden
May 1924

J. C. SQUIRE advised me *not* to change my novel, so I've decided not to and have informed Heinemann to that effect.

25. TO VERNON BARLOW, *an Oxford friend who had asked
Charles for advice on his writing.*

More's Garden
25 August 1924

FORGIVE me for having been so long. I read all your articles with pleasures some days ago, but have foolishly postponed writing from one morning to another.

I won't attempt a detailed criticism, for I don't think it necessary, but I can at least state my preferences. I like 'Sur le pont d'Avignon' far the best, because it is simplest, most straightforward, least strained for effect and has most 'matter' in it. It is, in my opinion, very good and interesting writing, and it leads me to believe that your true line is not so much to 'play with words' as to write upon a definite subject upon which you have something definite and personal to say. 'Hasdrubal' I like least, chiefly because I don't like such phrases as 'garments of apparel'. I believe that what is known as polysyllabic humour seldom comes off; at least it doesn't with me, though I know that Wodehouse and Darlington both use it deliberately. But it's the stuff of a broad jester, not of the true essayist. It's very tempting; we all fall into it now and then; even Lamb does and of course Tom Hood is always at it. But you won't find it in Addison or, I think, in Steele, and they are the perfect models for a writer who wants to be amusing and delightful without necessarily making a joke. But take all I say on this subject with several grains of salt, for I am no humourist or I should be a far richer man than I am ever likely to be.

'The French Riviera' is a good piece of journalism. As for the others — 'The Snowman' and 'The Swiss Spring' — I have this to say. Personally, I like them, but then I like Wilde's poems in prose and similar fantasies. But they're dangerous. Anything symbolistic, anything that has 'personifications' of Youth or Poetry or anything else is infernally dangerous. People think it dull; won't be bothered with it; and editors don't like it. The trouble is that it *is* dull unless it is extraordinarily well done, and then it's interesting chiefly to those who are interested in *style* rather than in matter. And the great world isn't interested in *style*, although I believe — I should hang myself if I lost that belief — that, given the matter, style does 'get it across' even to the multitude as no-style cannot. In short, if a good style is applied to a subject that interests them and which they can or think they can understand, then they are won by the style without realizing it. Goldsmith was a perfect stylist. As Johnson said, whatever he did he did better than anyone else. But, before the world his essays are dead because their subject no longer holds the world. But the *Vicar* and *She Stoops to Conquer* have a peculiar immortality because the world can't resist a great stylist when once he gains a hearing. You see, your personifications are half-way between an essay and a sketch — I mean by a sketch a very short story. I believe it much safest to stick to the essay or boldly use fictitious names and endow your people with a tiny personality by a touch of description — just enough to make your readers see your poet as an individual instead of an unseeable abstraction. And one other thing as regards everything you write. Avoid clichés like the plague. 'Phenomenally' is journalese; so is 'fared forth' and 'curiously arresting' and 'to pulse', used as a verb, and so are 'the vanished pomps of yesterday' — that is all right, but has been said too often. When you are describing, think with your eyes either tight shut or wide open: in other words tell simply what you see, or else meditate in your own heart on the spiritual significance of the things seen, and give them if you can an authentic, unborrowed phrase that comes out of *you*. You'll always know the authentic phrase when it comes. It gives you a stab of joy as no borrowed phrase can. But, unless the stab comes — and it can't always — keep to a rigid and austere simplicity of observation. 'The ruined bridge, with its seven arches, hungrily sucked by the deep current of the Rhone . . . ' — that is good, very good, a clear picture truly drawn. And be careful of pseudo-mediaevalisms such as went 'a-warring'. Hewlett could do it, but it's a dangerous affectation.

No, I wouldn't pay a penny for any 'course'. They are mostly uncultured men. They are useful to teach bank-clerks the rules of grammar, but they'll teach no Oxford man anything. Read the masters: that's the only teaching. Avoid eccentrics however brilliant. Wilde, Meredith, Stevenson are all good, but they are thoroughly bad models. Go to English at the fount and then make what you will of it with your own personality. By English at the fount, I mean Steele, Addison, Swift and Defoe and Goldsmith. AND THE BIBLE, in THE AUTHORIZED VERSION. AND THE COLLECTS AND THE LITANY. Use no word that is not contained in those writings unless it is a technical word used to express an idea which they had no need to express. Sometimes you may have to vary their constructions. For example, you may prefer with reason to say 'the same as' although the masters always say 'the same with', even down to Macaulay, I think. But nothing will ever make me write 'different to' instead of 'different from'. The rule is — if in doubt stick to the classical forms. The Fleet Street hacks would call it pedantry if they knew, but they won't know because they have no eyes and certainly no ears. And editors of some worth will notice it and say 'Good God, here's a young man who can write English'.

This is miles longer than I intended. I'm sorry. But I get wound up. And it's too hurried to be an example of any style at all, I'm afraid, except the slovenly colloquial. I envy you your round of visits. I haven't stayed in an old English country house for years and that, particularly if it is a farmhouse, is very near heaven for me. Tell me how you get on from time to time.

26. TO ANNE FREMANTLE (The Hon. Mrs. Christopher
    Fremantle).

More's Garden
28 October 1926

YES, I see your point. But there's journalism *and* journalism. To
write stories and articles on subjects that please you for papers that
please you is one thing. It's extremely good practice; there's nothing
against it and everything to be said in favour of your thus creating a
definite demand for your work and setting yourself a definite task.
Again, to write even on subjects that don't please you for papers that
don't please you is good practice and a first-rate lesson in the difficult
arts of compression and self-control. But this last should be done in
strict moderation and done deliberately for discipline's sake. The fatal
thing is to write what other people want for money *and to depend upon
it.* If you do it badly, you starve; if you do it well (as I hope I do!) you
get more and more work, and more and more paying work, of the
wrong kind. You get half proud of it; you begin to enjoy the quick
recognition, the instant audience, the power; and you forget *Henry
Brocken* [by Walter de la Mare]. That's what I meant. Journalism is
good as a discipline and pocket money, but not for bread and butter.
By all means put some of your eggs, but not all of them, into that vast
waste-paper basket. Unless of course you feel (and it is a reasonable
and by no means a dishonourable feeling) that journalism itself would
satisfy you. In its higher branches, it is a not intolerable profession. It
is a way to power, if you want power. But I don't think you personally
would be satisfied by it. I'm sure the way to choose a profession is this.
Ask yourself: should I be finally content to reach the top of it? Would
you be finally content to be Sir John Simon? — then go to the Bar.
Or to be Prime Minister? — then go into politics. Or to be Garvin
[Editor of the *Observer*] or Editor of *The Times*? — then go into
journalism. When I discovered, too late, after doing extremely well in
the Navy, that I didn't want to win another Battle of Trafalgar, I
promptly left it. I ought to leave journalism for a corresponding reason.
But I never did imagine that I wanted to be Editor of *The Times*. I
went into journalism, I thought, as a side-show to novel and play-
writing: now I am in danger of being eaten up by it. That's what I
want you to beware of. I don't know how much money you will

need to earn. Everything depends on that. If you must earn a good deal, don't journalise for it or you will write nothing else. If, on the other hand, you can please yourself, journalise by all means in moderation, remaining your own master. The test of being your own master is this. Whenever a job is offered you ask yourself 'Shall I be able to do this job and, if an idea suddenly burns in me, be able to *write* on no other subject for six months?' If the answer is 'yes', all's well. But, as an imaginative writer, beware of a job that *commands* your pen, for if one postpones a creative idea it dies. If a fairy comes to your window and asks for admittance and you have to say: 'Please wait until this set of articles is done', the fairy flies away and never returns. And when you have done that a few years the news spreads in fairyland and no more fairies visit you. That is the journalist's parable.

27. TO ANNE FREMANTLE, *on reading a poem of hers.*

More's Garden
29 January 1927

I LIKE it, though I dare say it *is* improper. Would it be possible to improve your 'mouldy' — an ugly word; also to avoid the assonances or half-assonances: 'Else*where* . . . *care* . . . I have you *here* . . . Here your eyes . . . You tear . . . Two thousand *years* . . . very *near* . . . breaks *here* . . .' Some of course stand but there are too many of them. Assonance is lovely when rightly used (*vide* Yeats), but dangerous. Read your poem aloud and you'll hear the trouble. Do you know the best line? It is: 'Nay, heart on heart.' Why? Because a natural generous emphasis falls here on *open* vowels. Open vowels are rare in English; their effect correspondingly great. In Italian they are so many that an Italian poet is in perpetual danger of being treacly. Do read Milton. You have most things, but concentration, austerity and (I think) a full sense of the grandeur of English. Stop reading French for a bit — greatly inferior language! Milton is the master for you.

28. TO ANNE FREMANTLE.

February 1927

TRY a sonnet. Try lots of sonnets. What you need is form. Once you can get that, it will automatically strangle such weeds as loose words and slack phrases. By the way, sensuous poetry has clichés of its own which simply can*not* be repeated. Scented hair and white limbs are two of them. Swinburne has them all when at his worst. Don't read him. Read Shakespeare's sonnets and Milton, MILTON, MILTON.

I am sorry to be such a wet blanket. But I'm not in truth. I shouldn't criticize at all what I didn't think very much worth criticism. You'll forgive me some day.

29. TO ST. JOHN ERVINE, *who had read an early draft of* Portrait in a Mirror, *then called 'First Love'.*

More's Garden
22 January 1928

FAR from 'minding' your criticism, I am extremely grateful for it. That you should trouble to read the book at all is strange; that you should write of it so fully and criticize it with so much attention is delightful and generous.

Yes, my reply is what you expected — with variations. I felt that in my last book I had been running before I could walk. 'First Love' is a self-imposed discipline in craftsmanship, an attempt to do a particular thing (a circumscribed thing) as well as I could do it. What I was aiming at was this: to show the world as Nigel saw it under the influence of his first love. Thus Clare is not, and cannot be, seen as you or I, cold observers of the general world, would see her. Nigel does not see the truth of her — and I have tried to suggest that the old man writing the narrative was aware of the distortion of his own youthful view. Now I suggest that under the influence of first love one sees not a woman, but some kind of goddess. The girl herself is relatively immaterial. She happens to have sprung up in the flesh to answer to the name of our own imaginative ideal. What we love then is not that girl, but a personification of our own passionate· aspiration. It's as if, walking with the sun behind us, we saw our own shadow thrown upon a bank of mist, but did not know it for our own shadow. Thus Clare is of necessity nebulous — though perhaps I have not made her nebulous in the right way; and thus the men, with whom Nigel is *not* in love, are seen clearly, as you and I might see them.

This is not a defence, but an explanation. I admit the limitation, but my point is that the limitation was self-imposed. What I hope for from this book is that, working on a small canvas, I have learnt the elements of my craft and discovered for myself the beginnings of a prose style. I have been, in short, making tools for myself and learning the use of them. Now, if I can get peace for it, I'm going to write something very different and, I hope, fuller and richer.

Thank you again, I do value both your praise and your damning — and the more because I know that we approach the whole business of writing from opposite angles and that therefore I'm probably a trying brute for you to read — just as Bennett and Wells are trying to me because their attitude of mind is foreign to me. I can admire, but seldom enjoy them. But that is wandering from the point into more chatter. All I really wanted to say was how grateful I am.

30. TO ROGER BARRETT.

Hotel Angleterre, Corfu
3 May 1929

IT'S good to hear you liked the *Portrait*, though I should like to have you near and hear you slash at its faults. Particularly I want to hear your and Margaret's comments on the conclusion. It is the only point that any reviewer has attacked. The Church papers — R.C., C. of E., and fancy religions — all praise the book, but put in a saving clause that the end is 'a pity' — simply I suppose because they were bound to be a little shocked. But the *Lit. Supp.*, the *Observer* and the *Quarterly Review* said either that the end was faulty, or that they didn't understand it. There is, I think, something genuinely wrong — not in the psychology, which appears to me to be true enough, but in my having permitted myself a 'set-scene' of high emotion in a book which elsewhere studiously avoids such scenes and the whole virtue of which is its evenness and quietness. I saw the difficulty before I wrote the 'bedroom scene'. But, since what happened in the bedroom produced profound psychological results, I could not avoid an account of it without leaving a yawning gap in the story. In other words, having advanced so far I was compelled to take the fence or obviously funk it. So I took it — I think successfully so far as success was possible. The bedroom scene seems to me to be a genuine *tour de force*. The fault lies in this — that, in this particular book, any *tour de force*, any fireworks, is out of place. However, it's not for me to pick holes in my own work. What I now feel about the book as a whole is:

(1) it is a successful experiment in small scale work.

(2) it has proved to me what I wanted to prove — that I can be a craftsman and preserve evenness of texture and avoid extravagance.

(3) it was a very valuable technical exercise as a corrective to the faults in *My Name is Legion*.

(4) that, though it has served its purpose, it is really only a minor work and that I must go beyond it into much deeper and more turbulent and less specialised water: wherein, God knows, I may drown as I did in *My Name*. But I have a better chance of sailing on an even keel than I had before I went through the discipline of writing the *Portrait*.

It is now in its 12th thousand in England. In America it has done no good and is still under 5,000, partly because the American reviewers, who have the minds of Sunday-school teachers quickened a little by an aphrodisiac, complain that it is 'too well written' and 'is lacking somewhat in primitive urge', and partly because the nearer one keeps to the classical simplicity of Goldsmith and Steele, the more difficult it is for Americans to understand you. . . .

What I have in mind to do now is a story with my days in Holland as a background. The point is that life in Holland then was, in the strangest way, a life within life — a sort of spiritual island, and so a delusion. I want to tell the story of an English officer (temporary), naturally a scholar and philosopher, who had all his life — for the sake of his responsibilities to his widowed mother and sisters and because he had to earn his living as best he could — denied his nature and been harassed by the solid, ordinary necessities and ties of the world. Living in the Dutch countryside, free for once of all responsibility and pressure of worldly circumstances, he thought he saw an opportunity to live the contemplative life that the ordinary work-a-day world had denied him. He was filled, moreover, for various reasons, with a feeling of guilt, of having in the past betrayed himself in a thousand timorous and worldly comprises. Here was his chance —

> *Be still, my soul, be still; the arms you bear are brittle* . . .
> *Be still, be still, my soul; it is but for a season;*
> *Let us endure an hour and see injustice done.*
>
> *Ay, look: high heaven and earth ail from the prime foundation;*
> *All thoughts to rive the heart are here, and all are vain:*
> *Horror and scorn and hate and fear and indignation —*
> *Oh, why did I awake? When shall I sleep again?*

And:

> Grant we beseech thee, merciful Lord, to thy faithful people, *pardon and peace*, that they may be cleansed from all their sins, and serve thee with a *quiet mind*; through Jesus Christ our Lord, Amen.

So here he is trying to establish within himself a quiet mind. He has a natural gift for languages. In the Fort he has mastered Dutch. The Baron had an old uncle, Willem van Kisten [changed to van Leyden], now dead, who was a recluse and generally considered half-mad. Willem left behind him an abundance of miscellaneous MSS., all in Dutch, some in plain Dutch, but the greater part (because the old fellow was extremely odd) in a variety of codes and personal short-hands. No one has troubled to decode them, all the van Kistens saying: 'Poor old Uncle Willem — of course he was mad.' But the MSS. are preserved in the Castle library, and Sterne [changed to Lewis Alison] — the Englishman — gets permission to work at them. His idea is simply to provide himself with a mechanical discipline for so many hours a day — to establish a routine on the monastic principle; but he discovers, as he decodes, that, though he may have been 'mad', old Uncle Willem was no fool. The MSS. — stories, essays, apothegms, random comments, fables, ravings — supply side-lights on the narrative as it unfolds and I shall quote from Uncle Willem when it suits me. Among the MSS. is a Dutch translation (in code) of *Paradise Lost* so that Sterne is continually in touch with Milton's poem — (you will see why presently).

Now, just as he is beginning to establish 'a quiet mind' within himself, he is gradually — gradually, for he is a mature, resisting man — drawn into love for an English girl much younger than himself: imagine a beautiful Madame E[lout] in her youth.

This girl's history is briefly this: Her father was an English country gentleman, her mother a Dutchwoman — a pretty, arrogant, snobbish creature of good, but not noble birth. The girl (Alison) [changed to Julie] spent her childhood in England until her father died, when she returned to Holland with her mother. The mother married Baron van Kisten van Evensvoort. He was much older than she; a widower with a family who was now marrying to please his own desire and marrying, by the van Kisten standard, beneath him. Hence the girl Alison was curiously isolated; an English girl among Dutch step-brothers and sisters and step-relations of all sorts who were mildly resentful of her because they disapproved of the old Baron's re-marriage. In this isolation she grew up. Shortly before the war she made, by her mother's snobbish and ambitious contrivance, a *marriage de convenance* with a young German aristocrat and officer named von Streumarck [changed to von Narwitz]; lived with him a few weeks; then, when war came and he went to fight and she was a strange English girl in a German community, returned at her husband's wish to her own people in Holland. So here she is in Evenvoort [Enkendaal] Castle again — a young grass-widow. Her German husband means very little to her; she knows that he is a gallant soldier and a great gentleman who (she has been almost surprised to discover) loves her; but she has never loved him, and, as time passes, he becomes more and more unreal to her. His letters from the front, full of suffering, seem to her the letters of a man she scarcely knows and will probably never see again. So she and the Englishman fall in love — but *not*, so to speak, 'with a view to a permanency'. The other two Englishmen go off to The Hague or somewhere, and when the cold winter comes the Baron invites Sterne to be his guest in the Castle (as we were at Roseneath).[1] So Sterne goes on working in the library in the tower; Alison's room is above the library in the tower; there is a connecting passage (supposed to be closed); and they become definitely lovers, saying to themselves: 'What we do now is cut off from exterior responsibilities. We are living a life within a life.' They imagine their love to be a completely detached thing. Someday the war will end. Someday the girl may go back to her husband, who will never know of this liaison. Someday Sterne will go back to being a solicitor. Meanwhile . . . They both realise that for them ever to be

[1] The dower-house of Rosendaal.

G

husband and wife is hopelessly difficult. They do not even contemplate it. They would not match each other in tastes or position in the ordinary work-a-day world. So to the girl this is a *temporary* adventure; to the man it is all of a piece with his dominant idea that life in Holland is detached — is 'bracketed in the narrative of life'.

And all this is, of course, a delusion. There is no escape from life. Life always catches you in the end. The German husband, broken by the war, a splendid, pathetic, tragic figure, with nothing in his life but his love for this girl who has become for him an idol and a symbol of that spiritual stillness which he has achieved at the core of his suffering, is invalided out of the army and comes to Holland. The isolation of 'life within life' is broken down; the lovers' false illusion is shattered; like Adam and Eve, they see their own nakedness. Two things happen: the girl, with every instinct of pity and protection aroused in her, wants to give a full answer to this husband who loves her and depends on her and has suffered so much; she is bitterly ashamed of her betrayal of him which, to the other side of her nature, has seemed so light, so detached a thing; she wants to confess, for her husband is on the edge of madness. And the Englishman, because the German has acquired an extraordinary spiritual quality by his suffering, becomes deeply attached to him. The point here is that the German, who is Suffering personified, the crucified being if you will, 'draws all men unto him'. The girl sees that there is no love except through suffering; the Englishman that there is no stillness of soul except it be stilled by suffering. Only anguish can temper the brittle arms of the spirit and only through crucifixion — not through a flight from life — is there pardon and peace. The German has won what they could not win. They must part, and keep their secret and inwardly profit by it.

But then the German discovers the truth. He says nothing, but she knows he knows. Then an incident occurs that forces him to speak — (the dramatic climax). His outbreak of despair; his spasm of cruelty which she suffers uncomplaining; then his relapse into silence. She wants to keep him; to make him understand that now she is wholly his; but she knows, with horror, that he is contemplating his own death. This is her agony. And at last, when the break up of the German Empire is added to his knowledge that his wife has betrayed him, the German kills himself, for all his hope is gone.[1] The lovers are left, free to marry, free to satisfy themselves, outwardly with a 'happy ending' and yet with the

[1] In the final version Rupert von Narwitz dies of his wounds.

life and death of this tormented man lying between them — their only
enduring riches being their knowledge of him. And so they go out to
face together a life of infinite doubt and danger — to try to bring their
'temporary', merely passionate love into line with the world and their
experience.

And this is where *Paradise Lost* comes in for the last time:

> *They looking back, all th' eastern side beheld*
> *Of Paradise, so late their happy seat,*
> *Waved over by that flaming brand, the Gate*
> *With dreadful faces thronged and fiery arms.*
> *Some natural tears they dropped, but wiped them soon;*
> *The world was all before them, where to choose*
> *Their place of rest, and Providence their guide.*
> *They, hand in hand, with wand'ring steps and slow.*
> *Through Eden took their solitary way.*

This has run to a terrible length, for I have added to my original note;
and even now it sounds crude and abrupt. But realize that the note was
written as a reminder to myself — not for other people's reading. I
like the theme of the book. It is rich and full. It will be for a long time
a very quiet story — light sketches of character gradually filled in as
the theme is stated and re-stated; then a very difficult central section
while the man and the girl are lovers — difficult because their love,
though passionate, must not be merely greedy, and, though 'temporary', must not be merely callous or lacking in a spiritual quality of a
peculiar kind; then a deepening and darkening of the whole narrative
when the German — who is the key to the book — appears; and finally
a conclusion that is at once ironic and gentle — a suggestion of the
extraordinary difficulty of the struggle that is before this man and this
woman when we leave them. I am sorry for many reasons to omit the
Fort.[1] It was a period of great fascination. But to begin so far back would
leave the book's theme unstated for too long and I am bound to sacrifice a direct narrative of the Fort. But some of it will appear in retrospect and some of it — the mental aspect of it — will be transferred to
a different scene. . . .

I won't continue this letter now. But I will write something less
damnably literary before I leave Corfu.

---

[1] C. M. changed his mind about this. The first part — i.e. the first five chapters
— of *The Fountain* is entitled 'The Fort'.

[Postscript.] Yes, I think your father might have liked the *Portrait* — anyhow the manner of it — though he would have argued against the end, I think.

31. TO HILDA MORGAN, *with further reference to* The Fountain.

5 April 1930

I'VE been worrying and worrying about the end of my book and un-certainty about it has been holding me up. I can't really account to my-self for their deciding to marry. It seems to me rather revolting in a way, with the ghost of the dead man between them. My theory was originally that in some mysterious way his death bound them together and made their marriage necessary, but I can't see it that way now. I have tried to think it out by asking myself: Why did he marry? Why did she? The answer in his case is fairly easy. He had always loved her subconsciously since he was a child; he saw her now isolated and miserable with the guilt of having allowed her husband to go to his death upon her; and he married her under a compulsion of conscience combined with a longing (not desire now) to fulfil the yearning of his childhood and early years. But why did she marry him? Had she grown, while his mistress, to desire him? If so, how do we reconcile that with her attitude towards her husband after he came from Ger-many? It looks to me as if her motives, if they are to be credible, must be pretty unpleasant. Will you try to meditate on the subject. You have a way of unravelling these tangles. When I think ahead, without a pen in my hand, I think in circles.

32. TO LOUIS GILLET, *a most active member of the editorial board of* La Revue des deux mondes.

More's Garden
13 August 1930

MANY things have prevented me, to my shame, from writing to thank you for your too generous letter about my book and for your gift of a volume from your own pen. I have been out of London for a week on the business of *The Times* and, since I returned, great men,

whose obituary notices it fell to me to write, have been threatening to
die; with this unhappy consequence that I have seldom left my desk
until three in the morning and have started work again at nine. With
this I have been combining an attempt, I think not unsuccessful after
many battles and failures, to make progress in my new novel — an
account of a man's endeavour to lead a life of scholarship and contemplation and of the assaults of the world and the flesh upon him.

   In the midst of all this, I have read nothing else but I have been reading your essays with the utmost enjoyment. I do not presume to praise
their style; I know only that their French delights me and has been a
joyful relief from too much English flowing and flowing day and
night from my own inkpot. Your essays on Shaw particularly interested
me, for I have often wondered what effect *Back to Methuselah* and
Saint Joan made on a French mind. My view of *Methuselah* is that the
first and last parts contain nearly all that is valuable in it; the caricatures
of Asquith and Lloyd George I found silly and tedious. And *Saint
Joan*, though the most popular of Shaw's plays and a brilliant aggregate of theatrical devices, has always infuriated me. Shaw knows much,
but he does not understand and is temperamentally incapable of understanding a mediaeval and Catholic saint. He thinks that the words
'saint' and 'reformer' have the same meaning, and his St. Joan is, in
essence, a political agitator from Protestant Ulster.

   But, in England, Shaw touches, or has touched, us all so closely that
our opinion of him is still in the melting-pot, violently stirred by our
own prejudices, and your calm, detached judgment of him, expressed
with so brilliant a spirit and a freedom from English hatred on the one
hand and English idolization on the other, is wonderfully refreshing and
satisfying. And you see Virginia Woolf in perspective. Here she is at
present either unknown or a 'cult' — and that is perilous to the
balance of criticism. Thank you for having given me so much pleasure
and enlightenment, and thank you again for your too generous praise
of my book.

33. TO HILDA MORGAN.

London
23 August 1930

I HAVE been working very hard at my novel. I have done practically nothing else, with the exception of my Malvern expedition, night or day. As a result the whole of the Fort prologue has been entirely re-written and the part about the tunnel and the leaving of the Fort, which I hadn't written at all, is written now all but a couple of thousand words or less. This re-writing has been a horrible labour and it has meant prolonging the Fort to 30,000 words, but it has been worth the trouble. Lewis is now twice the man he was; the philosophy has been deepened; and all the action and the minor characters (a few new ones have been introduced) are more vivid and lively and representative of the composite life of the Fort than they were. I have also succeeded by indirect wiles — principally the reports of Ballater who visits the Castle — in giving a preliminary impression of the Castle and particularly of Julie which will, I hope, provoke the reader by promise of a feminine interest and certainly is valuable as a preparation for what is to come. Also, as a result of having the book continuously in my mind, I have suddenly hit on an idea which has always been inherent in the story but has never clearly presented itself to me before.

This morning, when I was crawling into bed at 3.0 a.m., completely played out, I was thinking vaguely of the scenes between Julie and her German husband that lie before me — still distantly alas! — and I saw a scene in which the husband, knowing by now of her conduct with Lewis, has an outburst against her and then, with a sudden power of second-sight, reveals to her, and to the reader, the whole secret of Julie. What she is is a spiritual courtesan. She has a power of making herself the spiritual complement of whatever man she happens to be interested in, or attached to, or in love with at a given time. When she is at a tennis-party or a dinner among frivolous young men, she *is* frivolous and shallow; when she is married to the German, who is by nature a man whose whole life is concentrated in symbols, she becomes his symbol of all that he desires and honours in life; when she first meets Lewis at Ekdaal [later Enkendaal], she is just sparkling and vain because she still thinks of him as her 'schoolmaster' and he is nothing to her, but, as time passes and her own desires prompt her, she begins to take an interest in his work and an understanding interest (witness the scene in the library when they discuss the seventeenth century),[1] but, because she doesn't consciously desire him yet, she is still something of a dilettante and he is aware of her superficiality. But when she loves him and becomes his mistress, she becomes his full complement. He is a man of deep spirituality and deep sensuality and she responds to both aspects of him. Because she is a spiritual courtesan, he feels her to be, not merely the mistress of his body, but an inspiration of his work, a condition of it. She throws light on the dark places of his thought and he feels himself moving towards his goal as he has never moved before. Then, when her husband returns and the liaison is broken off, she responds naturally to her husband's necessities and her whole thought is to console and quieten and compensate him.

All this her husband sees in a flash of insight. And the view of her as a spiritual courtesan — that is, a woman who changes the depths of her individuality in accordance with the changing demands of men — connects up and explains the whole book. It explains:

> Why the German, knowing what he did, could yet think of Lewis with honour and compassion, not with angry jealousy.
>
> Why Julie could move from Lewis to her husband and from her husband to Lewis again.
>
> And, above all, why Lewis married her — not in duty merely (a dull reason that has always troubled me), not to save her from scandal (a conventional reason that has likewise troubled me), but because she had become a spiritual necessity to him — a kind of food of his mind. There is, too, the other reason, a very strong and good one, which was part of the original theme — namely, that Julie and Lewis are bound together by their guilt. This reason stands, but it is, I think, enormously strengthened by the idea that she has become spiritually necessary to him.

And the idea has other advantages. The fact that the German, instead of being blinded by physical jealousy, has sympathy and insight enough to perceive this profound truth of his wife's nature greatly strengthens my view of him as an almost Christlike being. His understanding is that of Christ and the psycho-analysts — 'neither do I condemn thee'.

And the idea knits together all the diverse phases of Julie, making her, I think, a unique and coherent character.

[1] *The Fountain*, 'The Castle', ch. IV.

And finally the idea strengthens Lewis — showing him, not simply as a would-be contemplative who surrendered to his pleasures, but a man who finds in Julie a new spiritual impulse by which he is fatefully bound to her.

I may be all wrong. It may sound nonsense to you. But at the moment I feel that here is a master-key to all the problems of the book.

A minor trouble of mine at the moment is that I have read and written so unceasingly that my eyes have begun to trouble me. So this afternoon, instead of going on with my work, I walked with Roger to the Tate Gallery. My eyes ached all the way there, but are rested and quite comfortable now. I went and looked at Walter Crane's 'Renaissance of Venus', which is extraordinarily like you. . . . It is lovely and so are you. . . .

I've suddenly remembered that you may be writing yourself, in which case all this about my book ought not to have been written to disturb you, but you did ask for news of the book, which I had been carefully abstaining from. You had better take warning by this. When you ask for things from which I have been carefully abstaining, you are in peril of receiving more than you ask or deserve!

34. TO HILDA MORGAN.

More's Garden
11 April 1931

IT is after midnight and I am going to bed so that I may keep to my routine of breakfasting at nine and doing three hours at least before lunch. . . .

For at last it flows. I didn't tell you, but I've had a wretched struggle, often not more than a page surviving of a day's labour. It was all stiff and awkward. I could *not* bring about or conduct the first meeting of Lewis and Narwitz as I wanted to; but tonight at last Narwitz began to talk. It is *just* talk. Nothing happens, and you being a real story-teller may object; but I think you will allow this; for unless I'm mad there's real substance in the talk — substance of the kind that would make Lewis think: 'Here is a man wiser and greater than myself.' The conversation, which is to end with Julie's coming from the house and the dramatic clash of their being together, all three, for the first time, is only half done, but I have in my mind pegs for its later development and unless anything goes wrong it ought to flow tomorrow. That's why I'm writing even your letter now — so as to have nothing else to think about but the book.

There's really nothing else to write of except my joy in hearing this morning that you were really feeling better and writing. . . .

I don't want a holiday yet. I'm quite content to wait for the autumn if things work out that way. I want to finish this book and you to have so far broken the back of yours that we can take a holiday without any kind of duty to write at all. I should probably write a little in any case — I can't be happy without it — but something off the track; a poem; some stories; not a big novel for a little while. . . .

35. TO HILDA MORGAN.

More's Garden
25 May 1931

MY father, who is at a loose end, has just rung up to suggest Lord's today, but we have decided that Bank Holiday is not the moment, so I am to stay and work today and go a-cricketing tomorrow, if fine. Wherefore, though I should like to chatter, I must follow Lewis and Julie across the moors, whither they are going on a hot September afternoon to a fire in the woods that has just been signalled by the church bell. It is several miles away and the fire will be almost out before they get there. On the way home, they are overtaken by the thunderstorm that has been threatening for days. They go into a dark pine wood for shelter and there, with the two of them driven together by rain, the Lewis–Julie theme, which has lapsed in favour of the Narwitz theme, is picked up again and the way is prepared for Narwitz's final illness and death — not so far off the end now, thank God.

Be as happy as you can and come back when you feel it's all right to come, bless you.

36. TO HILDA MORGAN.

More's Garden
28 July 1931

I HAVEN'T moved from my desk since last I wrote to you except for an occasional withdrawal to bed and I've seen no one but big Roger,[1] so there's little to write about except my book. I have almost entirely rewritten the prologue and think I've been rather clever about it. There are three things difficult to convey: the family retrospect; the nature of the history Lewis proposed to write; the appearance and geography of the Fort and the idea of a mixed crowd gathered within it. In the first version (which, incidentally, was already the second!), the narrative went heavy whenever I touched any of these things because I gave them to the reader in too large doses. Now I've let them come little by little, strung on to a string of scenes and incidents and conversations. I have still a nasty chunk to do before I get on to the tunnel. In this chunk my only important incident is the visit of the van Kesterens [changed to the van Leydens] and I have somehow to convey the passage of months without being dull about it. When this is over and the tunnel passage is written I shall then be complete (all but one tiny scene in Julie's tower music-room) as far as Lewis's going away from Enkendaal — i.e. the end of book one. It looks to me as if, in Roger's typescript, this would work out to some 60,000 words, which horrifies me. However, *Clayhanger* is 250,000 and the Clayhanger trilogy is 500,000. I've been reading *Clayhanger* at meals with the object of observing how Bennett makes the transitions from book to book in a trilogy. It is an instructive work, particularly to me, its method being so violently opposed to that of George Moore.

37. TO MISS WOOD, *an acquaintance from Charles's Oxford days.*

More's Garden
19 August 1931

MY experience is that a man who is going to write will have written a great deal (though he may not have published it) before he is 22, and I assume that Mr. Turner has done so. In that case, his first step is to

[1] Roger Barrett.

try to sell it — the practical course being to get a little volume called *The Writers' and Artists' Year Book*, published by Black at 3*s*. 6*d*., to study in it the particular requirements of each magazine, and to go on sending his typescripts in until some of them are accepted. To have had work printed in papers of repute is the beginning of everything and the attempt costs nothing but persistence and postage.

The next thing is for him to be clear in his mind about what he wants. Does he wish to be a writer of books or to be a journalist? If he wants to be a writer of books he must, unless he has private means or makes an immediate and very big success with a first novel, keep himself meanwhile. This he can do by entering some other profession and gradually emancipating himself from it, or, if he has the courage and confidence and no wish to marry, by living dead poor and just writing. Any profession will do which gives him any leisure at all. Mine was at first the Navy; then *The Times*. To me journalism is the bread and butter which enables me to write novels in my own way and without any thought for their sales. The Bar or any other profession would have served my purpose equally well.

If he wishes to become a journalist — either as an end in itself or as a means to other writing — then advice ceases to be of much use. I don't personally imagine that schools of journalism are much good. The difficulty is to get any kind of beginning. The series of newspaper amalgamations that have happened in recent years have greatly narrowed the opportunities and London is swarming with experienced journalists with nothing to do. Introductions are almost useless, for the jobs simply don't exist. When anything falls vacant it is snapped up instantly; you can get nothing except by being on the spot and knowing people. Further, I would say this. That journalism, as it is today, is no life for a *writer* or gentleman except on a few papers. *The Times*, the *Telegraph*, the *Sunday Times*, the *Observer* almost exhaust the list in London, though there are a few good provincial papers such as the *Manchester Guardian* and the *Yorkshire Post*. The only way for Mr. Turner to get in (unless he has a friend who can put him in) is to try to live by free-lancing and watch and watch for a staff job. It is all luck — the start; the rest is work and ability and more luck. And even the staff jobs, except on the three or four solid papers, are hopelessly precarious. Of course if Mr. Turner is set on being a journalist nothing will stop him. He will go on bombarding editors with contributions and live, however poor, in London until he can get his foot in. But unless journalism *itself* is his ultimate ambition I believe that he would do better to choose some other profession as maintenance while building up a reputation as a serious writer — partly because journalism is an unqualified profession and therefore wildly overcrowded, partly because (as I know) it needs a prodigious self-control to earn your bread and butter by one sort of writing and to satisfy your soul with another. Whereas a crossing-sweeper can turn to writing with relief at the end of a day's sweeping, it is very hard to sit down to write your novel at the end of a day's journalism.

If he can really write and really studies the requirements of particular papers he won't have any prolonged difficulty in selling his work. There is a great demand for stories, and publishers are shouting for novels and biography. I think these courses lie open:

1. To live at home and *write books*.
2. To live poor in London and *write books*.
3. To write books and meanwhile struggle to sell contributed articles and stories.
4. To have another profession for bread and butter.

No. 1. requires means and a vast self-confidence.

No. 2. requires nothing but devotion, poverty and genius.

No. 3 requires a little means; and courage and ability.

No. 4 sounds like cowardice but I don't think 'another profession' is, from the writer's point of view, any more disturbing or time-absorbing than journalism.

When I was coming down from Oxford, I was very proud of myself as a writer. I had had works published — chiefly poems! — in *The Times*, the *Fortnightly*, the *English Review*, the *Westminster Gazette*, etc. I went to see Garvin with an introduction. He said 'Yes, you have shown that you can write. Now go away, put your pride in your pocket, get work accepted by the magazine-page of the *Daily Mail* and so prove that you are a journalist.' Which I did. It was hard then; it is much harder today. The real question — the only question that matters — is: can Mr. Turner write (a) books (b) acceptable journalism. I don't believe anyone can teach him but himself. Why don't his people gave him a tiny allowance for a time and let him take a room in London and prove himself? If he has the stuff in him he will sell some of it. In a couple of years he will know in his own heart whether it is worth while going on. He might meanwhile take his Bar exams and be called to the Bar, which is of some value even if you don't practice. I'm sorry to have nothing but advice to offer; but writing is a profession in which one makes one's way and no one can help much.

38. TO HILDA MORGAN.

4 December 1931

I HAVE provisionally made arrangements for my after-Christmas escape and I joyfully imagine myself wandering through Buckinghamshire with you. I like it better in winter there for some reason. Icy going upstairs; but how good the fires are, and bare trees and road puddles, and what a delight is bed — when one (or two) gets there.

What is more I'm on the track of a new story that I want to think about and discuss. Goethe, I believe, used it in something called *Die Neue Melusine* and I have put Amie [Anne Fremantle], who is going to the London Library today, on to the job of finding out what Goethe did say. It's the old story of a man who fell in love with a beautiful lady of the dwarf kingdom. When she put a ring on his finger, he too became a dwarf and lost consciousness of his previous existence and was blissfully happy. Then slowly he became vaguely aware that he had once been a giant — that is, of the existence of an ideal or transcendent Self — Goethe's consciousness of his own independent genius — and so at last, as Goethe always did, though he loved the lady-dwarf, he broke the ring and escaped.

Now that seems to me to be one of the great legends of the world. Of course I may find that what Goethe has written makes my use of it impossible, but there are many ways in which it might be used. It might, for example, be used for its symbolism alone, in a modern story with no actual fantastications about dwarfs and rings. Or it might be both modern *and* fantastic, like *Lady into Fox*. And if it is to be this, one still has to choose between various treatments. Perhaps the man might start in our world and move to an invented dwarf world. Perhaps the dwarf world might be our world and he be conscious of a previous 'gigantic' existence. Perhaps he might move between the two. Perhaps it's a novel. Perhaps it's just a story that might go into a volume with my Portofino story about the Double-Headed Jewel. I don't know yet. But I think we are on a track — aren't we?

39. TO MRS. ROBERT MENNELL, *showing the beginnings of* Sparkenbroke.

More's Garden
22 February 1932

BLESS you! What a good letter to have. I do love people who tell me what *bits* they have liked and disliked. I can learn something either way.

What next? More pertinently — when next? I have a big American contract for three novels. One is matured in my head. It has been brewing there for six months. Another exists vaguely as a theme. Two or three more are still in embryo. Anyhow the 'mature' one is now ready to be begun. I'm struggling to get 2 or 3 weeks ahead with weekly articles (not for *The Times*). Then I shall cut myself off from domesticities for a fortnight and get the novel founded. That will be something. I can't describe it except in the crudest terms. It is to be about (1) a girl of character — solid upper middle class — not 'flighty', with a genuine sense of duty and responsibility. Not selfish or sensual. No frills. *But* devastatingly beautiful. I mean no less than that she is one of the great beauties of the world.

(2) A country doctor who loves her, whom she marries, to whom she owes a thousand things. An attractive, sound, unselfish man. Like her — without frills. Character for character they are splendidly in accord.

But

(3) There is a man of genius. A poet. Lord Sparkenbrook [later Sparkenbroke]. Something of Aldous Huxley in him; something of Lord Byron. Passionate, arrogant on the surface; underneath, deeply sensitive. He seduces the girl before she marries. Then, returning, seduces her again. In all else she is mistress of herself. With Sparkenbrook, helpless. But, having character, she does finally break with him, refusing to see him again. Then he, who had regarded her hitherto as a brilliant plaything or side-issue to be taken up and dropped at his pleasure, falls desperately, desperately in love with her. He comes back to her with a new proposition — to let his world go for her, to run away, abandon his wife upon whose wealth the preservation of his estate depends, in brief — to burn all his boats. Now what will she do — go or stay. I have a lovely final scene that you shall have some day.

It's really a study of passion as an insanity — the force that *can* sweep everything — the character of the girl, and the unscrupulousness of the man, right off its feet. Also a study of a girl of real integrity in the grip of it. Also a very elaborate study of the inward, secret lovableness of a man who is outwardly a cynical rake and of the psychology of a modern man of genius.

I didn't mean to write all this — but, having begun, I found that it was clearing up my own mind, as I went on. Forgive me!

40. TO M. LOUIS BONNEROT, *a scholar and an authority on Matthew Arnold, with whom Charles now began a lifelong friendship.*

> More's Garden
> 1 March 1932

I AM extremely grateful for your letter and for your suggestion that you should write about my work in the *Revue Anglo-Américaine*. I would most willingly give you copies of *The Gunroom* and of *My Name is Legion* if they were available, but both are out of print, and, since the success of my later novels, they have become 'collector's' pieces and are extremely rare. *The Gunroom* in particular is rare for two reasons: first that, as it is a criticism of the Navy and is officially frowned upon, many copies naturally went to sea, they have just vanished as books do that find their way into ships. To save you from error I may add that, contrary to a general legend, *The Gunroom* was not officially suppressed nor was it withdrawn from publication. What happened was that the book was selling and beginning to cause a stir when suddenly, in twenty-four hours, it vanished from the booksellers and from the circulating libraries. It was still possible for a persistent buyer to buy it from the publisher, but the ordinary means of distribution ceased to be available to it. How this was brought about I do not know, but, as the Navy has a Secret Service, I draw my own conclusions.

I hope you will regard *The Gunroom* and *My Name is Legion* as juvenilia and little more. I have deliberately refrained from reprinting them. *The Gunroom* is, I think, a good book in so far as it gives an account of the lives of midshipmen in the Royal Navy. These parts were written with blood and reflect my own experience. But the love-story was foolishly added and is extremely bad.

My Name is Legion is a curious book. I am proud of having imagined
it and of many terrible passages contained in it. But it is extremely
uneven and structurally imperfect. The explanation is that I took more
than four years to write it. During that time, I took my degree at
Oxford, which was a diversion, and — much more important — I
went through periods of profound personal bliss and misery. These
experiences changed my whole attitude to life and threw me into emotional turmoil, with this consequence — that the man who finished *My
Name is Legion* was not the same as the man who began it.

I am sending you copies of both books, but I beg you with all my
heart to return them at your leisure. They are the only copies I have
and I can obtain no more in England.

41. TO ROGER BARRETT.

More's Garden
1 April 1932

I HAVE thought often of you all during the troubles in Shanghai.
The feeling here is — thank heaven it's so far away that we needn't
trouble yet! — and even the Labour pacifists don't know whether to
stand on a Japanese or a Chinese leg. A certain smug complacency has
fallen on the country since the National Government took power and,
because gilt-edge are rising and the dollar falling, there are people
optimistic enough to think that we are out of the financial wood —
which emphatically we are not.

The Fountain prospers. The reviews were better even than I had
dreamed of and the book sells. It has now sold 27,000 — just double
Portrait in a Mirror. . . .

I too wonder whether I ought not soon to think of novels only, for
I am now dead certain of a minimum of £3,000 for any novel I write.
But I'm doubtful about it. I don't like *depending* on novels. It's so
damned easy to go out of fashion and anyhow I hate to feel that it
makes any financial odds how soon I produce a book or how unpopular its theme may be. I chose in *The Fountain* what I thought was inevitably an unpopular subject — philosophy, contemplation and
what-not. It seems to have touched some personal and religious streak
in people; so it sells; but that's chance — not to be relied upon. I am
getting masses and masses of letters from strangers. The interesting

thing is that *our* great fear — the priggishness of Lewis — hasn't troubled them. Some go all out for Narwitz; some for the Baron; but they all seem content with Lewis. Julie is the heart of the controversy. *Men* adore her; they write to me what are as near as nothing love letters to Julie! But women are divided. Some dislike Julie quite a lot.

42. TO MARGARET STORM JAMESON, *referring to her novel* A Richer Dust.

> More's Garden
> 5 April 1932

MY book may be a flash in the pan. I hope not; I don't think it is; but it may be. Whereas your great series is there to stand and last. I haven't read the latest book, but I must very soon — it shall be my first holiday book — for I am told everywhere that it is your best. If people still say that of me when I have had your experience as a writer, I shall have reason to be thankful.

As it is, I'm at a parting of the ways. What has happened to *The Fountain* in England, plus what is bound to happen in America where it is to be Book of the Month, plus a three-book contract with the Macmillan Company of New York, makes me in effect independent of journalism. Apart from anything that might come from serial rights, I am dead certain now — for three books at any rate — of £30 a thousand for any fiction I write, which is much more than journalism will yield. And yet I'm uncertain. I'm frightened of depending on novels for fear of being compelled to write them not in my own time and with care for the financial result.

Journalism is a guarantee against that and enables me never to spend a penny that comes from novels or to rely on them in any way. The question is whether it's better to keep this absolute independence and to write novels, as I wrote *The Fountain*, in holes and corners and scraps of odd time (which means endless rewriting to preserve continuity) or to throw up *The Times* and venture. I don't know. And I'm becoming desperate because I can't get a clear twenty-four hours anywhere to write even the first paragraph of a book that has been boiling in my mind for ages.

Come to London soon, please. I should enormously value a talk with you. Meanwhile bless you for your letter.

H

43. TO ROBERT MENNELL.   (*The essay on Emily Brontë, here referred to, appeared first in* The Great Victorians, *edited by H. J. and Hugh Massingham, and later in* Reflections in a Mirror, *First Series.*

Hotel Rubens, S.W.1
23 April 1932

I'M very grateful for your letter and extremely proud of your having liked *The Fountain.* Lately I have been studying Emily Brontë, because I have to write an essay on her, and have become so deeply interested that I have pursued the study far beyond the requirements of the essay. As I read her poems, I am more and more convinced that she was one of the rare people who had a secret, inner life in the midst of all her cookery and bread-making. If it's some time since you read her, I think her poems would interest you far beyond *Wuthering Heights.*

44. TO SIR HERBERT THOMPSON, C.I.E., *a contemporary of Charles at Oxford, who had written from Peshawar.*

More's Garden
27 June 1932

YOUR letter was very good to have. It came this afternoon in the midst of a pile of muckins from America. *The Fountain* has done very well in England — but America seems to have gone mad. It was the choice of the Book of the Month Club there. This means a lump sale to their members of roughly 40,000 to 45,000 copies and I was very glad of it, for, though the lump-sum bargain is such that it doesn't mean a fortune to the author by any means, I thought that, the slump in America being what it is, I should do well to take what I could get — for it seemed to me highly improbable that, outside the Book of the Month Club, there would be much sale. The book was published in New York on June 1st. The *New York Times* gave me a whole front page and the other American critics likewise went off the deep end. . . . Letters from Americans are pouring in — many of them send me their own books and I am buried in correspondence, paper and string. It would be a joke if it weren't so damned strenuous. And it's a very marvellous and significant and serious and revealing joke to me that America of all places should go mad about a book about the contemplative life. But when Americans send me their own books and write for pages about 'mechanistic esotericism' I feel like making a swift journey to Peshawar. . . .

I'm glad you like your job. It seems to me a job enormously worth doing — much less open to question than the writing of novels. Nothing is more conscience-searching than a sudden wave of popularity. I have always thought I was writing very difficult and austere books for myself and a very few others. Then, suddenly, I find myself being liked by people who like books that I despise, and I wonder what cheap trick I have unconsciously been guilty of. But your job isn't open to the same doubts. Put at its lowest, you administer a better justice than would exist without you. You may doubt sometimes — I should sometimes — whether the English ought to be on the N.W.F. at all, but given that — and I'm enough of an imperialist to believe it still — then your job is morally flawless, and, I think, easier to keep flawless than the job of an artist who appeals to public taste. For public taste is corrupt and your law isn't.

What a lecture! I didn't intend it when I began. But I'm always tempted to imagine myself into other people's shoes and I'm greatly interested in your job — particularly in Peshawar.

45. TO HILDA MORGAN.

Garrick Club, W.C.2
9 August 1932

LAST night I went with Jamie Hamilton to the Wagner night at Queen's Hall and — as I always do when I listen to music (or half-listen to it) — I got the unifying idea that *Sparkenbroke* has long been lacking. The idea is — it sounds crude and I won't expand it here — that Love and Death are in fact identical or, rather, two aspects of the same release from the finite to the infinite. As I write it now, it means nothing to you; but it tells me suddenly what *Sparkenbroke* is *about* (which I didn't really know before) and I think I shall be able to write it now.

46. TO HILDA MORGAN.

More's Garden
20 August 1932

THIS is one of those murderous nights in which the sky is full of remote lightning and pieces of paper suddenly whirl up into your face out of the gutter, but there's no thunder, no rain, only an electric air that fills the body with the tremors of fever and the mind with darkness.

I wrote some letters this morning — among them one to your father, but since then I have been steadily — or, rather, unsteadily — at *Sparkenbroke*. It was wrong to begin with him in the train. The two women, through whose eyes he was seen, having no part in the story, were a false trail for the reader — quite fatal. And the opening with the doctor and Lady Sparkenbroke won't do either. It delays *Sparkenbroke* and the girl too long. So I've started in the hotel, after father, girl and fiancé have been in Chelmouth two or three days. It is the day on which George is to call for them in his car, drive them out to lunch in his farmhouse, and then send them up to Sparkenbroke House as tourists. I start in the girl's bedroom in the hotel, establishing her character and her fiancé's bringing in George and Sparkenbroke by reference. Then George on the scene and the drive out. More of Sparkenbroke, through George. Then George's sister and old father introduced. Sparkenbroke House (and churchyard) seen from outside. Then from inside with the tourists. The girl breaks away from the rest. Loses herself in the wood. Meets Sparkenbroke. The effect that S. has on her is seen at first directly in their encounter; then, from a different angle, when she returns to the Manor Farm for tea and ultimately to the hotel.

I believe that marshals the opening pretty well. The question is where to start bringing in the retrospect about Sparkenbroke's boyhood and his adventure in the tomb. Such a superb scene that I should have liked to write it in my own language, not break it up and blunten it in George's account of it. But short of doing it boldly as a prologue, I don't see how I can work it in except at second-hand, and I'm afraid of doing it as a prologue. It would break the progressive unity of the book and it would strike too high a note at the outset. Wouldn't it? Anyhow there's time enough. My usual prolixity has prevented me from getting them out of the hotel yet! I shall go on and see how the tomb incident works in as retrospect. If it goes wrong in that way I shall write in a new prologue — just as I had to write 'The Fort' because the retrospect of that defeated me.

I think the present opening is good. That is, true of the girl, and promising for the future. But it is on the light side. Nothing majestic about it as yet; nothing to suggest the stature of the whole book as I dream of it. Still, perhaps it's not a bad thing to begin fairly near the surface and go deeper gradually so that, as in life, the reader finds that he is learning more and more of the people he meets.

I have been at it all day. At 10.30 I thought I'd take some air. So I put on a pair of white sandshoes and slopped round Chelsea feeling very wild and woolly and shaggy, like a character in Tchehov. I get less and less Morganish when I'm alone. If Mildred [Charles's sister] knew how I live now, she'd have a fit. If only I were sure the work was good. It's always difficult to judge the cautious opening chapters before there has been any big scene.

As I walked I was rather envious of the lights in people's windows. I wanted to get away from myself and talk.

47. TO THE EDITOR OF *EVERYMAN*.

London
29 November 1932

SEVERAL of your correspondents have lately discussed the passage in my story, *The Fountain*, which describes the death of Narwitz. The core of discussion has been the following sentence:

And he cried aloud and said in his own language: 'Into thy hands, I commend my spirit,' and when he had spoken thus, he gave up the ghost.

The connexion of this passage with St. Luke's gospel is so plain that I have not thought it necessary to reply to any accusation of 'plagiarism'. Unconcealed quotation is not 'plagiarism'. Nor can a writer usefully discuss his own 'sincerity'; his book must speak for itself in that matter; if a reader of *The Fountain* is not already persuaded that its faults and its merits spring from its having been written with blood, I cannot now persuade him.

But I am troubled by the courteous letter in which Mr. D. M. Gordon says that in the passage I have quoted I have sinned as an artist and that, because I used 'ready made phrases', I 'never really visualized the scene'. Mr. Gordon adds that I have done worse than borrow phrases — I have borrowed the action itself.

There is no action described except the act of death. Narwitz dies. Jesus died; but death is common to all men; the action is borrowed from Nature, not from the Gospel. The real ground of Mr. Gordon's criticism is that I borrowed two phrases (1) 'Into thy hands I commend my spirit' (2) 'And when he had spoken thus, he gave up the ghost.' The first has been for centuries a very familiar phrase on the lips of dying men. Here it was Narwitz who quoted, not I. It was because I did so intensely visualize the scene and, while I wrote, was so deeply present in it, that I heard him say these words; and I was bound to record them. Having recorded them, I had then to state the fact that he died. Those who saw the facsimile of my MS., which was reproduced in your columns, will have noticed that at first I made this statement in words of my own. I exchanged them for those to which Mr. Gordon objects because Narwitz, by quoting from the gospel, had set up an emotional association so powerful that I was bound by it. 'When he had said this, he died' is a plain, honest sentence which would have held its own in different circumstances; so would a dozen other sentences that I might have written. But, following Narwitz's quotation, nothing would do except a sentence that deliberately and openly followed the gospel. To have done otherwise than I did would have been presumptuously to challenge the gospel, and, if I may so express it, to break the emotional and associative continuity of the prose. I hope Mr. Gordon will believe that the passage is governed by Narwitz's words. When they had been spoken, I was compelled, as an artist, to use, at the risk of every sort of misinterpretation, the sentence that the gospel's supremacy made inevitable. In the circumstances, to have chosen another would have been cowardice and affectation. An artist must obey the voices of his people; if they lead him to the gospel, he must not be afraid to follow them.

48. TO LOUIS BONNEROT.   (*The translation referred to
was of Donne's poem 'Going to Bed', made by A. Morel in* Le Navire
d'argent.)

More's Garden
22 December 1932

I WAS delighted to have your letter and the translation of Donne and
the copy of the *Revue Anglo-Américaine*. I don't feel that I am competent to criticize French verse because my ignorance of the language,
though it gives me the meaning, denies me the rhythm, and in verse
rhythm is everything or almost everything; it is indeed part of the
meaning itself. So I will say nothing of the translation except that it is
extraordinarily close and that I have read it again and again with increasing interest and appreciation; but I can say something of your
article in the *Revue*. I was astonished by its perception and depth. It
told me things about myself that I didn't know I knew; but an instant
afterwards I knew that they were true and that I had subconsciously
been aware of their truth all my life. I mean, particularly, the connexion
that you discover between my books. Of course I know that they were
all at root autobiographical and that they sprang from a common
source, but not until you pointed it out did I realize how intimate the
connexion was.

I know how great the danger is that writers of my sort may gradually
come to avoid the coarse-grained stuff and so limit their vision of the
world. It is dangerous to write always of people who do not have to
earn their own living or who earn it by the arts. I am afraid the big book
I am now working on stands in that peril as much as *The Fountain* but,
I feel that I must say what I have to say on death, on the desire of man
to return to the womb — his desire to lose himself that he may find
himself, a desire that connects the impulse to love, the fascination of
the tomb, and the longing that we all have for our own childhood, even
though that childhood may have been materially unhappy. That is the
theme of the new novel, *Sparkenbroke*, and Sparkenbroke is a noble-
man and a poet. The philosophical and emotional story is itself so
complex that I cannot further complicate it with Arnold Bennett
realism. But there is a strong connexion with earth in the fact that the
girl in the story is married to a country doctor, who is a plain, hard-
working man. I rely upon him to preserve the human balance. . . .

The book will take long to write. I had a six weeks holiday during October and November. I was very exhausted by work when I began it and for nearly ten days I wrote nothing. Then I wrote 25,000 words before coming back to London. Since then I have not touched the MS. But I go into the country for six days after Christmas and shall work hard there. That is how I have to write. If the book is written by the end of 1933 I shall be surprised and happy. . . .

I don't think Priestley's idea — 'some kind of dramatic symbolism, in narratives that would move in more than one world at once', will, in Priestley, lead to much. Of course I am temperamentally opposed to him; I may not be a fair judge; but I think he is making the mistake of imagining that he has found something new where nothing new is. Strindberg has done it in the theatre and Emily Brontë has done it in the novel. I tried to do it myself, 'on a spiritual plane'; in brief, to make the essences and not the appearances, of the characters, the protagonists of the story. Emily Brontë brought it off. No one else has. She succeeded for the very reason that she did what she did intuitively, without theory. She didn't know she was writing about essences; she didn't trouble about dramatic symbolism; she wasn't self-conscious; she worked a miracle, unique in literature. But if Priestley starts playing with dramatic symbolism, he will be lost in a muddle of self-consciousness. I am sure of it. I know precisely why *My Name is Legion* is a failure as a work of art.

49. TO LOUIS GILLET.

More's Garden
7 January 1933

I HAD not become distressed by the silence of the *Revue des deux mondes*. To have an essay on my work in it at all is like the coming true of a dream and one is not surprised if dreams delay their fulfilment a little while. Thank you for still having the possibility in mind.

My wife and I called on George Moore on Christmas morning, not having seen him for a long time. I shall never forget it. The front door was opened by a little man with red curly hair and a bowler hat who was carrying a small black hand-bag. He was spoken of by the housekeeper as 'the surgeon'. He was, in fact, the man who does, with tubes and other appliances, what is now necessary to do for G. M. His morning work was just done and we were admitted. G. M. was in the sitting-room downstairs, propped up in a chair — his feet up and covered with a rug — a surgical pan at his side. Behind his head was a window; the light holland blind was down; the white lace curtains were drawn; the light of the December morning filtered muddily in. Over him was a cut-glass chandelier, blazing with unshaded electric light.

'My dear friends, I shall soon be going away — not from this house only, but from the world.'

Then, suddenly, he began to entertain us with stories of Vizetelly,[1] with discussions of *Lady Chatterley's Lover*. And when we were going, he begged us to come again, singly or together. 'All day, I lie here alone. All day. All day.'

He does not *look* ill, but he is very ill. His housekeeper has been warned that he may die. Personally I did not feel death there — not yet.

50. TO HAMISH HAMILTON, *who had passed on to Charles a letter from Fr. Bede Jarret, O.P., criticizing* The Fountain.

More's Garden
22 February 1933

I HAVE been in bed with a cold or I'd have answered sooner. Thank you for letting me see the letter. It is an extraordinarily good one. But he has, as you say, missed the point about Narwitz's renunciation of Julie. He wasn't repelling or condemning her. On the contrary; he was, by deliberate self-abnegation, making it possible for her to work out her problem and establish a new life. And of course I am far from being able to accept the superiority of the Christian to the Greek ideal.[2]

---

[1] Henry Richard Vizetelly was an English publisher of Italian descent, fined and imprisoned for publishing Zola in translation, and involved otherwise with questions of literary indecency around the turn of the century. He published four of George Moore's early novels.

[2] For the changes in C. M.'s thinking, compare this letter with the earlier no. 3 (of 27 May 1917), and the later letters no. 129 and no. 132 (of 27 July 1949 and 16 June 1950). No. 145 (18 September 1953) makes it clear that C. M. had reached the Christian idea of 'The Grace of God'.

Plato, not Jesus, is to me the summit, and when Father Bede Jarrett
likens me to the Greeks I ask no more — except to understand Jesus's
greatness better than I do. If you have an opportunity please tell
Father Bede Jarrett how greatly I value his letter even where, partly
in ignorance, partly in temperament, I differ from him. I am delighted
to hear you are becoming a new man. That is splendid. I expect you
will begin to see the wisdom of making a clear cut from the past. I
believe only in that way can you become really happy again, which is
what I — an unashamedly interfering friend — want.

51. TO C. D. MEDLEY, *George Moore's lawyer and literary executor.
This letter, with the appended draft of a letter to* The Times, *shows
Charles's attitude towards an important point of literary conscience.
The remainder of the story is given in the Appendix to this volume.*

More's Garden
28 February 1933

FOR the past month my secretary and I have been hard at work, for
five mornings of each week, filing and docketing material for G. M.'s
biography. As a result I have reached the conclusion that my labour is
being thrown away; that I am entering into an investigation which will
occupy many years of my life, making other work impossible; and
that, even if I were to continue this, I should continue in vain, for a full
biography of G. M. cannot, and ought not to be written until many
now living have been dead for a generation.

The alternatives as I see them now are:

(1) To write, on the basis of imperfect information, an avowedly
'full biography', which would, inevitably, have a scandalous
character and do harm to Moore's memory and to me.
(2) To write an evasive and decorous record, full of suppressions
and omissions. Any pious compiler of facts could do this; I
think it is valueless; I know G. M. would have hated it; and I
would rather not attempt it.
(3) To send to *The Times* a letter, such as is suggested on the enclosed draft (Enclosure I). This is, I think, the right course.

I can only summarise here the reasons that have forced me to this conclusion. Among them is Lady Cunard's refusal to grant access to the Cunard correspondence, which emerges from Enclosures 2, 3 and 4. When she first refused, I told G. M. that without it the biography could not be written and he agreed. I asked him to release me. He said: 'No. Go on working with me. She may change her mind.' So I went on. Now the obstacle stands firm. Professor Tonks wants me to continue nevertheless. So does Colonel Moore [G. M.'s brother]. But what is the use? Other women, if I approach them, would take precisely the same position as Lady Cunard, or, worse, would give me their own discreet selection from their correspondence. I don't blame them or her. But the effect upon a biography is destructive. To dig secrets out of people, especially women, is a thankless and distasteful task. To labour in Ireland, where nearly every informant is bitter with prejudice or vanity; to make researches in Paris; to copy and file and cross-reference thousands of letters — nearly all undated and most of them trivial, for all but the trivial are withheld — is a life's campaign and, as I realise now, a campaign in violently hostile and secretive country. I believe that, for fifty years, the difficulties — apart from Lady Cunard — will remain insuperable. Moore used to say: 'I have had two interests in my life — art and women — and, though no woman has directly influenced my art, they are woven together. You must weave them together in my Life.' I have, as yet, scarcely touched the fringe of his personal life, but I have learned enough to know that it cannot be described at this range. It doesn't in the least shock me. It was part of the nature from which his art sprang, is continually reflected in his writings, and is therefore of the utmost importance. But even to suggest publicly to what extent he was a voyeur and tactilist and the special coldness or detachment of his sexual approaches would be to raise a British outcry. And what is the good of representing him as he was *not?* Better to leave it.

Since I reached this conclusion one thing or another has prevented me from talking to Professor Tonks about it, but I have corresponded with him, for I greatly value his opinion and I am anxious not to act in this matter without the approval of such old friends of G. M.'s as you and he. I think I represent his view when I say that, while he recognises that the biography may be impossible for many years, he wishes me to allow it to lie fallow and not publicly abandon it, for he is unwilling to lay open the ground to less desirable biographers. The answer to this is, first: that no biographer could act without your authority, your control of copyrights giving you an absolute veto; and, secondly, that to go about the world as the prospective writer of a biography which in all probability cannot be written by me puts me in a false position. It will involve me in a continuous correspondence. I shall be bound to accept, copy, file and analyse such material as comes my way, and a great quantity comes unsought. I shall be asked continually why I don't go to Paris, why I don't spend time in Ireland, why I don't do a hundred things that a purposeful biographer ought to do. And I shall have no answer. In any case, I have my own life to lead, my own work to do, and to do the spade-work for a biography that cannot be written is too hopeless and discouraging an occupation.

Therefore, I want to be released, if you will release me. The letter to *The Times* is no more than a draft for your consideration; it can be amended as you wish. A critical and personal appreciation, that does not pretend to be a full biography but embodies my personal recollections of G. M., can follow at leisure, if you think it desirable. In it I can do him real honour with an easy conscience and represent aspects of his character, brilliant, charming and generous, of which the public knows nothing. But it must, I think, first be made clear that I am not attempting a biography or I shall spend my life in those troubled waters. In any case is it not better to abandon the larger project publicly and at once on the excellent ground that certain sources are not available than to allow people to wonder, as the years pass, what discreditable cause there may be for the failure of a biography to appear?

I put these arguments before you because I care very much that you, as G. M.'s representative, should approve of what I do before I do anything irretrievable.

To the Editor of *The Times*

A clause in Mr. George Moore's will, in which he spoke of me as his biographer and asked his friends to give me their assistance, was recently published in your columns. I should be grateful if I might be allowed to make my own position clear.

Some years before Mr. Moore's death I began, at his suggestion, to collect material for a Life. When I pointed out that conversations with him, however elaborate, could not be the only source of such a volume as we contemplated, he agreed and introduced me to friends of his. At this point, access to certain indispensable sources was denied to me, and I asked to be relieved of my task, offering to hand over the material I had collected to any other biographer whom he might choose. He wished me nevertheless to continue, thinking that in time the necessary material might become available.

Since his death, I have found that this material is still inaccessible. Without it no full biography can be written. It is still open to me to investigate other sources, but I feel that I should not be justified in asking the help of Mr. Moore's friends in accumulating material for a biography that may not be completed in this generation or by me. An overwhelming correspondence forces me not to rest upon indecision and I have decided, therefore, with the concurrence of Mr. Moore's literary executor, to put out of my mind as presently impracticable a full Life of George Moore. I hope nevertheless to write in time a critical appreciation of the man and his work which shall make my material available to other biographers.

52. TO HILDA MORGAN.   *Written from a house to which the Morgans had moved in June 1933, and recording the further development of Sparkenbroke.*

16 Campden Hill Square, W.8.
1 August 1933

I HAVE made some real progress this morning. What I have been wrestling with all this time is the rescue of Piers from the tomb. (How many days ago was it that I said to you: 'I shall finish the prologue this morning'? and cursed you because you gave me letters to write instead!) It is done at last in exactly a hundred pages of MS. My trouble was the little scraps of broken dialogue and description after Piers's coming from the tomb. To make it real! To convey what he had been through! To discover the single comment — the queer, natural saying — in which a boy might communicate, or suggest, that he had just come through a complete mystical experience. As you know I can't think ahead. I depend on my pen for suggestion. And I have written and written and crossed out and crossed out and crumpled. Nothing would come right. But it's done. Enough now for you to put right. It's not what I wanted it to be. I suppose that was impossible. But it will serve.

Now on. All the next section about Frances's[1] coming to Chelmouth is written. It needs revision. The meeting of F. and Sparkenbroke needs completely rewriting. That is the next job. Then what remains is

(1) His seduction of her. His leaving her. Her consent to marry George.
(2) Her married life with George. Her going with Helen to Pisa and the Lucca episode.
(3) Her married life with George again. Sparkenbroke's return.
(4) Her 'running away' and Sparkenbroke's death.

No. 4 is done for the most part. The other three remain — about 300 pages of MS. probably. I say to myself in a dream five pages a day for sixty days would finish the book by the end of September. But that is only a dream. It is, however, possible that I might be finished, omitting the Lucca episode, and I ought to be able to finish that and revise the whole before the end of the year. But one never knows. Now theatres are quiescent. Nothing breaks into the book. But soon they will begin again. . . .

Shall we both aim at having a solid chunk of new work done by the end of September? . . .

It's rather melancholy this big house all solitary. Strangely enough, I miss Roger and his bed-time story; and I miss you at tea-time and late at night when work is done and I should like to talk. But I'm doing too much work to be miserable. . . .

Do you remember that ages ago I sent you in a letter some '18th Century Verses' that I had composed? I wonder if they would be among your letters still. They might suit Sparkenbroke in a light mood.

53. TO HILDA MORGAN, *anticipating 'Canterbury week' in a heat-wave.*

Campden Hill Square
5 August 1933

I HATE the thought of the journey today and I expect I shall be bored to death with Canterbury before I've done with it; it will be

---

[1] The heroine's name, after many doubts, was finally changed from Frances to Mary.

intolerably hot; still, at the moment I rather welcome the idea of a change; I'm tired of my own company completely undiluted, although there has been the reward that *Sparkenbroke* has begun to flow. For the last two days I have had a very large output, but, alas, not the output of which I think you would approve. Having finished the prologue, I felt that the proper thing to do, instead of plunging into Frances direct, was to link the prologue with what was to follow by opening my scene with the Doctor, already known to the reader as a boy, and, what is more, opening with him in the churchyard, where the reader had been left twenty years earlier. So what I have done is to use, and re-write the scene, written and rejected long ago, of his going to the nursery of Sparkenbroke's son, Richard. This scene was good in itself, with a touch of humour and humanity useful to me, but we rejected it *as an opening* because, with nothing else before it, it gave too light, too trivial an impression of the book. Now it has a hundred pages of TOMB before it and is good in its place as a contrast, I think. It is short: then, when George leaves the nursery, he goes down to Lady Sparkenbroke's morning-room (passing impression of the interior and *size* of Sparkenbroke House) and she walks with him down over the terraces and orchards to the churchyard. What has happened is that their conversation — about Sparkenbroke — has expanded and taken charge of me. I suppose when you get at it it will have to be drastically cut, but I found I couldn't stop, for two things happened — first Lady Sparkenbroke came alive, I saw all round her, she became a distinct and extra-ordinarily interesting human being whom I'd never met before but suddenly knew all about, and, secondly, I found that this was a wonderful chance to suggest what Sparkenbroke had become in the intervening years and, so to speak, to prepare his entrance. What's more I learned more about George than I'd known before and found that in the conversation between these two — both of them fond of S., both of them opposed to him temperamentally, both approving of 'the regularities of life' and yet, almost to their own surprise continuing to love and admire him — I found that I could get over what his special power was and why, though he was outwardly callous and sensual, women fell for him. Also I could state rather subtly — because George and Lady Sparkenbroke almost stumbling on the truth don't really understand it themselves — the triple theme of the whole book: I mean, the idea that the great artist is like a god visiting the earth, that what he wants (e.g. incarnation — the Christian legend, the Greek

Jupiter-myths) has no relation to the earthly values of the Georges and
Lady Sparkenbrokes of this world; that what he wants in a woman is
something that he himself creates in her and that, therefore, to him no
woman is commonplace or contemptible or impossible, all of them are
potentially Danaes or Ledas or Virgin Marys until he finds that they
aren't. Therefore, to be loved by him, though pretty frightening and
from the woman's point of view impersonal, is like being visited by a
god — and that to a woman is exciting. And further: just as no woman
is too commonplace to be (for his purposes) possible, so no material is
too commonplace to be the subject of his works of art. It depends, in
both cases, not on what they are, but on what he can put into them,
what he can make them receive, what he can make them reveal to him.
The analogy between the woman and the work of art is thus made
clear. And what is the other dominating factor in Sparkenbroke's life?
George knows intuitively, though he doesn't know why, that the incident of the tomb is somehow connected and, standing on the ground
where it happened, he tells Lady Sparkenbroke about it. He is just
gathering facts together. He has not perceived the synthesis of them.
The purpose of the book is to make that synthesis clear — to make
clear that the seeming 'inhumanity' of a great artist is a godlike attribute.
He is a god visiting earth, seeking incarnation. He is seeking, as Jesus
did, death in order that he may 'ascend' or be born again or return to
the absolute divinity from which his sojourn on earth is a separation.
And there are three forms of death: the mystical ecstasy, love, art —
all forms of self-annihilation. I want the old Rector or someone, later
in the book, to say that Sparkenbroke is the only person he has ever
known who was capable of *feeling* the idea of the resurrection; others
believed in it or didn't believe in it, but he felt it.

Anyhow, part of all this is being hinted at and felt towards in the
conversation between George and Lady Sparkenbroke. It is an extraordinarily subtle piece of dialogue and to me at the moment wonderfully alive. But it may not stand. I may be saying what I want to say
too soon. Time will show. But I think it is valuable apart from all
this because it shows what George's own attitude is towards women;
how he believes himself (rather complacently) to be exempt; and
so prepares the way for the flash that strikes him when he meets
Frances.

By the way I must think of yet another name for Frances. It can't be
Mary because 'George and Mary' won't do. But I don't think it can be

Frances because I have an idea that Mrs. Thomas Hardy's name is Frances Hardy — or is it Florence? I hope it's Florence.

Don't attempt to cope with this long rigmarole or to discuss it. It's much too long and muddled and your job is to go on steadily with your own book. It just does me good to write it, and it may interest you over breakfast for a moment before your own day's work begins. The time for you to discuss and criticize will be when I produce the completed manuscript. God knows when that will be. I often wonder how I finish a book at all, for the more I do the more ideas thicken and expand, and the longer it gets. However, thank God I'm never floored for ideas. The awful thing would be to have a scene go dry on you and find that really you hadn't got enough to say to fill the paper — the kind of feeling one had as a child at Christmas time when one had to write letters of thanks to one's aunts and uncles. My trouble is precisely the opposite. Either nothing happens at all or, if I do get into the swing of it, the scene thickens and thickens — which is dangerous because until later, when I can see the proportion of that scene in relation to the whole, I never know whether I am writing something really necessary to the whole or merely over-elaborating a part.

54. TO HILDA MORGAN.

Campden Hill Square
16 September 1933

I AGREE with all you say about *The Fountain*. Much of the Lewis–Narwitz–Ramsdell dialogue is out of character, or, at any rate, not strongly enough *in* character. I think that, if one is developing a philosophic theme, one is bound to have passages of suspended action, but the ideal is certainly to weave the theme and the incident together wherever it is possible. I did it fairly well in *The Fountain* — better, I think, than it has been done before — (consider the chunks of inactive philosophy in *Marius* and *Inglesant*!) — but still I didn't do it well enough. You see, the tennis tournament scene isn't encumbered with the theme at all. It develops, in a parallel action, the emotional crisis of Lewis and Julie — precisely like the race-course scene in *Anna Karenina*, though I was unaware of this at the time, and anyhow the tennis scene is yours in origin. But it *isn't* philosophical — that's the

I

point. It has nothing to do with the contemplative aspect of the story except very indirectly. And what I have to do is to discover some way of 'getting over' these abstruse ideas without letting the dramatic movement freeze. The same trouble arises from Sparkenbroke's peculiar kink — his identification of death, poetry and love. To get that over without direct exposition is the very devil. But you have your finger on the nerve of the problem. The struggle is almost too wearing to be endured. Still I'll fight it out in *Sparkenbroke* and my next novel shall be just about men and women observed and watched as accurately as Flaubert watched them, but more deeply searched I hope — but searched, not for their thought, but for their feeling. Now I'll get back to Sparkenbroke's wood. No scene has ever given me more trouble.

55. TO HILDA MORGAN.

19 September 1933

I'VE never really felt before what God was. Now I think He's the imagination. So much fits in. (1) In us only the imagination is inescapable. We can't stop imagining ourselves. We can by will kill our bodies, but there is no suicide of the imagination. (2) The Kingdom of God is within you. (3) The imagination is both good and evil — God and Devil. (4) To be good is to have a good image of oneself for we become what we imagine ourselves to be — a sort of spiritual Lamarck–Shaw idea. (5) If we imagine well enough we create our own Heaven; if badly we create our own Hell. (6) What is wrong with man is that, in general, he allows his imagination to congeal. (7) The value of Art is that it fluidifies the imagination. This idea has it every way. I have always felt with Wilde that 'all Art is quite useless' in the sense that it is not informative, doesn't make men more happy or instruct them. And yet I couldn't accept the Art for Art's sake formula.

Well now it is Art for God's sake, which is the same as Art for the imagination's sake. Tell men stories, not to impose my opinions upon them, but to fluidify their imaginations. It unfreezes the river. After that the river flows on to God or Devil. The artist can't imagine for another man. He can only enable him to imagine for himself. This is the link between Art and Religion. This is the DIONYSIAC principle of release. This is the Aristotelian principle of catharsis. This is the whole teaching of Jesus. It fits everywhere. I should like to write a great work — as big as the *Golden Bough* — on the Human Imagination. One chapter (or volume) would be: The Defence of Story-telling. Others: The Notion of Death; Imaginative release from the brake imposed on it by the body; The Nature of Love: The same as death in another form. In the erotic act — a form of ecstasy — everything else is shut out. For a moment we leap with free and absolute imagination. And so on.

(Note.) Conversion — e.g. Francis of Assisi — is the same as love, the same as death, a plunge into the absolute imagination, free of body, free of intellect.

All nonsense perhaps, but I am burning with it and can't judge yet. I like the idea of the book you suggest. I'll get it: when I read anything again. At the moment I am writing. O, the joy of not being interrupted — of being left alone with the struggle.

56. TO LOUIS BONNEROT.   (*Pauline Fourès was a Carcassonne milliner who accompanied her soldier-husband to Egypt and there became Napoleon's mistress. Charles was contemplating a play, to be written by him in collaboration with W. Bridges-Adams and based on her story; but it came to nothing. 'He was in search of grand passion,' wrote Bridges-Adams, 'but there was neither much passion here, nor any grandeur.'*

Campden Hill Square
31 January 1934

I AM still plodding on with *Sparkenbroke*, but it breaks my heart to think how much still lies before me, particularly because my mind is yearning for new things — vague ideas for new stories rise continually in my mind and I dare not turn aside to any one of them. There is the story of Pauline Fourès; there is my old idea of a new story in prose of Tristan and Iseult; there is the miraculous story of the coming of Volto Santo to Lucca — a marvellous tale of how the image was carved in the Holy Land and how it came across the Mediterranean in an empty ship, without helmsman or crew. Nothing is more mysterious and provocative of the imagination than an empty ship on the high seas — and, strangely enough, the same idea occurs in one version of the

Tristan legend, when he, being wounded and helpless, is put into a
ship on the Cornish coast, and is carried over to Ireland, where he
meets Iseult, the wind and the waves being themselves the agents of his
destiny. But I cannot now write these tales, and I have fathered them on
Lord Sparkenbroke. They are what he is writing—the Lucca story in
verse, the Tristan legend in prose — so that, vicariously I have the joy,
if not of composing them, at least of thinking about them and feeling
their mood.

Otherwise I have no news. Except to a theatre and to *The Times* late
at night, I seldom go out of that little top room which you visited.

57. TO HUGH GIFFARD, *who shared the Dutch internment.*

Campden Hill Square
February 1934

IN my book a girl has been walking in a wood. Time: June. Place:
Dorset. In the evening the following dialogue occurs between her and
her father:

'Father,' she said, 'you know about gardens. What is the thing
with bluish-green leaves, spotty-mottled, and a yellow flower?'
'What is that, my dear?' said her father, coming out of his newspaper. She repeated her description, adding to it. Rue, probably, he
told her.
'It was in the wood,' she said.
'Then it can't have been rue. Unless it was planted there.'

The questions are: Where does rue grow? Is there any possibility of
its growing wild in an English wood in June? If *not*, do I correctly get
out of the difficulty by suggesting that it may have been *planted* there?

I should be immensely grateful for your help. You are my horti-
cultural mentor. I want rue, if I can have it, because of the symbolism,
but if it is *wrong*, I'll just cut it out.

58. TO ANNE FREMANTLE.

Campden Hill Square
13 March 1934

IF you have time to spare for such things, I should be eternally grateful if you would give me your sterner comments on this translation which, if it has any merit, I should like to father on my Lord Sparkenbroke.

> *Iucundum, mea vita, mihi proponis amorem*
> *hunc nostrum inter nos perpetuumque fore.*
> *di magni, facite ut vere promittere possit,*
> *atque id sincere dicat et ex animo,*
> *ut liceat nobis tota perducere vita*
> *aeternum hoc sanctae foedus amicitiae.*
>
> CATULLUS, CIX

> *She that is my life doth promise love*
> *Joyful and deathless. Grant that she*
> *Speak from a certain knowledge of her heart.*
> *So against Time may yet sufficient prove*
> *This sacred vow of loving constancy.*

Notes:

1. I have deliberately dropped out a foot from my pentameter after *deathless*: to get the effect of a 'rest' in music. Approved?
2. I have deliberately kept to half-rhymes so that the contrast with the unrhyming Latin may be less. Approved?
3. I have done my damnedest about *amicitia*. My view is that it is neither 'love' nor 'friendship' here. Am I right?

My blessing upon you — all three.

59. TO HILDA MORGAN.

Campden Hill Square
21 August 1934

SPARKENBROKE is in Pisa, walking along the Lung' Arno under our hotel windows, with time on his hands, remembering how Etty and Richard came out a year ago and how she (Lady S.) and he (S.) had discovered their different view of the nature of love. Soon he will see Mary. Next page, I think. This really is daylight. The actual Lucca episode might be finished in a week. Then there will remain:

1. The intervening period while S. discovers he is really desperate for Mary and returns to England.

(To be written.)

2. The scene in which he asks her to run away with him.

(To be written.)

3. The night of crisis. Her flight and return.   (*Written!*)
4. Sparkenbroke's entry into his tomb.   (To be written.)
5. George finding Mary pretending to be asleep in her bed.

(Very brief — to be written.)

Say:	The Lucca section	10,000
	The bits just set out	15,000
	The gap before the marriage still left to be filled in	5,000
	Total to be written	30,000

As I am writing now about 2,000–3,000 a day all kinds of miracles might happen before the end of September, but I really put it at 'before Christmas', what with revision, etc. The book wants a lot of chopping and pulling together. The bits I have been re-reading in typescript seem to me good, but even the best of them — e.g. the bandstand scene — is a little *over*-written in parts and needs chopping of romantic adjectives. I have to beware of being too glamorous and struggle back towards a more classical plainness which is, emotionally, much more powerful if one can bring it off. . . .

PS. 1.30 a.m. Sparkenbroke has met her. They are just going into the hotel where Helen is ill. 2,400 words today.

60. TO HILDA MORGAN.

Campden Hill Square
25 August 1934

YES, I know Mary must be miracle-minded, but it's damned difficult to do — especially in combination with the solid aspect of her character. There was a bit of it, I think, (1) when she played Sparkenbroke's 'invisibility' game with him at their first meeting in the wood and (2) in the bandstand scene. And I am working up now — today I hope — to a scene which came to me suddenly as I walked over to Amie's[1] at 9.30 last night. They are in the palazzo at Lucca. S. working late. He finds that having M. in the house is not an interruption but an impetus (this is one of her differences *to him* from other women). He is writing at the top of his bent, all worked up and excited, in a condition of creative ecstasy comparable to his tomb-ecstasy. The night is passing. It is very early morning — all thrilling and ghosty. The door opens and M. comes in — in a white night-dress. She has wakened from a dream — a dream that he was her lover — and, awaking, has been afraid to move, feeling that in her bed is his body — dead. She has lain still in her bed, afraid to move. Then, awaking further, has found her bed empty. Then, wide awake, has understood that she was dreaming, but has been possessed by the idea that she dreamed what she did because S. had in fact died. So she has rushed down to see. He has not died; but he has been in a corresponding creative ecstasy; this has communicated itself to her; such is the communion of their minds. And there they are set for their love scene — a physical ecstasy — or not — I don't know yet and don't want to know.

61. TO ST. JOHN ERVINE, *commenting upon his book* If I were Dictator.

Campden Hill Square
(undated: probably August 1934)

CHARLES MORGAN, with his humble duty, is very far from taking no interest in these things. Bless you, I believed in liberty when you were still a Socialist.

[1] Anne Fremantle.

I think the book is a good and valuable book; there's a real political philosophy of the middle path which the world, afflicted on the one hand by the Laskis and on the other by the Hitlers, is beginning to re-discover. It wanted re-stating and you have re-stated it with an energy I envy.

Why do you think that, because I don't go about reforming people, I have no interest in these things? To put it at its most personal, I want to be allowed to tell stories slowly and in peace — not to be bullied into propaganda or silence. It is true I don't want to reform the world. I believe that every advance produced a retrogression. Man learns to fly, then allows flying to be a menace. He misuses vilely everything that he uses well — drugs, leisure, everything. He always — in the mass — cancels out his own progress. Except in the very long run. The world is a bit better because Plato and Shakespeare lived in it. But theirs is the only kind of 'reform' in which I believe. You can't directly persuade mankind to teach mankind. But it is possible for someone with the force of Plato to deflect a little the course of the human imagination. Nothing else matters. The statesman's job is to keep the machinery ticking over until great genius appears and to prevent hot-heads from throwing things into the works.

If I hadn't always hated him, I should have learned to hate Hitler during my tour of Europe. What England doesn't understand is that the Germans mean war and soon: that nothing on earth will stop them except the certainty of defeat; and that they believe, as they did in 1914, that we shan't come in until it's too late. If by any means we could persuade them to the contrary, there would be peace for another twenty years anyhow.

All of which divagation proves that your book has stirred me — and I am very grateful for it.

Shirley has whooping-cough in Wales; Roger probably will; their own nurse is a crock so a hospital nurse has been moved in. H. is coming up next week-end and returning to Wales till the end of September. Meanwhile, in a lull of playgoing, I live like a monk, writing. I wish you'd walk in one day.

62. TO ROGER BARRETT.

Campden Hill Square
16 September 1934

MY own news is pretty various but not very exciting. In the middle of May I set out for Oberammergau, to write on the Passion Play for *The Times*. It was a kind of preliminary performance before the tourist season began so we had the village more or less to ourselves and enjoyed ourselves — Hilda and I, and Darlington (of the *Telegraph*) and his wife. The play itself lasts from morning to evening and one sits on hard seats. What is more, at the time when other people had a break for lunch, I had to go without lunch and spend the precious hour writing like hell. Then I took paper and pencil into the performance and wrote on my knee whenever the chorus was giving tongue. In order to save the expense of exchange on so expensive a message I had told *The Times* to ring me from London at a fixed hour, so I was tied down to the moment, and had the utmost difficulty in getting my copy into order in time, for they wanted a full turnover — about 2,200 words. And when the call came through I was on that wretched line dictating for more than three-quarters of an hour. Nothing destroys me as completely as telephoning.

When Oberammergau was done, we went on a tour of Europe, Munich, Vienna, Prague, Paris. The idea was that I should stay four or five days in each place, go to all the theatres I could and write a turnover on each. The only trouble was that I was too conscientious and didn't give myself any time for leisure. I went to twenty-three plays in twenty-one days and did the journeys by air. I don't mind a couple of hours in the air, but seven and a half hours from Prague to Paris did me in. I felt next day as I did on the day after the Antwerp retreat. However it wasn't boring, and I saw a lot of plays and people, and learned a lot of politics, and enjoyed Vienna and loathed Munich, which is like a prison camp. The great point about the Germans, which no one seems to realize is this: whereas in other countries, all the gilt is off the war-gingerbread and everyone thinks of war as perhaps inevitable but certainly sordid and vile and useless, the Germans take the opposite view. To them war is still the opportunity for romantic splendour. It has for them still the glamour that it once had for us. They desire conquest as an end in itself — as we did when our nation was young — and the men have an almost Japanese view about the splendour of dying for one's country. It is this that makes them formidable and war, sooner or later, certain. Not yet. They aren't ready. But still, it's coming, and the best that we can hope for is to postpone it. A clear alliance between us and France would postpone it so long that the whole condition of Germany might have changed meanwhile; but as long as foreign policy is clogged by our continued adherence to the League, nothing can be done. But I gather that you don't agree about that. You do still believe in the League. To me it is nothing but a thing that has failed — the dead body of an ideal tied to Europe and preventing her from working towards any settlement on different lines.

63. TO LADY CROMER, *who had asked Charles to criticize a book of hers in typescript.*

Campden Hill Square
8 October 1934

THE book seemed to me to become more clear and definite where you reached the Egyptian section and again approached more nearly to direct narrative. Nothing is harder than to express pure emotion; only the greatest lyrical poets of the quality of Shelley and Blake have succeeded in this; for that reason any sentence in prose which ends or might end in an exclamation mark is to be distrusted. My advice would be that, when you revise the book, you should do so with three chief purposes:

(1) To connect your sketches as far as possible on a thread of consecutive narrative.

(2) To increase their solidity wherever you can by giving direct descriptions of persons and objects seen.

(3) To do a thing which I always do myself when every other revision is complete. I take a pencil and go through my typescript pointing to each word in turn and considering it separately. I ask myself

(a) *Is it necessary?* Thus I detect and cut out many adjectives which are not, so to speak, pulling their weight. Their going adds to the austerity and clearness of the prose.

(b) *If necessary, is it the best possible word?* Is there, perhaps, a word less often used, less rubbed, more precise?

(c) *If it is the best word I can find, is it in the best place?* This involves consideration of the rhythm of the sentence in which it occurs.

You will feel, I am afraid, that this is to ask too much, but I believe that it is only by infinite labour that good books are written. I think there is no passage in anything of mine that has not been read and re-read forty or fifty times and re-written in my own hand five or six times. One is a pupil all one's life and I remember that George Moore used to say that nothing of his was readable until the fourteenth draft. I feel that behind your work is sensitive perception and feeling which you sometimes cloud or permit to fall loose and which, if you bound yourself by the hard discipline of consecutive narrative, would be clarified. When I was a very young man someone said to me: 'Write what you see. See nothing except with your eyes tight shut or wide open', and the whole discipline of art seems to me to consist in deciding within oneself what has been, so to speak, 'half-seen', or seen under the influence of others, and rejecting it.

Forgive me if all this seems to be demanding too much. I am a fanatic on the subject of writing. A book takes me four years of work; nothing seems to me 'good enough' in my own writing or in anyone else's.

64. TO ERNEST SHORT.

Campden Hill Square
13 November 1934

MY latest task has been to re-read — not fully perhaps! — the entire works of Brett Young, that I may write in the *Lit. Supp.* on the Severn Edition of his novels. Today, after a break of more than a fortnight, I got back to my own tale. I have stared at the page all day, re-reading, writing a little, trying to entwine myself in it again. It will come. But how I hate these efforts of return, these struggling, barren days. You are right. I ought to leave the paper, but, as it is, excluding book royalties, I am living almost without margin. If I left the paper, I should be under necessity to earn by novels £1,500 a year and, though the earnings would *probably* average much more than this at present, I should hate to depend on novels or to feel that I cared at all whether anyone bought my books or not. As it is, I don't care. Royalties make no odds to me; they just accumulate for my children to inherit or the Government to take away. It is a choice between two liberties — the liberty to write novels only; and the liberty, which I now have, to be completely independent of them. I may be choosing wrongly. The choice certainly means that I shall write *few* books — but perhaps there are enough in the world.

65. TO JAMES AGATE, *who had written to* The Times *hailing as 'the best bit of dramatic criticism since Montague' Charles Morgan's notice of* The Old Ladies.[1]

Campden Hill Square
9 April 1935

IT'S odd that you should have liked this notice of mine for I spent Sunday morning in fierce dispute with you on the subjects of death and poetry and old age. De Senectute and the younger Tennyson! To me death is one of the three supreme ecstasies, together with love and poetry — but I won't trouble you with that theme now. There will be trouble enough, I fear, when you find it in the novel that I have been writing for the last three years.

66. TO JAMES AGATE, *who had an extreme horror of dying, and commented on the preceding letter that he could not let people tell him 'at nine in the morning that death is an ecstasy!' Acknowledging the following letter from Morgan he wrote, 'Your case would have utterly failed had you not boldly said: " I do ask you to be excited about the pre-natal state." That was crucial, and when I put the question I had no idea it was so very near the heart of your mystery. Now the thing holds together, for my intellect lets me believe in a continuum open at both ends but not in one which starts with birth, like the starting gate in a horse-race, and then goes on for ever.' (From* Ego 2, *Autobiography of James Agate.)*

[1] Rodney Ackland's play, based on a novel by Hugh Walpole.

Campden Hill Square
14 April 1935

THANK you for a very good letter — but it's the hell of a letter to answer; I've been trying to answer it, in the book, for over three years — and here is the last hour of Sunday morning! But at the risk of being crude, I'll try to be precise and answer your direct questions.

'*Of what kind is "my Ecstasy"?*' I don't mean ecstasy in the sense of pleasure or, even, happiness. The word means 'out of, or beyond sensuous perceptions'. I *do* ask you to be 'excited about the pre-natal state' — my idea being that there is a real and continuous life from which sensuous experience in the body is a divagation. We are shut up in a house; we came from the outside air and shall return to it. Whether the condition after death is pleasant or unpleasant isn't the point; whether it is a personal survival or an absorption 'in the eternal mind' I don't know — possibly it is both; but I think I know it is more real and, in a profound sense, more natural and less divided against itself than our present experience. If you ask me for algebraic proof, of course I have none, but there is presumptive evidence in the lives of the saints and the mystic poets and, if you will accept it as evidence, in my own experience. The interesting facts are that in love and poetry one is aware of an extraordinary transcendence of oneself — of self-loss; from which one agonizingly falls back. Secondly, that the complete mystical experience appears always to be describing the *same* transcendence. Thirdly, that the emergence from one life to another by the route of death is continually repeated in Nature and in the principal beliefs and symbols of a thousand religions that differ in all else. The thing seems to have the authority, not of algebra, but of necessity.

'*Am I looking forward to a final ecstasy because I think the future holds something to be ecstatic about?*' Again with the reservation that ecstasy is not a synonym for happiness — yes . . . My book, you will be relieved to hear, has nothing to do with the fusion of twin souls. The woman is alive when the book ends. The man is one who, having had a partial mystical experience early in his life, struggles for its fulfilment — in love unsuccessfully, in poetry less unsuccessfully, in death perhaps successfully. Please believe that I'm no more didactic than you. I am telling a story and asking questions.

Time limit. '*How much fun is Hannibal getting at this moment out of being dead?*' Except in 'the house', there isn't any time. That is our particular unreality. Hannibal has just died and will always have just died . . . I don't expect 'a hell of a fine time on my death-bed' — more probably agony. But since you quote Montaigne, wasn't it he who said in the Essay on Cruelty something to the effect that, though he didn't envy the dying, he envied the dead? I believe that where at root we differ is that you do not willingly distinguish between the physical act of dying and the state of death. I have no particular love for the act of dying; but all my understanding leads me to believe that the state of death is, in fact, vital and real; that even in life some of us sometimes have direct apprehension of it; and that two of the occasions of these imperfect apprehensions are poetry and love — precisely because they also lead a man 'beyond sensuous perception'.

I know that this letter is a scrappy note on a vast subject. Anybody with your wit can pick it to pieces and ridicule it. I suppose if I were cautious I shouldn't send it. But there seems to me just a chance that, though you and I pretend to be miles apart, our philosophies are less opposed than our outward showing would suggest. You have a great capacity for enjoyment of many things; I envy you that; but I refuse to believe that you are complacent about experience here or feel it to be complete. To me life is exciting because it is incomplete. We are born inside a house — often very pleasant and well lit by artificial light — and we live inside the house all the time. There are windows, but the lamps and candles inside are so near and powerful that everything outside the windows looks black. If by some means we can put out the candles — i.e. die, even for a moment, to sensuous perception — all the night outside becomes brilliantly visible. Love and poetry are two of the possible means. But still, there we are, always inside the house. Death puts out the candles and opens the windows — that is the idea I am driving at. And as you won't deny that there are stars because I have no astronomy, so you won't deny that there is an ecstatic condition, called 'death', because Vaughan and Traherne and Crashaw and Emily Brontë have all tried and failed to describe it. The point is that they were under necessity to *try* to describe it because they knew well enough that there was something to describe and knew that it was of transcendent importance. It isn't fair to fasten on Keats; his 'ceasing upon the midnight' etc. was personal despair — not metaphysical doctrine. Personally I don't believe in 'just ceasing'. If I thought it was as simple as that I should have killed myself long ago — on the various occasions, not infrequent, in which life has seemed to take more than she gives.

67. TO MRS. ROBERT MENNELL, *with allusion to a notable production of* Tristan and Isolde, *conducted by Fürtwangler.*

Campden Hill Square
27 May 1935

HOW nice to have a human letter! Everyone who writes to me nowadays is either mad or wants something (often both) — the kind of letter that one stares at in despair; and it was good to have yours by way of sane contrast.

That was my first experience of *Tristan*, except orchestrally and in bits. The consequence was that, being unfamiliar with the action, I had to look at the stage, which (God protecting me) I will never do again. What a ship! What dresses, wigs and acting! Grossly, offensively, quite unnecessarily vile. Surely, even if one is a *prima donna*, one need not stand with one's feet a yard apart and wave one's arms like a drowning policeman. However, opera is a corrupt aesthetic medium and one must go prepared. I like my music pure and when I could I forgot the large walruses on the stage and listened to the orchestra and watched Fürtwangler. He did profoundly impress me. So different from Beecham. Beecham gets between me and any music. He is vain, selfish, worldly, without humility; he is, among musicians, what Somerset Maugham is among writers — though Maugham does at least create while Beecham only interprets. Fürtwangler conducts with devotion and without self-exhibition.

Still — to my surprise, though I felt a deep admiration and though even my musical ignorance knew that I was listening to a very exceptional performance of *Tristan*, I was surprised to find how seldom it 'made my heart turn over'. I don't know why. The theme is very close to me; the identity of love, poetry and death, three aspects of the same transcendence or ecstasy, is the theme of *Sparkenbroke*, my book now near its end. That was why I went to hear Tristan. I wanted to hear what Wagner had to say on my subject. But he seemed to me to be talking about something else and it was only a lyrical passage here and there that *got* me.

68. TO PATRICK MALIN, *an American active in academic and public life and a Quaker.*　　(*It was to him that Charles entrusted the care of his wife and children in 1940.*)

Campden Hill Square
29 December 1935

YOU must think me very discourteous in not having written sooner to thank you for your letter and your William Penn lecture. I was abroad when your letter came, as my secretary will have told you; since I returned I have been more than busy in correcting the final typescript of a new novel, and, alas, in illness, and in my regular work for *The Times*. Now, after Christmas, there is a lull in playgoing; my novel is at the printers; and, until proofs begin to come in and new plays to appear again, I have time to breathe. I could have dictated a reply sooner, but I wanted to answer your letter in my own hand, for it gave me genuine and deep pleasure.

I myself am not, in any social sense, a crusader at all. I was baptised in the Church of England, but it has long ceased to be of any account in my life, partly because I hate priestcraft, partly because there is so much of the Church's doctrine that I cannot accept, partly because the Church of England is, to me, an uncomfortable, timorous compromise. If I belonged to any sect it would be to the Quakers, but I am debarred from that, though I have many Quakers among my friends, by two facts — first that, in England, Quakerism is profoundly exclusive; you are born a Quaker, you are not encouraged to become one; second that, in England, Quakerism has become more and more associated with the militant section of the political Left. I am not a politician; I shrink from militancy and propaganda in any form. What is more, I am by nature a solitary; I distrust collective social action for the betterment of the world. I have only two talents, to imagine and to write, and, unless my writing is unconsciously a crusade, I live without crusading, and, in that sense, selfishly.

That this is one-sided I see clearly. I like the balance and moderation of your Penn Lecture. But one-sidedness is another word for single-mindedness, and, unless I can remain single-minded, I am lost. I believe that men cannot be helped by what others tell them or what others do for them. They can only help themselves by imagining themselves and re-creating themselves in the light of that imagination. To imagine

Membre de l'Institut de France, November 1949
Photograph by Roger Morgan

as from 16 Campden Hill Square
London W. 8

Tuesday, June 10
1941

Dear Eddie,

The Horace you sent me has March 18 on its flyleaf. Only your friendship can pardon so long a delay of my thanks for a book that has seldom, during three months, been out of reach of my hand. When it came I read it to myself & read it aloud at all times of the day and night and I wanted to send you a telegram of gratitude and excitement; but I didn't — wisely? foolishly? and planned a long letter, but I was forever finding new delights, the letter waited for them, day followed day and — well now, at last, I write about a book that has touched and stirred and enchanted me far more than any that

First page of a letter to Sir Edward Marsh

oneself deeply and intensely enough is, ultimately, to see God. The purpose of art, as I understand it, is not to instruct men or persuade them, but so to impregnate their imaginations that they begin to imagine and re-create themselves, and to preserve the unity of all ecstasies and transcendencies. This is what I have been driving at for four years in the new novel, *Sparkenbroke*, just finished. Love, poetry and death are three aspects of the same transcendence. 'I am certain of nothing,' Keats said in one of his letters, 'but of the holiness of the Heart's affections and of the truth of Imagination. Imagination may be likened to Adam's dream — he awoke and found it truth.'

As for my personal way of life, it is, I suppose, a kind of fanaticism. To write and re-write; to write and re-write; and to accept for my own use as income no profit from imaginative writing. I live on my private income and what I earn as a journalist; what comes to me from novels is at once invested — my family gets the interest — and so I have the safety of knowing that whether I take four years or ten years over a book and whether it succeeds or fails financially will make no odds to me. The history of my books is very strange to me — particularly of *The Fountain*. As far as I knew I was writing, in an age of materialism, a book about the contemplative life which might have an obscure interest for a few people of like mind with myself. That it became *popular* is still to me incredible. It was some freak of public taste which is not likely to repeat itself.

I feel always, in my sphere, as you do in yours, that the end of the world as we understand it is very near, but I do not attach your importance to the prevention of war. I think people are obsessed on that subject. Are we not in danger of attaching too much importance first to our lives, secondly to our decision — to fight or not to fight. If one is imprisoned, perhaps unjustly, perhaps justly, it is neither important nor a matter of spiritual principle whether one obeys or disobeys the warder's command to perform certain tasks. What matters is not whether we accept or reject the rules of the prison but whether we live in such a way, and with such inward independence, that the tasks we perform do not corrupt us and the iron bars are not our cage. War is, in many respects, vile. I should hate it because it would prevent me from doing my own work. It is to be avoided, if it can be avoided without grovelling and cowardice. But to think of it, as many do nowadays, as the epitome of all evil is, I think wrong. Peace is not an end in itself; only 'the peace of God' is that; and the peace of God is by no means inconsistent with political war — indeed, often springs from it.

The doctrine of non-resistance is a beautiful doctrine, but why do men, even Quakers, interpret it so narrowly? The command is: resist not evil. War is a form of evil. The order of the government to take up arms, if we consider it a form of evil, is not to be resisted. We are creatures of the spirit and our actions, unless they corrupt that spirit, are not bad, and, unless they increase that spirit, are not good. If we kill in wrath or malice or for personal gain, then we sin; but if we kill in submission to Caesar we do not sin.

That, at any rate, is a point of view. It seems to me to carry the quietist doctrine a step further than it is ordinarily carried. I remember using as an epigraph to an earlier book, *My Name is Legion*, a saying of the Persian, Kabir: 'He is the true saint who teacheth thee to be still amidst all thine activities.' Why not in war? Is war, accepted in unwilling submission, a greater peril to the soul than lust or greed? Why does the modern world single out war as a supreme evil? Only, I think, because it is an obviously unpleasant and uncomfortable vice, not because it is, in fact, supremely vicious.

You will have had more than enough of this. The extreme interest of your letter provoked me to it. I hope we shall meet some day. I doubt whether I shall come to America. They want me to lecture there, and I don't think a lecture tour is an artist's job. If only I could come without anyone, except a few friends, knowing I was there, then I'd come gladly, for I want to see the American theatre and afterwards go to the Southern States. Perhaps I shall *have* to go some day as dramatic critic of *The Times*. Meanwhile, please tell me if you are in England. Not only what you say and think, but that you are a Quaker and admit to being happy as a husband, as a father and in your job makes me eager to meet you. There aren't many happy people to meet. . . .

[Postscript.] . . . I think you'd like London still. It's very old and one feels it, through all the noise and racket. I have a tall house; built in the year of Waterloo,[1] at the top of a high hill — the square is on the slope of the hill. My workroom is at the top of the house. Really silent. Vast views over London to green fields beyond. And a flat roof for sun and air. I sleep and mostly eat in this room and seldom come out of it except for plays at night.

[1] The building of the square was, in fact, begun in 1827.

69. TO LOUIS BONNEROT, *with a first mention of the factual
seed that later grew into* The Voyage.

Campden Hill Square
30 December 1935

SUCH a pleasure and relief to have French verse that I can read easily
and really understand! De Musset I know and even Baudelaire; Rim-
baud I love laboriously in anthologies, but I had begun to think that
all French verse written in my own time was too difficult for me, and
the volume you sent me has given me real joy. I read it very slowly and
shall continue to do so — as I have been reading also a new arrange-
ment of Shakespeare's Sonnets. You, who are much more scholarly
about English Literature than I shall ever be, are probably familiar with
this. The original edition of 1609 gave the Sonnets in a certain order
which has been followed by most editors ever since but which was
obviously a bad jumble. Then in 1925 appeared a book called *The
Original Order of Shakespeare's Sonnets* by Sir Denys Bray. This drew
attention to a 'rhyme-link' between those sonnets which are beyond
doubt *pairs*. By applying this rhyme-link to the other sonnets a new
order is obtained — a new order which depends, not on choice or
opinion, but on this purely mechanical process. This new order has
been used in the New Temple edition which I shall send you in a day or
two. It answers almost miraculously a dozen or more tests, but *above all*
it makes sense! Never have I understood the Sonnets so well. I who
hate the pedantry of most Shakespearian scholarship am persuaded by
this. These poems, each one a masterpiece, have now become *one* poem,
and the effect of reading them straight through is overwhelming.

I have been enjoying a little leisure, though I am cursed by dentist
and doctors. *Sparkenbroke* is really finished and I am dreaming of new
books — and new themes.

Did you ever hear this remarkable story of your country? It
appeared in *The Times* two or three years ago, having been sent over
from our Paris office. A man was brought to trial on a charge of having
converted public money to his own use, and this was the story revealed:

Somewhere in the French provinces — some remote village — this
man was *in charge of the local prison*. He was on good terms with his
prisoners, whom he treated almost as members of his family; but he

was a poet, and liable to forget and neglect them. Anyhow, the need to look after them disturbed his poetry and his having to shut up his fellow human-beings disturbed his conscience. So he let them all go. But he had to pretend they were still there and was thus forced, though by nature honest, to continue to receive from the Government the money intended for their upkeep. Time passed. No one suspected anything until, at last, one of the liberated prisoners, finding his liberty difficult and expensive, complained to the authorities that he had been unjustly turned out of his comfortable prison.

Is not this a perfect parable of a saint (a humble and slightly ridiculous saint) in the modern world? I want to use it as the subject of a gently ironic novel and have written to the Paris office of *The Times* to try to obtain more particulars. I can't imagine under what legal system it is possible for a prison to be controlled by one man, not checked by inspectors and so on. It is a lovely story. Anatole France would have liked it — Alphonse Daudet even better. I see the little man as a saintly Tartarin! But how on earth was the thing possible in France? That's what I can't understand.

70. TO ROGER BARRETT.

Campden Hill Square
25 January 1936

I HAD meant long ago to say how sorry I was to hear that the *Critic* had fallen down. It seemed to me a remarkably good paper, though I must say I always wondered how any weekly could be made to pay in Hong Kong, seeing the difficulties they all have in London. I doubt very much whether any of the high-class literaries pays except the *Spectator*, though of course *Punch* is a gold-mine and I dare say *Truth* does pretty well. What happens to you now? Tell me your news, even if you have time for only half a sheet. I shall be anxious until I hear. . . . On the day of my return from my holiday, November 22, I published a little book — only about 20,000 words — called *Epitaph on George Moore* — to explain why I had abandoned the big biography (I couldn't get the Cunard letters) and giving a combined character-sketch and critical survey. Really no more than an elaborately worked essay. It has done me a great deal of good I think, and, though a little book addressed to a highly specialized audience can't mean money, the Press has been generous. I hope it is a good omen for the big novel, *Sparkenbroke*, which, after four years of sweat, comes out in April. I have just finished the galley proofs and this letter is written in the interval between then and the coming of page proof. The point is the same as it was in *The Fountain*, but I find to my horror that there will be 560 instead of 450 pages. I have read the thing so often that I simply am without judgment. English Macmillan's haven't read it yet — they sent the typescript straight to the printer; but American Macmillan's, for what they are worth, are bursting with enthusiastic cables. No one else has read it except my secretary, who typed it and whose judgment is as dead as my own; Hilda, who approves; and two doctors whose eyes have been bent on medical detail — so I don't know what to think. Probably the chief character, Lord Sparkenbroke, has too much of Byron in him not to be hated; but the girl, very young and simple, and *not* a minx, is lovable and so, I hope, is her plain, straightforward, wise doctor-husband — like a younger and much fuller version of old van Leyden who was one of the *solidest* characters in *The Fountain*. The book contains verse and runs every sort of risk. It is a marvellous target for my enemies. What a mocking, damning review I myself could write on it! And yet I think it has character and glamour, so I pray to God, and glamour is precisely what most modern novels are without.

I'm wondering now what to do next. I have four stories in my mind and I can't choose between them. The one I like best involves a scene in France about the time of the Directory and I funk working against an unfamiliar background. All the research in the world won't supply those tiny pieces of personal observation that are the breath of life to me. Anyhow I'm in no hurry to choose. I can't begin to write until the *Sparkenbroke* proofs are disposed of.

The King's death postponed first-nights and gave me a let up for a bit, but on Tuesday I have to describe the funeral from outside Westminster Hall and then all the banked-up plays come in a torrent.

71. TO LOUIS BONNEROT.

Campden Hill Square
28 January 1936

I HAVE a long article to write on the King's funeral and I must now write a letter to thank you for yours. . . .

As for the Sorbonne — of course I should be greatly honoured by an invitation to lecture. I wonder what kind of subject? And length? I should like my text to be the saying of Keats: 'Imagination may be compared to Adam's dream — he awoke and found it truth.' In other words, an essay on the creative power of imagination in life and art. This becomes more and more, in small things and in great, the key to my personal life and I believe it is the key to the life of nations. 'Without imagination, the people perish.' And though I am Platonist rather than Christian in any ecclesiastical sense, I believe it to be the essence of the teaching of Jesus, who speaks always of the sins of the spirit (or the imagination) and very little condemned the sins of the flesh. 'He that looketh after a woman to lust after her, hath committed adultery with her already in his heart.'

But, to the woman taken in adultery: 'Go thou, and sin no more.' Not that I intend these quotations for the Sorbonne!

72. TO LOUIS BONNEROT.

Campden Hill Square
14 February 1936

FOR a month I have been buried in the proofs of *Sparkenbroke* and so your delightful long letter has gone unanswered except by a tiny note, nor have I yet read thoroughly *La Poésie d'Angellier,*[1] which you so kindly sent me. During the immense labour of proof-reading — a terrible labour for me who examine every word as if it were the text of the Code Napoleon — I read very little, but each night I fall asleep with Cousine Bette, to remind me that there was once another man [Balzac] who sat at his desk for sixteen hours at a stretch.

[1] A. Angellier was the author of *Sonnets à l'amie perdue*. Professor of English at Lille University and an authority on Burns.

When next I come to Paris — whether it be in the excitement of a lecture at the Sorbonne or just for the pleasure of sitting at a café and having a drink at an hour when Englishmen are forbidden by law to drink (except in private) — I shall particularly look forward to meeting Monsieur Madaule[1] — and, as for the student at the Sorbonne who is writing on *Le Platonisme de Charles Morgan*, I love him already. My heroine, in *Sparkenbroke*, tells Lord Sparkenbroke that when, not long ago, she was at school, she and her fellow-pupils used to recite poetry in class, as part of their English Literature lesson. It was, she says guilelessly, 'part of English Literature, of course'. — 'Did you all stand up with your hands behind you and say verses in turn?'

'We stood up. Why?'

'I was picturing you. It must make a poet shout in his grave when he sees English school-girls stand up to say his verses aloud. Then he's "English Literature of course". Westminster Abbey is nothing to that!'

And I feel that burial in Westminster is nothing to the honour of being the subject of a student's thesis at the Sorbonne. In America it would mean nothing, but in Paris — and for an Englishman! It makes me smile — and feel humble.

Thank you for the trouble you took about my 'saintly Tartarin'. I know so little about him at present that I don't know what to ask. So I shall not trouble you with him for a long time, but imagine him instead, and come to you later for revisions and suggestions if I may. The idea grows. I thought of it at first, as you did, as a long short-story, but since then a woman has come into my head — a beautiful creature of no morals who sings in the local café, whose only virtue is that Tartarin delights and amuses her. And Tartarin writes songs. To him they are almost hymns. To her they are a new kind of mock-innocent material — and so she becomes more and more famous and Tartarin, left behind, remains Tartarin.

I don't know. This is all vague. I knew very little of the lady when I began this letter. I have been making her up as I go along.

[1] Jacques Madaule. Professor of History and author of a standard book on Paul Claudel.

73. TO LOUIS BONNEROT.

Campden Hill Square
20 February 1936

BLESS you. The copies of *Savez-vous* have just arrived and I am most grateful for them and for the trouble they must have caused you. What is more, I learn from them for the first time that Louis Gillet has been elected to the Academy! I ought to have congratulated him long ago. I have done my best now to make up for lost time. I am very glad that he has been elected. He did so passionately desire it and what men want as much as that ought to be granted them. He had the gift of imagining himself as an immortal, and what a man imagines passionately enough does come true for him. There is a difference between wanting and imagining a thing. Thousands of greedy women want thousands of silly things — and they don't obtain them, for their wants are scattered, not single-minded, and so of no effect. But imagination — whether it be Bonaparte's of a world-empire or Gillet's of a seat in the Academy — works like a spell; and the spell is broken if imagination falters; that is why Napoleon fell — because, after 1810-11, he found that he had fulfilled the creative imagining of his life and he tried artificially to extend it. Before, he lived by faith — his 'star'; afterwards by will and will alone is no damned good.

One has to be a fanatic to succeed — Bonaparte, St. Paul, Balzac; but the moment poor St. Peter began to wonder *why* he was walking on the water, down he went; just as, when Napoleon said to himself 'Why am I in Russia?', Moscow instantly burst into flames. What an essay! 'A very questionable doctrine!' you will say. But then, you see, I am dreaming of my prison-keeper, who didn't worry about the outward appearance or names or reputations of men or women but knew an angel when he saw one.

74. TO LOUIS GILLET, *after his election to the French Academy*.

Campden Hill Square
20 February 1936

I HAVE always envied France her Academy and I envy her the more now, for she has shown again that she knows well how to preserve a great tradition. In England, though we are strong in the traditions of government and Law, we have never learned how officially to do honour to the arts. In painting, our Academy, though founded by great men, has fallen into contempt; no artist of the first rank joins it until he is so old that he has become more interested in his pensions than in his art. In Literature, we have tried to create immortals by conferring on them the Order of Merit, and, for a few years, it was honourably conferred; but lately it has become entangled with politics and the social graces; Kipling and A. E. Housman have stood aside from it; Moore was denied it; it has been given to Barrie and Galsworthy — that is, to men who are approved by the special snobbery and sentimentality that one associates with *Punch*; and even the Order of Merit has declined in repute. I rejoice the more that l'Académie has given a new proof of its wisdom.

75. TO M. RENÉ LALOU, *a distinguished French critic and an influential friend to Charles for over a quarter of a century. (He wrote prefaces to the French translations of* The Fountain *and* Sparken-broke. *The essay mentioned was on Rudyard Kipling.)*

Campden Hill Square
22 February 1936

THANK you again for your essay. I am glad you pointed out that Kipling's love of France came a little late in life and sprang from hatred of Germany. His intellect was not *naturally* French. I always feel that I have a better chance of being instantly understood by a French mind than by an English. The English refusal to count beforehand the cost of their emotions, their extraordinary habit of 'hoping for the best' until the inevitable worst is upon them, their whole attitude towards women, their incapacity to find *pleasure* in art as such, their deadly reticence — all these things make me feel foreign among them. Kipling on the other hand was at home among the English. He understood and sympathised with their fecklessness, though he was not feckless himself.

You see, the key to the modern English is that they are afraid of being called 'mean'. They will forgive a spendthrift anything. They will gamble with courage; when a crisis comes, they will throw in all their energies passionately, as a gambler throws in his all in the hope to recover his fortune; but neither in private life nor in public affairs will they systematically make provision for the future. This is called 'meanness'. If they do save (and they *do*), they save secretly. It is bad form to talk about money or to appear to be interested in it. Your T.S.F. is full of Bourse quotations; as far as our B.B.C. is concerned, there is no such thing as a Stock Exchange. The English therefore think that the French are mean: they loathe the small, careful *rentier*; in their hearts they envy him and dislike him the more for that reason. He is the tortoise of Aesop's fable; they are the hare. They can always save themselves at the last moment, in armaments, in private life, in everything, and, if they fail — well, isn't that better than to spend all life in cautious endeavour? That is their point of view. I think it mad and hypocritical; Kipling knew it was mad and pleaded for armaments, and yet, by one of the marvellous inconsistencies of the English temperament, he loved the English for the fault he condemned. The French were to him *allies* — but they were strangers. He had the English schoolboy's insularity. A part of his work will, I think, live as long as people remain historically interested in his period — and no longer. The same is true of Shaw. Was it not Napoleon who said of Sheridan that he made the mistake of treating love as a subsidiary subject, whereas it ought never to be treated at all except as a principal subject. The same is true of Kipling, and bitterly true of Shaw. In spite of the fault which Napoleon perceived, Sheridan lives by one play, *The School for Scandal*, and by one scene in it: the screen scene. A woman behind a screen is a subject for all ages; it gives Sheridan his immortality. But Shaw's women are all intellects; they have no bodies; they were born in their clothes and will die in them. Kipling's women, except in the romantic and passionate relationship, are alive and conspicuously female; that is something; but I remain persuaded that the enduring interests of man are the love of women and the fear of God (or the absence of God). What one remembers about the *Iliad* is Helen. And Kipling has written an imperialistic *Iliad* — but he has forgotten Helen.

76. TO MME DELAMAIN, *then engaged in the translation of* Sparkenbroke.

Campden Hill Square
21 March 1936

MANY thanks for your letter. A copy of *Sparkenbroke* will be sent to you on April 1.

I was very interested by your version of the first poem. It seemed to me an admirable rendering of the sense. The difficulty is that some of the poems in the book are rhymed and in strict metre. This is one. It is an inscription on a tomb and has a sound of eighteenth-century rhyming precision. Probably the verses of Corneille are the equivalent in French? But the attempt to translate rhyme into rhyme is so difficult — almost impossible I think — that I believe the *formal* verses at any rate ought to be left in English, with a French rendering of the *sense* added as a footnote. But there is time enough to think of that.

[The poem enclosed was:

> *We also moved, as thou dost move,*
> *With pride of youth and quick in love.*
> *Have pity then, who drawest near,*
> *That love and youth are ended here.*
> *Though in sweet April thou dost shine,*
> *December waits for thee and thine.*]

77. TO RENÉ LALOU, *on the publication of* Sparkenbroke.

Campden Hill Square
14 April 1936

I AM deeply touched by the extraordinary generosity of your letter — its generosity of time, of thought and understanding. It came this morning to console me for a fierce attack in the *Daily Telegraph* by a detective-story writer who uses Francis Iles as a *nom de guerre*. A woman, I believe.[1] It was inevitable, after the success of *The Fountain*,

---

[1] A mistake. Francis Iles is one of the *noms de guerre* of the writer Anthony Berkeley Cox.

that there should be critics lying in wait for me. I am fortunate in having been so little attacked. Besides the *Daily Telegraph*, only two papers have been hostile. The rest of the Press has been with me and has given great prominence to the book. It is, moreover, being sold very fast. But I have, as you know, an obsession about French opinion, and that you should like *Sparkenbroke* means all the world to me. What I shall write next I do not know. I have many themes but none has yet asserted itself above all others, and I shall wait a little while. The theme I love best requires a French setting — in the French alps[1] and in Paris, the period that of Dégas, the central feminine character an actress or *diseuse*, the chief masculine character a kind of saintly Tartarin! But the difficulties of background are very great; for an Englishman, perhaps insuperable; but my thoughts turn so often to France that I feel more familiar there than in fact I am.

78. TO ST. JOHN ERVINE, *who had submitted a play* (Robert's Wife, *produced in 1937*) *for Charles's consideration. It portrays a 'career woman' with a mission, wife of a clergyman, and the conflict between them in which a bishop intervenes.*

Campden Hill Square
27 April 1936

I CAN'T imagine why the managers have been so stupid about your play. For me it ranks in interest with the early ones, which, as you know, I have always preferred to *The First Mrs. Fraser* and *Anthony and Anna*. It may be a limitation in me, but I always prefer your serious to your lighter passages; and this is true even within the present play itself. But undoubtedly the play as a whole would hold the stage and is concerned with a subject that greatly needs discussion. Thank you very much for sending it to me.

Your letter about *Sparkenbroke* interests me enormously. Some people take the mystical view of death and some people don't. It is, I suppose, largely a matter of temperament. I knew that I was running the risk of that sharp division of taste when I used the subject for this book. I am only sorry that it should have, to that extent, spoiled the book for you. But it does seem to me curious that you should object

---

[1] This was changed to the country of the Charente.

to the attempted suicide. Suicides, nowadays, are always labelled 'melodramatic', but I think the label is a dangerous one. Anyhow, for me the scene was by no means artificial, but in many ways the most moving and inevitable in the book. People who write to me about *Sparkenbroke* seem to fall into two camps. You like Mary but hate him, whereas one young woman has just written saying that Mary is the one defect in the book. Part of her objection is that the poor girl wears a nightgown instead of pyjamas. Such are the miseries of novelists.

You must at all costs go to see the Parnell play[1] at the Gate. As a work of art it is not first rate, and if you expect a political piece you will of course be disappointed, but it is deeply moving and I think up your street, and the acting, except a minor part here and there, is superb.

79. TO GEORGES COUTANT, *a French student.*

21 May 1936

I WAS very interested in your letter, but the questions you ask are those that men have been asking themselves since the world began and it is impossible to give even an adequate personal answer within the scope of a letter.

For example, you ask 'what is the connection between the contemplative and the common life'. My view is that contemplation should be regarded rather as a passive than as an active process. The art of contemplation, and that part of it to which an intellectual, philosophical process can best contribute, is the art of putting oneself into such a condition that God (if he exists) can enter in and make himself known. If you are finally decided that God does not exist in any form; if, that is to say, your mind is intellectually closed against the possibility of un-intellectual apprehensions, then it would appear to me that the contemplative state, even if you could attain to it, would be useless to you — it would be, as it were, the opening of a room to admit a visitor known not to exist. If, on the other hand, a philosopher, while confessing his present ignorance of God in any form, is intuitively aware of spiritual powers external to the senses, which may perhaps make

[1] *Parnell*, by Elsie Schauffler, first seen at the Gate Theatre in April 1936. During that spring and summer C. M. was much concerned with attempts to lift the ban preventing its public performance.

themselves manifest to him, then it would appear to me to be tha philosopher's duty to induce a contemplative condition in himself so that the spiritual powers may make themselves known.

This brings me to the practical question: is the attempt to attain a contemplative condition to be regarded as part of the common life or as being separate from it? The answer is, I think, that both alternatives are possible. To some men it has seemed necessary to enter an enclosed religious order. To others, among them the Indian philosopher Kabir, it has seemed that 'he is the true Saint . . . who requireth thee not to close the doors, to hold the breath, and renounce the world: who maketh thee perceive the supreme Spirit wherever the mind resteth: who teacheth thee to be still amidst all thine activities'.

I think, if I may say so, that you are creating difficulties for yourself and putting chains upon your philosophical investigations by a too rigid decision that there is no God; for it has always appeared to me that one of the chief purposes of philosophy was to decide, first, whether there is a God, and, if so, what is his nature and what is man's relationship with him. It is this sense of philosophical awe which enables a man, whether he is a believer or not, to put himself 'in the second place absolutely'. If he is without faith, he has no image that he can worship, but the absence of faith need not prevent him, unless he is hardened and made barren by spiritual pride, from being aware of powers, as yet mysterious, greater than his own, which cause him to kneel down in a humility of intellectual curiosity long before he is capable of uttering a prayer of assured faith.

80. TO ROGER BARRETT.

Campden Hill Square
26 June 1936

ODDLY enough, your two letters, May 2 and 12, came in reverse order. I'm immensely interested in them both, particularly by what you say on the Temptation theme. And I see what you mean when you say there's a danger of my caring too much for technique — the opposition between the elaborate and the simple. My trouble is that, as far as my *intention* is concerned, I am innocent of elaboration. I have very complex metaphysical ideas to express: what I want is to be precise, not vague — above all lucid; and the only way I know to be lucid is to use my tools (words) with deadly accuracy and somehow or other by sound to enchant (or hypnotise) the reader into a condition of receptivity. I want to cast a spell under the influence of which readers will apprehend what they cannot understand — and what cannot be expressed — in terms of dry reason and intellect. To be *clear*, requires of me a special elaboration, granted my subject.

But I see the danger. And just as *Portrait in a Mirror* was written as a corrective to the wild hysteria which marred *My Name is Legion* so, I hope, my next book will have a subject which will liberate me from the excesses of my present style — a subject *with its feet firmly on earth*. I haven't begun to work yet. I hover between three or four possible stories.

Meanwhile, *Sparkenbroke's* fate has been interesting. The subject of death is one of those subjects — like incest and shooting foxes — that make Anglo-Saxons go off the deep end. I expected controversy and I've got it, particularly in U.S. In England the book has had a smooth passage, has sold 27,000 and is going on steadily and gently. In U.S. it has been attacked in a good many papers with hysterical fierceness and the pro- and anti-*Sparkenbroke* have almost come to blows. Letters pour in. One lady sent me six photographs of her extremely beautiful daughter, who, she said, was exactly like Mary — and so she is! Forty-five thousand were sold in seven weeks. Then, after that, the book became steadily the top instead of, as hitherto, the second seller in U.S. and has remained top for four weeks (they have regular weekly statistics from all booksellers). What the sales are now or what they will become I don't know. At present the thing goes on like a prairie fire. — It *is* very odd. I said to myself: 'Well, anyhow, this death-theme interests me, but it will finish me as a *seller*', but there's something in the book that drives people who *do* like it almost off their heads — particularly women.

I think I shall write now something as solidly earthy and naturalistic and non-metaphysical as *Madame Bovary*. It will do me good — damned difficult, particularly for me — therefore good to try.

81. TO STEWART HUNTER, *a Scottish writer and engineer.*

Campden Hill Square
3 July 1936

MANY thanks for your letter which has greatly interested me. The problem you put does of course lie at the root of all my work and has continually engaged my mind.

The answer to your question appears to me to be that, though it is not necessarily wrong or contradictory to love or to practise an art, and though to do so ought not to be spoken of as imprisoning oneself, it is extremely difficult to do either of these things without allowing the higher self to become 'attached' to the desire or ambition of the personal self. It seems to me that either one must spend one's life in endeavouring to avoid such 'attachments' to the results of one's activities or one must renounce action altogether. The problem of this choice you will find discussed very fully in the *Bhagavad Geeta* (translated by Purowit Swami). In this, the doctrine of Krishna is set out more clearly than the corresponding doctrine in the Gospels of Jesus, and I think the answer to our common problem is there, if we have the wit to find it.

82. TO LOUIS BONNEROT.

Campden Hill Square
3 July 1936

I HAVE had a strange letter from an American woman in Ohio. She says that her daughter, Carol, precisely resembles Mary in *Sparkenbroke* — the same turn of phrase, the same intonation, the same appearance. And she sends me photographs of the girl! I opened the packet with every kind of misgiving! But there she is, my Mary, in the flesh, as I had imagined her. How miraculous! Ohio too!

I have begun the book about the French prison. What its title will be, I don't know. It must be English, I suppose. There is an air of affectation in giving a French title to an English book. But I want its sub-title to be: '*Fantaisie Simple*' — because it is a fantasy about a 'fool of God'. You will be able to tell me when we meet whether *Fantaisie Simple* has the meaning that I want it to have.

83. TO HILDA MORGAN, *recording progress with* The Voyage.

Campden Hill Square
8 August 1936

I HAVE been making steady progress with Barbet. It *is* a queer book. My trouble is to 'profundify' him and make him interesting while avoiding complex introspection. I must keep him simple at all costs and not permit him Sparkenbrokish meditations. There is the difficulty, too, that I have never lived in any of the scenes I have to depict. There is none of the analogy with my own childhood that there was in *Portrait in a Mirror* and in the Rectory at Sparkenbroke Green. It is all to be imagined — like the scene of a fairy-tale; from which there *ought* to spring a kind of freshness and freedom — that is the hope. It is too early yet to say how it will be fulfilled or denied. Everything as yet is undetailed. It is the beginning of detail — the struggle to give the feeling: 'this really happened' — that will test me.

84. TO LOUIS BONNEROT.

Campden Hill Square
22 January 1937

THE novel has been making progress, but I am held up because, as yet, in spite of many advertisements, I have been unable to buy copies of *L'Illustration* for the relevant years. What I want is anything I can get of *L'Illustration* between 1883 and 1887, but if I can't get them, I shall have to come to Paris and consult them in a library. But that is always rather difficult and hurried.

You ask me a question about Plato's influence on me. As you know, I am not a Greek scholar, and read Plato only in translation. I think he is to be regarded rather as a seed and stimulation than as a philosophical influence in the true sense. The only texts of his that I have ever really studied with close attention are the *Republic* and the four Socratic dialogues. Apart from that, I have depended hitherto upon bursts of reading here and there and upon an extremely valuable book on the whole of Plato by A. E. Taylor. You, who are a devoted and thorough scholar, probably would have difficulty in believing how casual my

L

reading is. I drift from book to book, clinging only to what is of immediate value to myself and letting the rest go. That, to a scholar, must
seem very reprehensible, but for me it is the only way.

85. TO LOUIS BONNEROT.   (*W. G. Moore, Fellow of
St. John's College, Oxford, wrote an article on 'Mr. Morgan's*
Sparkenbroke' *for the* Hibbert Journal, *January 1937.*)

Campden Hill Square
14 April 1937

WHAT a strange life we lead — we write so much for other people
that we have little time to write to each other, and even tonight, when I
have leisure, I am tired, for I have been writing all yesterday and today
a long article for the *Times Literary Supplement* on Eugene O'Neill.
So if this is a bad letter, you will forgive me. . . .

What a good article you wrote and what a memory you have. I
couldn't quote from my own works as you quote from them. I have
read your last two paragraphs again and again, genuinely trying to
profit by them, but it is hard, for 'ce paradoxe qui est inhérent à ce
roman' is inherent also in my own life at its present stage. Will Moore,
I think, does not state the position quite accurately. His error is in the
phrase: 'men are *brought to ruin* by qualities we all admire, by ecstasy,
imagination, etc.' I will not admit by any means that *Sparkenbroke* is
'brought to ruin' and, as for Mary, what brings her to the point of
suicide is not ecstasy and imagination, but divided imagination, a
failure of synthesis, a falling away from singleness of mind. A world in
which imagination brought men and women to ruin would indeed be,
as Will Moore says, godless, but my point is that imagination and
ecstasy, themselves godlike, are, in common with all godlike attempts,
as perilous to man's weakness as they are necessary to his glory. I have
not condemned the godlike attempt. I have said only that failure in it
and the consequent division of mind are agony. And that is true.

You are right in saying that *Sparkenbroke* '*n'est qu'une expérience
purificatrice*'. It is, like all my books, and all my writing that is any
good, confessional. By that I do not mean that it is, in any ordinary
sense, autobiographical — only that it is an imaginative purge. I could
not write if I did not suffer. That is the common experience of artists.

That is what Wagner meant in the passage you quote. But it is equally true of me to say that *I could not suffer if I did not write.* That is the key to my life, my peculiar madness which every 'expérience purificatrice' is an attempt to outgrow or, as you say, 'une étape sur la voie du mysticisme idéal' or, as I would say, a struggle towards singleness of mind. Until I attain singleness of mind I can never write the book you speak of in your last sentence — at least, I think not, though I am not altogether sure what your last sentence means, what kind of a book you have in mind.

86. TO HILDA MORGAN.

Campden Hill Square
October 1937

I HAVE been at work on Barbet all day without stirring from my desk except for a meal and for a few words with your gardener, who is to train the creeper in the way it should go. . . .

I seem always to be feeling my way in this book. I have thought of it always, not as naturalism, but as a kind of 'fable with its feel of earth' and the tug is always: how much fable and how much earth? How am I to treat what would naturally be naturalistic, almost Balzacian scenes, such as Victor's scheming and devilish interview with Anton's wife, Bette? What I am trying for is to avoid photography even here, to simplify my moral outlines, to write of Victor in a perfectly simple, descriptive language appropriate to naturalistic story-telling and yet to imagine him myself with the kind of imagination with which one used to imagine the people of a fairy-story. It is a perilous balance and to me rather an agonising one. It would be such a relief, for example, to allow Barbet to fall into elaborate, self-interpretative meditation, but I know I mustn't; he must be discovered in his words and acts, none of which must be spectacular or emphatic; he must be *felt* in a thousand small unexpected clashes between his way and the world's way; and what he is must *dawn* on the reader; all the little clashes must become a unity that is Barbet. Oh God, but it's unknown territory for me! In some ways a happy book, but so *difficult* that when I have done a day's work on it I turn away with a sigh of relief and go off and look at my apples, or read the *Bouvard and Pécuchet* you gave me when

Barbet was begun, or wander down to the drawing-room and listen to
Bach's 'Jesu, Joy of Man's Desiring', which has *done* what I'm trying
to do.

87. TO LOUIS BONNEROT

Campden Hill Square
29 November 1937

SINCE you wrote, French criticisms of *Sparkenbroke* have been pouring in, and appear to be all extremely favourable. In fact, I haven't
come across a bad one yet. I wish my own countrymen of the Left
liked me as well!

Your question about the title of *Sparkenbroke*: the name was based
on various noble names in England, such as Bolingbroke; but certainly
it was also designed to contain the sound of water, which I always like
to have in any titles if I can. For the same reason, the play I have
written, and I think sold for production probably next September, is
called *The Flashing Stream*.

88. TO LOUIS BONNEROT.

Campden Hill Square
25 December 1937

HUXLEY has been struggling towards a mystical outlook for years;
it was perceptible in the extreme end of *Those Barren Leaves*, where
someone went off to lead a contemplative life; but Huxley is held back
— he has too much *knowledge*; he reads too much. . . .

About the play. It is called *The Flashing Stream*. I wrote it almost by
mistake. I have long had two thoughts in my mind: (1) that modern
English dramatists never write a play *about* love; they use love as a
counter; they tell you that A is in love with B, and then write a play
about murder, marriage, economics — anything on earth except the
passion and exaltation of love. I wanted to write a play about a man and
a woman of first-rate minds passionately in love from first to last;

(2) that no background to drama is so interesting as that of skilled men doing their own work — lawyers, tradesmen, what you will. I am tired of people on the stage with no *work* except to hand tea-cups. The job I know about is the Navy. I wanted a naval background. As long as I thought in terms of ships, I could see no way of combining a love-story with a professional naval setting. There are no women in warships — anyhow not women with a job. This difficulty persisted for years. Then I said to myself: Why not a naval station *ashore?* A group of specialist officers working on a secret anti-aircraft invention, a highly mathematical invention. No women. A community compulsorily celibate. One of the officers, a rare mathematician, is killed in an accident before the play opens. Who shall replace him? The work is urgent and is stopped. Someone must be found at once. The dead man's sister has come to visit him. Her mathematical genius is equal to his. Ferrers, the chief, reluctantly accepts her as a member of his staff. He and she love each other at sight. For the sake of the work, for the sake of the other celibate officers, they are bound to behave, not as lovers, but strictly on service. That is the tension — a man and a woman desperately in love, refraining from love because to them the work, the mathematics, is an absolute ideal, comparable to the ideal of the great *religieux*. I need not trouble you with the rest of the story. . . . The thing has happened, almost without my seriously planning it. If I become a frequent playwright, I shall abandon criticism. Whether I ought to abandon it when this play is performed, I am not sure.

I think it is good in its kind. I believe it as good as I can make a play *without breaking the frame of the ordinary theatre*. Really it is for me — as far as form is concerned — a technical exercise, a discipline, a deliberate submission to three acts, one scene, naturalistic dialogue. I wanted to see how much passion, how much of the relationship between love and mathematics, how much of the nature of love and genius (both these are *The Flashing Stream*) I could express within the accepted limits of the theatre. I wanted to learn to *draw* before I dared to distort in this supremely difficult medium. If this play succeeds (and its extreme intensity may prevent it from succeeding in England) I want to make experiments.

Meanwhile the story of Barbet continues in tranquillity. I love it. No one else will — not even you, perhaps. The play delayed it. Christmas theatres have delayed it again. But it goes on slowly and almost secretly. Nothing on earth is so difficult as to simplify and this tale must be told simply without philosophic analysis, almost without introspection. It is almost intolerably hard. I have to throw away all the weapons I have learned to use and learn to use new ones — to make new ones.

89. TO ST. JOHN ERVINE, *in reply to his criticism of the long essay 'On Singleness of Mind' with which Charles prefaced the printed edition of* The Flashing Stream.

Campden Hill Square
September 1938

BLESS you for your letter which, as all your letters do, encouraged our breakfast table.

As you're going to write on the book, perhaps I ought not to say anything meanwhile, but I have your own horror of single-track minds and I can't bear your thinking *that* is what I am applauding. I know there is a danger of confusing 'single-trackedness' with single-mindedness, but I have tried to make the distinction clear. To me a single-minded man may have a thousand interests — e.g. Leonardo whom I give as one instance, or Goethe, who was a very human human being. The point (and I try to bring it out at the end of the preface) is that what matters to the single-minded man is not the 'event', the material result. Leonardo doesn't despair if his picture is destroyed as long as he paints it. It isn't selfishness or egotism. It is devotion to an ideal — a selfless devotion that doesn't reckon in rewards or even in success. Karen makes it clear that this was true of Ferrers. He *wanted* his invention to succeed; he did his utmost to make it succeed; he was not such a nincompoop as to be indifferent. But it wasn't the success or the material effect that deeply mattered to him. He would work with devotion as selflessly as an old gardener plants an acorn with full knowledge that he will never sit under the resulting oak-tree.

St. John, don't think, as many do, that I am aloof or a prig. I value work and competence passionately. But I believe the only way to live with real independence is to try to do one's job for its own sake and not for the sake of its results. That — roughly — is all.

I won't go on. You have had enough of my writing. But I couldn't resist this one point.

90. TO M. LOUIS CARETTE, *in connection with an enquiry instituted by the Brussels Catholic review* Cité Chrétienne *into 'Literature and Christianity', and in particular into the relationship of a writer towards his own work and its influence on others.*

26 September 1938

I AM not a Catholic and it would be arrogant and foolish in me to express an opinion on subjects that directly touch Catholic faith and morals. My thought and my work have their root in my belief that though a man, in his capacity of citizen, may, without self-betrayal, acknowledge loyalty to his country, his Church or his party, he must not, in his capacity of artist, submit his art to the influence or the service of any group. From this the answers to two of your questions directly follow: An artist's choice of subject must be limited by no other consideration than the suitability of the subject to his genius. Secondly, an artist must not allow his work to be influenced by any consideration of its effect upon men's actions. If his art is pregnant and fertile it will indirectly affect action, but that is not his concern, for art and propaganda are different in kind.

You ask further whether I consider a Catholic literature possible or desirable. My answer is again that an artist must not be limited in his choice of subject. If Catholic beliefs are the eyes through which he sees his God, he must write on Catholic subjects; if the philosophy of Plato occupies his spirit, he must write on Platonic subjects. It appears to me that in this sense only is one subject more desirable than another.

91. TO HUGH WALPOLE, *written while Charles was still at work on* The Voyage.

Campden Hill Square
18 November 1938

I CERTAINLY didn't mean to drag you into a reply to my note. It means much to me that you should have liked *The Flashing Stream*. It's odd; I wrote it honestly and as well as I could, and I enjoyed writing it as one enjoys a kind of holiday exercise, but I think of it only as a swerve from my novels, whereas *Sparkenbroke* meant all the world to me. But it *was* a labour. No holiday exercise about that!

And I expect it went heavy in consequence. Whether the delight of writing is always a good test of what is being written, I doubt. If it's true, then I ought now to be writing a masterpiece, for I am enjoying myself as I have never enjoyed a novel before. But one can never be sure. That's why I envy painters and draughtsmen; they can see their finished work all of a piece; but people in our job never can. After the hundred and first revision one wants never to see one's book again and in fact never reads it. And yet I can go to my play with interest again and again. God knows why!

92. TO LOUIS BONNEROT, *who had commented upon the Preface to* The Flashing Stream. (*The misunderstanding referred to could easily arise from the following passage:* '*It must be understood by whoever loves singleness of mind that* "*a sense of humour*" *is his enemy....*')

Campden Hill Square
9 December 1938

I AGREE with a great part of your criticism. In the first place I would rather have left my play without preface. I don't like explanations of imaginative work. But I wanted above all that the play should be *read* and not only seen in the theatre and it is a fact, which has to be faced, that no one will read a book that contains *only* the script of a play. A preface was necessary to make the thing a *book* for the library.

But you misunderstand my attack on humour. I am *not* attacking humour. I am attacking that tendency to decry and sneer at all boldness and greatness which, in England, 'is MISCALLED a "sense of humour"'. It is miscalled a sense of humour because the people who use it like to attach an attractive name to their vice. But my use of the phrase has caused confusion. People have not observed my word 'miscalled'.[1]

---

[1] 'That acidity of derision and self-derision which is miscalled "a sense of humour"'.

93. TO HILDA MORGAN, *written after Charles had passed the opening months of the war in intelligence work for the Admiralty.*

Campden Hill Square
4 December 1939

I THINK I am going to leave the Admiralty. Except now and then my work there could be done as well by others and I could do more *good* outside. What is more, you were right and I believe it is my job to write. What is more, I think I shall go mad if I don't. I starve and starve for that one unchanging agony-bliss.

94. TO PATRICK MALIN, *who had proposed the 'refinement of preferences' in the course of personal experience, as a third source (alongside theology and humanistic philosophy) of individual and social ethics.*

Campden Hill Square
27 September 1940

YOUR Baccalaureate Sermon was good to read and will be good to keep — particularly, by my choice, the paragraph on 'the refinement of preferences' — a new and a newly illuminating phrase for a thought which, I think, runs through all your thought. It will be good to talk of if you come to England or I survive to come to America. At the moment, I feel rather *désœuvré*. I had a commission to edit and write an introduction to a book on Plato but I have cabled to Longmans in New York trying to release myself from it. They have answered neither my cable nor my previous letter; I do not know why; perhaps they are offended; and indeed it must be hard for them to understand the stress in which we live. In any case, I cannot now face the quiet, solid re-reading of Plato and the writing of a scholarly essay. I must write what is new; I must have the stimulus of creating or I cannot write at all while living from hour to hour as we live now.

As yet I have not begun a new book. I hope I shall soon. It will be something to live in, but whereas, in the past, it seemed worth while to tell a story if one struggled to tell it well and truly and to pour one's being into it, now I look and look for a subject greater than any I have attempted and greater than contemporary events. To see this *war* except as a tragic *episode* in the spiritual history of man is to make art meaningless and life intolerable. Therefore it is necessary to imagine a greater river in which what we are now passing through is no more than a rivulet — and such subjects as that of *Paradise Lost* are not easily come by. One would have supposed that the extravagant madness of our daily life would have driven a writer to choose ephemeral subjects and to snatch at the hour; but it is not so; the less chance I have of being alive tomorrow morning the more my thought turns to epic subjects which may need many quiet years to mature.

95. TO HILDA MORGAN, *in America with their children, Shirley and Roger, and under the care of Patrick Malin. (Charles was sharing his home with Christopher Arnold-Forster and Rache Lovat Dickson.)*

Campden Hill Square
9 October 1940

DON'T worry, dearest, about US IN ENGLAND. I don't feel that the future is utterly bankrupt, either personal or national. This business has caused me to write off a great deal of worldliness and anxiety and I believe that life needn't be intolerable *as long as there is no compromise on the war.* However great the losses, we can face them as long as, at the end of the war, we know what they are; but a patched-up peace and the threat of new German aggression would be utterly intolerable. And I think that, if I live, you will like me better when this is done. One does have to compose one's soul in order to live through it because what is necessary is not to be heroic or to make war-time jokes or think consciously about spiritual things, but simply to acquire a *habit* of assuming that the bombs are not going to hit you so that, when the blitzkrieg gets going each night, you do really go on writing your letter or playing your Mozart as if the bombs were not dropping.[1]

[1] 'There arose among the people a stubborn and ancestral madness which, carrying them beyond their urgent fear, enabled them to see these days in retrospect. They did not doubt that the time would come in which they or their children would say: "The enemy did not land" or "The enemy landed but in the end we got rid of him." ' From *The Empty Room*, published 1941.

96. TO ROGER MORGAN, *then aged fourteen and at school at Andover, Massachusetts. (Written from the home of the Earl and Countess Cawdor.)*

Raitloan, Nairn, Scotland
1 November 1940

AS you know, I am not in love with the American way of life, and I don't wonder that you find Andover rushed and difficult. . . . I do ask myself whether I was right or wrong to take you from Eton. On the whole, I still believe it was right, for, though Eton continues, it cannot be what it was, a place of leisurely and quiet humanities. Much of their life must be lived in air-raid shelters and, above all, their *minds* must be on the war, its uncertainties, its living from hand to mouth. But perhaps you would have preferred even this. If so, I'm sorry, Roger, but do not imagine that even now — and still less in a few months time — England is the place you left. It is pretty grim and it is hard to have any long perspective. It seems to me possible, whether we like it or not, that the things we care for will, if they are to live, have to be born again to Europe *through* America. Your long view of your own life might well be to forward and even to direct that process. At the moment I believe your particular power is to make friends. Choose them; make them; keep them. It is through them that you can gradually make your own influence felt. My habit has always been to be too much self-absorbed. You get on much more easily with people, and it is a great gift. Obviously, this mingling of English and American life is going to have an effect on the future of the world, and you, as a statesman or an artist or a man of business might guide that effect, whether your ultimate headquarters is U.S. or England. Begin to imagine on these lines; what one deeply imagines, comes true; . . . Don't even despise business. It is, in a way, the American means of self-expression.

Every country and every age has its own means of expression and one has to use it. For example: I am pretty certain that what Shakespeare *really* was, was a poet — not by choice a dramatist. His Sonnets have his personal genius in them even more than his plays. But it happened that, in his day, people *wanted* plays. It was through plays that a man of genius could make certain of an audience upon whom to exert his power. The theatre was 'the means of expression' at the time, so Shakespeare used it. In my time, novels have been the means of expression. I would always rather have written poetry, but novels were the way to an audience and novels it had to be. In America, business is the chief way, or one of the chief ways — of influencing men, of making yourself felt and heard, and it is obviously not impossible to take a very long and imaginative view of business and to work *through it* towards whatever political or humane ideals one may hold. It may not be your way. But don't rule it out. Don't necessarily despise it. Try to see how it could be used. . . .

I don't think I like my life at the moment much better than you do yours. But you will have a lot of years in which there will not be a war, and in some of them I hope you and I will do good things together.

97. TO HILDA MORGAN.

Campden Hill Square
25 November 1940

YESTERDAY, while at Mortimer,[1] so vast a scheme of novel-writing floated into my head that I don't know whether to laugh at and reject it or take it seriously. I thought of a great series of novels beginning in Periclean Athens and ending in the Renaissance — 2,000 years. The central theme would be that civilization, as you and I understand it, is imperishable; that it survives even the downfall of Greece and the Dark Ages; that it crops up continually — in the cathedrals, in the monasteries, in individuals, and, periodically (perhaps only once in 2,000 years) flowers. And since a series of novels cannot consist in variations on the same theme, each novel would have to have a separate theme of its own. What a project! Am I already too old to attempt it? And, if I did, would my heart fail me in midstream. To set out *now* on such a labour seems a kind of madness, for tomorrow morning I may not be alive, and yet the very desperation of material day-to-day existence makes a vast work like this appear, in the long view, as the right boldness — a kind of balancing sanity. I don't know. I wish I could walk with you in the country and sit by a parlour fire and talk about it.

[1] In Berkshire, with Denys Kilham-Roberts and his wife.

98. TO HILDA MORGAN.   *Written from the Buckingham-
shire home of Sir Arthur Bryant. (The 'Discourse' referred to,
'France as an Idea Necessary to Civilisation', was repeated at the*
Institut français *and later printed in* Reflections in a Mirror,
Second Series.)

The White House, East Claydon
30 December 1940

I THINK life ought to be good and peaceful. The floors are so old
and uneven that it is the devil to persuade any table to stand evenly on
them, but I have established a good table in my bedroom where there
is one electric fire. Ordinarily I work downstairs in the sitting-room by
an open fire while Arthur goes off to his own study, but there is always
my bedroom to fall back on.

My immediate job is to write the 'Discourse' I am to deliver at the
Royal Institution on February 25th. Meanwhile my staple reading is
the Verney Memoirs, the whole domestic history of the Verney family
from the end of Queen Elizabeth to the beginning of Queen Anne —
the perfect background for the seventeenth-century novel first hinted
at in *The Fountain*, which you and I have so often talked of together.
It would be good to lay the foundations of such a novel here, for this
house is a part of the Verney history. How to tackle it as a *story*, I don't
yet know. I think the thing to do would probably be to make my
principal characters fictitious (perhaps cousins of the Verneys) and use
all the authentic Verney material as background. A great deal of the
material is gathered into the Verney Memoirs, but, if I want to elaborate
any particular point, all the original letters are at Claydon House and
Sir Harry Verney would let me use it. I think of this book as a kind of
long, slow magnum opus — the stress and beauty and thought of
England for a hundred years — to be written slowly and with no
thought of critics or public. Other novels might be written concur-
rently with it if they were different enough in kind. I don't know. But
certainly that the Verney Memoirs should fall into my lap seems a kind
of omen and there is a certain comfort and reassurance nowadays in
contemplating a work that would need YEARS to complete.

99. TO HILDA MORGAN.   (*The new novel referred to became* The Empty Room, *and was in fact dedicated to Patrick
Malin.*)

East Claydon
20 January 1941

YESTERDAY and the day before I began and finished the first
chapter of a new novel, provisionally called 'The End of the Tunnel'.
To write in London has become very hard — the depression and ruin
are overwhelming (I don't mean doubt of the outcome. I mean the
depression of the whole way of life there) and, as spring comes with its
lighter nights and as the whole war tightens and intensifies, to write
anywhere will be an extreme battle and in London most of all. Still, I
will go on. If I can't do *that* in any circumstances as long as I am alive,
there's nothing I can do; but for what world or future I am writing I
don't know; it's a strange feeling; and yet, so powerful is the influence
of the writing itself, that for two days I have been happy, living in my
'fictions', longing to read my bit aloud — with no one to read it to,
for Arthur is absorbed in the beginning of his own book on Disraeli.
So I don't look far ahead and only hate having to upheave myself at the
moment of beginning. How I hate unsettlement and wandering. It is
like being at school again — whenever you get into a corner and begin
to read and feel civilized, some hulking lout comes and knocks the
book out of your hand. — All this, my dear, when you are upheaved,
even out of your own country. God give us a little Rectory on the
Herefordshire border and food and fuel and ink! . . .

Now I shall go back to the novel and introduce my heroine — a
woman who can heal life and enable others (and so the world) to be
re-born. And so my love to you for whom the book, if written, will be
written.

100. TO HILDA MORGAN.

Campden Hill Square
7 February 1941

WHAT I am doing and have made some progress with is a much
simpler *Portrait-in-a-Mirror*-like story about a girl who had the

quality of giving peace to 'perturbed spirits' — her father and the man
she loved, and, at last, her mother — I won't go into the 'plot' yet; it's
a bit too new to me; but the theme is, roughly, whether human beings
and nations have the power of regeneration or renaissance. I just go on
with this quietly and that is what I should *like* to do, but the feeling
that it is my job to go to sea and describe this naval war as no one else
can gnaws at me. . . .

Yesterday I had a diversion. I went to the High Court and gave
evidence in defence of the Sitwells who had been libelled by a scurrilous
paper called *Reynolds*. I have never given evidence before and was
rather alarmed less the K.C. who was against us might, in cross-
examination, reveal my quite astonishing ignorance of the Sitwells'
works; but all was well; I actually enjoyed myself in a battle of wits.
Our counsel and solicitors told me afterwards that I was a superb witness and that my evidence had done more good than any other.

101. TO HILDA MORGAN.

Campden Hill Square
10 May 1941

I THINK that, in many ways, what you have been through may have
been more trying than my experience. . . . But certainly our life hasn't
been pleasant. Bombs, which most people suppose to be the worst, are
for me the least of its evils. The worst of it is the long, long stress, the
abnormality of everything, the terrible monotony of conversation, the
utter boringness of the subjects that everyone talks of, the everlasting
difficulties in the way of doing the simplest things — and the knowledge that for ages and ages these restrictions will continue and increase. Oh for the days of the Victorians in which, if you wanted to go
to Timbuctoo, you just got into a train with a cheque-book! However
— and that's the point — it does teach a stoical patience and an absolute habit of 'judging not'. I shall find it damned hard ever to
condemn anyone for anything again; humanity suffers too much.

102. TO CHRISTOPHER ARNOLD-FORSTER.
Written on board ship while Charles was on his way to undertake
American lecture tour on behalf of the Institute of International
Education.

30 August 1941

THIS from my bunk — Saturday August 30, 1941 — the first night
at sea, a pretty spacious cabin which I share with a Hungarian-
American named Friedmann.[1] He has a professional name, too; Capa
or something like it; a star-photographer, I gather, who, together with
Jean Forbes-Robertson's sister,[2] has put together a book on the
London blitz, to be called *The Battle of Waterloo Road*. He is the
oddest mixture of Hungarian pathos and American toughness. . . .

It was a godsend that you and Rache came to see me off. Ordinarily
I like being *met*; being seen off matters less; but it mattered this time;
and a black curtain of unreasoning loneliness descended upon me when
you were gone. I am a good traveller in some ways, but moods of bleak
panic strike me when all I want is a cheerful companion — or a nurse
— and I began to be sure that everything would go wrong. . . .

[The ship] turns out to be not a C.P.R. but a small Norwegian, with
a blond captain out of a saga. Ten passengers, I think: my photographer; a man who arrived on board completely blind and was seen
to everyone's delight climbing into a life-boat and going to sleep in the
sun — ten minutes later he was asleep again in the photographer's
bunk and had to be moved on again; a man bound for Shanghai; a
French commandant who *looks* half Chinese and is already so sea-sick
that he forgot that pawns take diagonally; and a batch of American
ferry-pilots. I feel a certain affection for the ship. She is a ship, not an
anonymous hotel, and there are sheltered places where I hope to read
and write. I was pleased with myself this afternoon — I found that I
could still read the escort's morse; not that it meant anything when
read — presumably groups of flags or some kind of alphabetical
code. . . .

[1] André Friedmann (Capa). Born 1913 or 1915 and considered one of America's
top photographers. A friend of Hemingway and Steinbeck. He was killed in the
fighting in Indo-China while working for the magazine *Life*.
[2] Dinah Sheean, a daughter of Sir Johnston Forbes-Robertson, and wife of
Vincent Sheean, the writer.

As a result of sitting in the sun and *not worrying* I am beginning to imagine — no eruption yet but premonitory rumblings in Vesuvius. It is the pleasant mood before you come down to brass-tacks or are committed to any particular tale, in which scenes of novels and scenes of plays make an inconsequent appearance. There's an idea long in my mind, with its root in the story of Tolstoy and his 'wicked' brother Sergei, which is kindly presenting itself in the form of scenes in a play, as yet completely disorganized — the period and place as vague as a dream, the problem of nationality (for I can't write about Russia) un- solved — but bits of dialogue jump out excitingly and the thing has already an inchoate life without, as yet, having imposed any responsi- bility on me. . . .

I find that my Hungarian photographer's name is CAPA. Rache will know about him. He has been showing me his photographs of the Spanish and Chinese wars which appeared in *Life* and elsewhere. His camera has an extraordinary sense of the humanity underlying war; his talk is good where you can understand it; and I like him, though in the early morning he recalls Baudelaire's poem about the lamentable occasion on which he found himself in bed with *une affreuse juive*. It is an alarming race before breakfast. Capa also talks of American im- perialism as a powerful and increasing force. This is only the second time I have heard of such a thing — first from Malin, now from Capa. It's odd to reflect that Roger, at my age, will probably think of little else. I do not remember at all when I first heard the name NAZI.

Monday, September 1st, 9.30 p.m. The American ferry-pilots are playing high-poker. From a winning position, your sad opponent has just been beaten at chess. An empty day, grey, with a slow, moderate sea, and good visibility for the yellow-haired Norwegian boys, who stand by the guns and occasionally crackle off a few rounds to make sure the things work. It is thought that, if we are not already, we shall, during the night, get beyond the range of enemy aircraft, which alarm the Captain from the saga more than the prospect of submarines. The argument is that at 15 knots, rising to 17–18, we can get away from a stern chase and that anyhow a single, fastish, small ship is not good bait. It is an argument that doesn't convince me any more than it en- courages me to be told that the ship has made 34 Atlantic passages. In the last war, on November 10, 1917, in Rotterdam, the Captain of the *Lapwing* spoke to the same effect and next day we sank in seven

M

minutes. But one is much more concerned by the variation in one's comforts than by the chances of being sunk. To keep the cabin breathable at night is the chief problem. We haven't dared to open the scuttle in case we should wake, forget and turn on a light. However, if all goes well, we should make Montreal by Sunday afternoon. I have written nothing and read little. Flaubert's *Education Sentimentale* is, in period and subject, too near the knuckle for me at present; I lay it down and can't bear to go on. *Cage me a Peacock* is easier reading and I am grateful to the wise giver of a book that I shouldn't have been wisely frivolous enough to buy for myself. Tonight three years ago was the first night of *The Flashing Stream*. . . . It was good at dinner this evening to hear something I wanted to hear. One of the ferry-pilots believes America will come in and ought to come in now. Another, very young, talking to the Norwegian captain about the prospect of revolt in Norway, said: 'Then we shall have a jumping-off ground.' It's the first time I have heard an American use that WE, as if his countrymen were already fighting. Ordinarily these pilots, some of whom are fighting pilots also, make me understand (and I don't mean this disparagingly at all) what the mercenary soldiers may have been like in the past. They don't talk about the war, strategically or politically. They are entirely professional and fight in this war, just as they fought in Spain, because they want to FLY and it earns them big money. Flying men are becoming a race apart. They have courage and toughness and skill, but nothing in them, except that one word WE, has suggested that they are in the least partisans or even interested in the war. . . .

It was good to wake this morning in calm water off Newfoundland. Sunshine, too. Very cold — icebergs and whales — but still, sunshine, a deep blue sea and a sky of pale violet streaked with horizontal bars of deep blue ink. I ought, I suppose, to be thankful to be in safe waters; so I am, in a way; but I have found on this voyage that what has, in fact, presented itself to me as a thing to be dreaded has not been death but the discomfort of an open boat and the inconvenience of losing my gear. I have pictured myself in U.S. bothering about a new passport and visa; I have imagined myself cabling to Rache for the numbers of the old ones. Such is the angle of my absurd anxiety. Fortunately I had no manuscript to lose!

103. TO ROGER MORGAN, *in Massachusetts.*   (*This and
the following four letters were written in the course of Charles's
American lecture tour.*)

Ohio
[undated: 1941–2]

I'M very glad the work is going better and that you contemplate that
essay competition. Here is a note or two that might be of use, worked
in with your own ideas.

1. *Crime and Punishment*

One of Dostoevsky's dominating ideas was the validity of suffering
as a saving force. Modern materialists believe that suffering is an un-
mixed evil. Dostoevsky thought that it purged the soul and tempered
the mind — not that it was good and desirable in itself; (he was not a
MASOCHIST who *seeks* pain) (look up in dictionary); but that out of its
evil good comes.

Compare with this the Christian idea as expressed in the Crucifixion.
You will find in the Communion Service (I can't quote accurately)
something about the Crucifixion having been 'a full and sufficient
sacrifice for the sins of the whole world'.

Compare with this the key passage in *Crime and Punishment* — one
of the most beautiful in literature. Rashkolnikov kneels before SONIA
and says:

'It is not to you I kneel but to suffering HUMANITY in your
person.'

(I quote from memory. Verify.)

The line on this book is to compare it on the one hand with the
Christian idea and on the other with the modern idea of avoiding discomfort and suffering.

If you are writing on Shelley, a good thing would be to read his
Defence of Poetry (a prose piece). You will find that though he often
wrote political and moral poetry himself, he believed that poetry lost
value when it begins to moralize and you can point out that he was
always at his best in his purely lyrical passage — except, perhaps in the
Prometheus where he does moralize and is *MAGNIFICENT* — particularly at the end.

104. TO CHRISTOPHER ARNOLD-FORSTER.

Carleton College, Northfield, Minnesota
2 February 1942

I AM now as far west as I shall go and begin to work my way home-ward. Four more week-ends will find me in Cambridge, and that will be near the end of one-night stands. Thank God. This week-end by Heaven's grace there has been a break. This college has given me a large and comfortable guest-suite and I have a chance to sleep FIVE nights in the same bed and to get laundry done. And I have luck, too, in the weather. Ordinarily at this time of year they expect three feet of snow and anything from 20 to 40 below zero. Now there is no snow and the temperature is 20 above. Even that nips an unaccustomed ear.

I thought that during the five days I should write a lot of letters and perhaps other things, but affable students, men and maidens, come and call and ask me what a boy or girl shall do to be saved — in brief, how to be a writer. They are odd. In most cases what they are thinking about is just how to get writing accepted by the magazines, which is, indeed, in a sense, how we all begin, but to them the magazine standard is the final standard; they haven't got a personal standard at all; they really and truly do not know that there is, or can reasonably be, any difference between a successful book and a great book. For the same reason every newspaper invariably refers to Singapore as 'the $400,000,000 naval base'. This is the measure of importance. . . .

America is thoroughly alarmed, which is all to the good if it were not so helplessly fluttering. They know they aren't doing enough, but they don't know what to do. They think that, except on a voluntary basis, general rationing is impossible. To prohibit the sale of tires is one thing and possible; to ration them or petrol or anything else is, they say, impossible because the law just won't be kept, because it will be killed by graft, and because vast numbers of cars are driven without a licence anyhow. As for grand strategy — they are still pathetically asking where the Pacific Fleet is and expecting the conjuror to repro-duce it out of his hat. In general, life goes on just as it did. The Uni-versities and Colleges are abolishing their summer vacation in order to rush their students through a full course in a shorter time. Apart from that, nothing is changed. There is masses of food; there are masses of students taking the degree of B.A. in journalism or B.Sc. in 'poultry-husbandry'; life is real, life is earnest; in this college, there is a Kellogg Endowment of half-a-million dollars for the study of International Relations. It is studied without reference to military or naval history, although the DISARMAMENT Conference is part of the syllabus; Mahan is not read; the head of the department is a Welsh Nonconformist minister from the University of Bangor, who was a conscientious objector in the last war. Hence, indirectly, Pearl Harbour.

105. TO CHRISTOPHER ARNOLD-FORSTER.

as from Institute of International
Education, New York City
2 March 1942

THIS is written on Monday, March 2, in the train from the University of Buffalo, where I have spent the week-end, to Rochester, N.Y. As the train moved out, the train-conductor shouted: 'Next station-stop BATAVIA.' I looked round at my fellow-passengers to see if the name had anywhere rang a bell. It hadn't. Neither their minds nor their hearts are in this thing. They feel that they have been bamboozled into it and scarcely know who has bamboozled them — the wily British or the 'dirty little Japs'.

As for me, I'm tired in my bones but not ill and I am near the end of the worst part of my journey. My feet have always been bad since Antwerp. Now they have given out rather badly. I live mostly in slippers and galoshes. But otherwise I have survived marvellously. I have been extremely lucky in avoiding extreme cold. Two feet of snow in Buffalo but the temperature all right. Here we are in Batavia, which may for a moment improve my handwriting. . . .

Wednesday, March 4, in train Rochester to Schenectady. Rochester was rather an adventure. I stayed in the house of the President of the University. He turned out to have gone to Balliol just after I came down and to know all my Oxford people. His wife was young and almost beautiful and brought up in France. The house was astonishing. There was one Eastman who made a Kodak. Also he built this house for himself and gave it to the University as a presidential residence. He had enough taste not to use his own and someone has made the house good. A really large and well-designed English country house.

Flowers, wood-fires, porcelain from John Sparks, pictures by Reynolds (portrait of a Miss Hoare), Romney, Raeburn, a grand Gains-
borough; Daubigny, Maris and several lesser Dutchmen, and doubtful
Tintoretto. A hall with superb wrought-iron and two organs! My bedroom a beauty with eight long windows; my bathroom like Alma
Tadema; my clothes-cupboard nearly the size of the cabin at no. 16.
And then, for the first time, I was protected from people.

My host and hostess and I dined alone the first night, a really good
small dinner with good, though Alsatian, wine. That night it snowed.
How it snowed and all next day (yesterday). Twelve new inches and a
blizzard. Motor-cars everywhere became fixed sugar cakes. A great
part of the work of the University was immobilized. A lecture that
night seemed hopeless but there was no way of cancelling it so we went
for the sake of the possible two or three just men. Somehow nearly
200 turned up — men looking like Captain Oates in the picture, girls
in ski-trousers, old ladies carried pick-a-back through the drifts. A
gallant band. I hope they thought it was worth it. I gather they did.
This morning there was brilliant sunshine. Spade and snow-plough
had cut tracks and I had another audience at the Assembly (voluntary!)
at 11.25. I was sorry to leave the civilization of Eastman House. It was
really civilized, materially and personally; much my best break yet.
To find a good, scholarly, youngish Oxonian living in the circumstances of a Scottish duke is very rare and odd. The poor scholars I
have met and the very rich merchants I have met, but here was everything — with an American edge and the very best Henry Jamesian
edge. Well that's past. In four hours I arrive at Schenectady. . . .

About the masterpiece. I haven't got it into the incubator yet. Indeed
there are more than one applicant for the incubator and none has
established his claim. The most frightening is: 'Forty Days and Forty
Nights' of which the Gospels tell gloriously little — Jesus trying to
decide *in which way* to do his job, recalling bits of his past, foreseeing
bits of his future, discarding the 'temptations' one by one and at last
seeing clear. But it does frighten me. It might flatter my faults. But I do
happen to know that now. Anyhow the idea persists pretty stubbornly.
Then there is what I call provisionally 'Fifty Years' — Victorian
childhood, *The Gunroom* (very different!), both wars and death before
the end of the second. What I mean is a NOVEL on the whole stretch of
my own life. The object here is that I have it fixed in my mind that a
novel covering *many* years doesn't stand. One is inclined to imagine

that *War and Peace* covers many years, but in fact it doesn't. Then thirdly there is the bit of me that wants a smaller, more intense canvas — I mean: *Portrait in a Mirror* rather than *Sparkenbroke*; Turgenev rather than Tolstoy. But the real indecision that makes me hesitate is: shall it be a close-to-earth masterpiece, as deadly and unsparingly TRUE as I can make it, or shall I let go completely and write the novel that never was on land or sea? What I want is your intuition about the KIND of masterpiece. Roughly: Sane or mad? Eyes wide open — or tight shut? You taught me that phrase ages ago. One thing I do know. I'm pretty selfless and humble about this book. It will probably be my last, so publishers and booksellers and newspapers and C. M. and all that can bury their heads. Of man's last disobedience and the fruit of that forbidden tree whose mortal taste brought death into the world and all our woe . . . SING HEAVENLY MUSE! and shut up everyone else, except C.A.F. when slightly drunk if ever. The *N.Y. Times* says whisky costs thirty-five shillings a bottle and that one can't get a tolerable meal in London for less than a pound. What have you chaps been doing since I went away?

106. TO HILDA MORGAN.   *Written after Charles's return*
     from America early in July.

Campden Hill Square
26 July 1942

I AM tired and sad today. . . . The week has been full of too many things. B-W[1] wants me to do work for *The Times* again, but the nature of it and the conditions are still undefined, and will not be defined until early in the coming week; that has been uncertainty no. 1. I have dined with Courtauld and RAB,[2] and what he wants of me is still completely indefinite and that also is to be discussed again early this week; that has been uncertainty no. 2. Then I have had frequent discussions with my former war-time chief, who wants me to return to him, but on a different basis and to do a much more independent and

[1] Barrington-Ward, editor of *The Times*.
[2] The Right Hon. R. A. Butler.

better job than before; that has been uncertainty no. 3.[1] What I have longed to do is to refuse them all and write, but that, in our present state, is the one impossible thing, and suddenly on Thursday an order was published requiring men of my age to register on Saturday, yesterday. So at 1.30 yesterday afternoon, feeling that all reason had gone from the world, I took a bus to Shepherd's Bush Green where I filled in a form at the local Labour Exchange. I was 'an author' and I was 'working on my own'. People who have no better protection than that go to factories and it was evident that an instant choice between my uncertainties was imperative. Numbers One and Two were not within my immediate grasp; number Three was, and I happened to have an appointment with my former chief at 6.30. So I made my decision. Tomorrow I take the oath. From August 1st I shall be on duty again. There are certain rifts in the clouds. As long as I do the special work required of me, I do it at my own times, so that apart from a brief 'daily meeting' I am not bound by routine, so that I shall be able to write in the old, not-impossible way — that is, against the ground of a different job, but with the joy and incentive of being hungry for the quiet hours and of writing being a consolation, not a sole profession. Perhaps it is for the best. I shall try to make it so. But I confess that the prospect of spending in this way these precious years of maturity depresses me. There is the added compensation, however, that this job won't tie me to the office. . . . So there it is, a little good mixed with much wastage, but everyone else who is an artist is being equally wasted. It is one of the ironies that, while a journalist may be reserved, there is no reservation of poets or painters or story-tellers if they 'work on their own'. But it is, I suppose, inevitable. This is, indeed, total war. The shortage of man-power is extreme. One must not allow oneself to be made unhappy or one's ultimate purpose to be destroyed. In a way this throws me back upon my basic determinations and patience, and so, if I can see it rightly, strips me of prides and prosperities, and makes me a young man again, beginning from the beginning. . . .

Wednesday 29. Two busy days have passed. I have spent a morning at the Admiralty and been introduced to many people and to the room in

---

[1] His final choice. It was 'special work' of which Admiral Godfrey writes, 'Charles Morgan returned to write what I think was his finest, but alas unpublishable work, a wartime history of the Naval Intelligence Division with all its strange ramifications.'

which I shall work. Chris and Rache and I had a pleasant dinner with
Osbert Sitwell in his little house in Chelsea, where conversation was
still what conversation once was and it was possible to forget the war.
Yesterday I had another long conversation with *The Times*: I won't go
into details of it because it is still inconclusive. What is undecided is
not the money (which is little and of little account) but whether I can
get my function so defined as to leave me a little leisure. . . .

People always ask me whether I am glad to be back. The answer is
no. The tunnel is very long. I know the only cure for it in me is to
write, and so I shall as soon as I can begin to adjust a routine. . . .

107. TO JOHN RAGSDALE, *a young American writer from the
University of Michigan.*

Campden Hill Square
23 August 1942

I WANT to clear up another point which might be the basis of misunderstanding between us. You say: 'about resignation I cannot agree
with you . . . although I admire A. E. Housman as a prince of poets, I
think his resignation is a drug and a slow poison. If American thought
came under his influence, a long span of human effort would have been
wasted.' Let us for a moment leave Housman out of the argument, because we may be interpreting him differently. What I want to make
clear is that though resignation, in the sense in which you use it, is
certainly evil, there is a distinction between resignation (analogous to
despair) and acceptance as it appears in the teaching of Jesus and
Tolstoy and certainly in the *Bhagavad Geeta*. Acceptance is as it were a
cloak that enables a man to *be* himself within the furnace and to pass
through it, whereas resignation is a surrender of one's own integrity
and even of the desire to pass through the furnace. I think the same
distinction reappears or ought to reappear in the endless arguments
about what is called 'escapism'. The word is often fastened, as if it were
a badge of cowardice, to works of art which are accused of running
away from life because they do not choose the subjects which occupy
newspapers; whereas, in fact, what they are doing is transcending and
passing through the journalese of existence (the furnace, if you will)
into a clearer atmosphere.

I will not go on writing for ever, but I wish you would write to me. You sent me a poem which began: 'How strange are the folk who have died in our hearts, and return . . .' I wonder whether you have read 'Smoke' by Turgenev? Why do people of your generation reject Turgenev? It is quite inconceivable that they should continue to do so for ever.

108. TO HILDA MORGAN.   (*'Gordon' is Gordon Alchin.*)

Campden Hill Square
4 October 1942

I AM writing this at a desk perched on a model-throne in Gordon's flat. He is doing an oil portrait. I said I could sit only if I wrote at the same time, and so it has been arranged. It gives me a little company that I am glad of, for life is ordinarily very flat. My office is in a basement; the artificial lighting allows no difference between morning and evening; it is always a surprise to come out, as I did sometimes last week, into a mellow, sunlit autumn day and to remember that things were different once. There is no hardship in our way of living. There are enough material things — enough food, enough clothes if you don't mind being shabby, not enough fuel but the weather is not yet cold enough to make that shortage painful. What is lacking is two things: variety and prospect. I look forward to Saturday because I don't go to the office; then I look forward to next Saturday; but there is nothing else except your home-coming and the hope that then we may be together in this wilderness and no more alone. Often, in the mornings, as I walk from St. James's Park Station across the corner of St. James's Park to the Horse Guards, I stop by the lake where the ducks and pelicans are; or I go by another route with Rache — into Kensington Gardens at Notting Hill, diagonally across the Broadwalk, past the Round Pond, down to the Albert Memorial, and I see people at leisure in these places and remember how we would sit and plan books and dream dreams. I am starving for that companionship and hope — and for small things, small surprises. . . .

Meanwhile, like a lost animal who remembers his old home, I contemplate always, deep within me, the one book I want to write before I die. . . . Could we not, you and I, so shape our lives that each of us struggles to write one more book, and aims at nothing but its greatness. Probably the audience for it will be gone. Never mind. The book is still worth writing. The alternative is mere existence and negation. . . .

I think it is, oddly enough, the loveliness of the weather that has saddened me. Everything, a good book, good music, even the autumn sun, seems to be out of its context, to belong to another age, and the intensity of emotion which, nowadays, every pang of happiness produces is exactly the aching intensity from which a great book might come in a later tranquillity. That is the hope. . . .

I want you to make a future plan — where to live and how to live. I feel that a consecutive work in quiet country would be unspeakable bliss. To go for our afternoon walk and return to tea at a fireside, in a room that became darker until at last one lit the lamp. And I think the man to read would be Goldsmith.

109. TO DR. ORLO WILLIAMS, *who had sent Charles a spare proof of his article, published in the* Criterion, *on the novels of Romer Wilson (1891–1930)*.

Campden Hill Square
17 January 1944

I AM most grateful for your having let me see this. It lights up a lot for me, and tempts me to get the books I haven't read. What I chiefly remember of her work was that it had that quality without which (for me) story-telling IS NOT: the only word for it (now scarcely usable) is glamour. The supreme example is *Anna Karenina*. Then Turgenev's *Torrents of Spring* and *First Love*.

The odd thing is that it is different in every author who has it and yet is always unmistakably the same glamourousness. Stendhal had it, but none of his imitators had, for they imitate only his dryness. Dickens had it — and Thackeray — and Scott (but *not* Trollope) and *not* Jane Austen. But there, God knows, perhaps she has — but J. A. is my blind spot. E. M. Forster has not, and Rosamund Lehmann has — or had. What is the root of it? Sex? Looks like it: Tolstoy — Dickens — and NOT Pater.

110. TO LOUIS BONNEROT.   (*Charles's lecture at the*
University of Glasgow, '*The Artist and his Community*', *was later*
published in The Liberties of the Mind.)

Campden Hill Square
27 April 1945

THE lecture went wonderfully well in Glasgow. I expect it will be
some time before it is printed. Then I will let you have a copy.

Meanwhile, thank you for your letter. My visit to your house was
my holiday in Paris — the rest, however pleasant, was hard work![1]

There is very little to tell you about my link with France *before*
1914. I went to France first when I was six for the Paris Exhibition of
1900. I remember nothing except Panhard motor-cars (and motor-
cars were then VERY new) and a pearl necklace, said to be worth
£80,000 — or was it 80,000 francs. I expect there were other little
visits, but they were certainly short and few, for you must remember
that after the Boer War the English were not very comfortable in
France.

My real French contacts began during my imprisonment in Holland
during the last war. In our fortress were three French officers, Coutis-
son, d'Humières, and Chauvin. Chauvin was in fact a sergeant but he
was a cultured man and was rightly treated by the Dutch as an officer.
He held classes in French. I attended them. You know, I am not a very
national person. My emotions suddenly swing my life. Quite simple
childish things — some wonderful piece of drama, some magnificent,
phrase, takes me by the throat. What won me to France first was that
story of Daudet's — is it called 'The Last Lesson' — about the
schoolmaster teaching his class in the Franco-Prussian war. If this were
said in a serious essay, every Frenchman would say: 'Well, there's a
fool Englishman!' — every Frenchman except perhaps some wise and
gentle one who knows that artists are not brain but heart. . . . Then,
when I left the fortress and lived on parole near the Castle of Rosendaal
in Gelderland, I came under another French influence. Have I told you
of her? Strangely enough she was Hollandaise, née Baroness de
Pallandt. She had married a Scot named LOUDON, and so, when I
knew her, was Madame Loudon. She eighty-six and the mother of two
daughters (still living) — one Constance, who, having married her

---

[1] C. M. was in Paris for the opening night of *Le Fleuve Etincelant*.

cousin, was then the Baroness de Pallandt de Rosendaal and lived at the Castle; the other, Helen, was a widow and was called Madame ELOUT DE SOETERWOUDE, and she lived with her old mother at Rose-neath, the dower-house of the Castle. We three English officers were received at Roseneath as if we had been the old lady's grandsons and the point was that, though Dutch by nationality, she was in thought and feeling FRENCH.[1] She had the manners and language *d'une grande dame de l'ancien régime*. She had danced to Chopin's waltzes with, as she said, '*Monsieur* Chopin playing them'; she had known everyone — people who, to me, were historical personages. She had the gift of the great saying. When someone asked her why she treated us so inti-mately, for certainly we were not of the great European aristocracy, she said: 'It should be enough for you, my dear, that they hold the King's commission and that they are my friends.' One day a rather pert young *bourgeoise* was brought to see her and treated her, not rudely, but rather casually and cheekily. Those who stood near ex-pected to hear her utter some biting reproof, but she remained gentle and affable. When the young *bourgeoise* was gone, the old lady was asked why she had been so forbearing? why had she not put the cheeky young woman in her place. She answered: '*Elle n'est pas à la hauteur de mon dédain.*' All this will seem odd to you. You, my dear Bonnerot, are French, and the French I think believe in *Egalité* more than in Liberté. I don't. I care for aristocracy that justifies itself by responsi-bility, learning or elegance. I adored that old lady and first *loved* France for her sake. In her presence I felt I was on a stage, playing a part in a very great play, and that is something in this life. In her I have lived imaginatively in the France of the mid-nineteenth century.

You will think perhaps, that I am wrong, but I believe that France is never happy except when she has a great man leading her and that she has a genius for preventing him from becoming a Hitler. Napoleon

[1] Perhaps a misapprehension. A grandson of Madame Loudon, Mr. F. W. H. Loudon, writes, 'It is not, I think, true that my grandmother received any educa-tion in France although she was certainly a lover of things French, which was probably her main medium of communication and very likely of thought.' Children of the van Pallandt family, like others of the Dutch nobility, learnt their languages from foreign tutors and governesses. But ties with France — not alone through the House of Orange — were strongest; French literature and thought dominated. It was with European culture, of which France had been so long the leader, that the young C. M. fell in love.

was not a Hitler. However, that is very personal to you. I must never speak of French politics.

What are you going to do with Pétain? A difficult problem. Why not condemn him to death and then let the Head of the State immediately grant him a free pardon 'on account of his age'? This would give it to you every way. You would be merciful to the old gentleman personally; you would condemn his policy; and you would leave yourselves free to hang Laval and all the rest. Personally I think that to deprive Pétain of his bâton and exile him from France would meet the case and draw the teeth of his partisans. It is always a political mistake to make martyrs. I shall watch what France does with extraordinary interest. Much of the future depends on it.

III. TO RENÉ LALOU.

21 May 1945

I AM making good progress with a new short novel. It hoped to be 30,000 words, but already I have written 100 of thin pages — roughly 25,000. I hope to finish in 40,000. It is called at present *The Judge's Story* but that title is not final. I hope, if it does not become too long, to serialize it in America, where they pay one a dollar a word — and that, even after taxation, leaves more than a shilling a word. Are there any French papers which publish serials of short length? The *Revue des deux mondes* would have done, but it exists no more.[1] Is there not a *Revue de Paris*? . . . Anyhow, I think it is a good and unusual story on the theme that some men exist only as effects — i.e. great business men, and some live in obedience to some inner loyalty: i.e. their art, their religion, their love, or their science. There are men with a core, a root, an earth, and there are coreless synthetic men. The coreless men will always try to force or beguile or tempt the others to be false to their inner truth. . . . This sounds a very moral story. So it is! But it has a good, clear action as well and is, I hope, a good story *qua* story.

[1] *La Revue des deux mondes* ceased publication in June 1940. It began again in January 1948.

112. TO RUPERT HART-DAVIS.

Campden Hill Square
29 March 1946

I DON'T think I have ever been far from revealed religion but I am a very long way from any Church, except (as an ancient loyalty sprung from childhood) the Church of England *when* it sticks to the Book of Common Prayer. You see, I'm a revolutionary conservative! So I doubt whether any pew will find in me a regular occupant, but as it happens I have to deliver (on April 1st and 2nd) *in* Winchester Cathedral two 'Discourses' on the Human Experiment, keyed to my old theme of Nicodemus — 'Except a man be born again'.

113. TO GEORGE BERNARD SHAW, *who had referred to Charles a stranger's enquiry concerning his doctrine of Creative Evolution.*   (*Charles's lecture 'The Creative Imagination' — reprinted in* Reflections in a Mirror, Second Series *— had suggested a connection between this doctrine and modern materialistic totalitarianism.*)

Campden Hill Square
14 August 1946

YOUR letter and a copy of the World Classic, *Back to Methuselah*, were good to have at this morning's breakfast table, and have sent off my wife (Orinthia–Jemima) in cheerful mood to continue the writing of one of those 'heartbreaking novels that Shaw is afraid to read'.

I had indeed read the World Classic even before you so kindly sent it to me. Hence the enclosed article in the *Sunday Times* welcoming your collaboration with St. John (The Divine) in quest of the unanswerable Whys.

But surely to God I *was* right in saying (in my lecture on the Creative Imagination, delivered at the Sorbonne in 1956 and now quoted by your correspondent) that the idea of 'willing' was an essential part of your doctrine of Creative Evolution as originally set forth?

You say in your letter:

'The extension of life to 500 years occurs, not to its advocates, but to people to whom it comes as a complete surprise and have never dreamt of willing such a thing.'

But the Preface says:

'Among other matters apparently changeable *at will* is the duration of individual life. . . . If man now fixes the term of his life at three score and ten years, he can fix it at three hundred or three thousand.'

The point was — wasn't it — that man *can fix it*. That was the doctrine of the original preface, which was what was available in 1936, and that was why I then attacked its 'materialism'. It seemed to me possibly true that men can by will produce a change in their physical condition but completely untrue that by will alone, unaided by spiritual forces, they can produce a change in their spiritual condition. I felt that, in the original preface, you had discounted the mystical element in the affairs of men, just as the economic materialists discount it in their interpretation of history.

But now something very remarkable has happened. The original Preface has been re-interpreted by you in the Postscript. I say 're-interpreted' rather than 'modified' because, as I recognized when the play was first performed at Birmingham and I wrote of it in *The Times*, the mystical element was magnificently visible in the last act, which moved me profoundly. Nevertheless, the materialistic aspect of your doctrine — 'man can fix it' — was left bare in the Preface; it is not left bare by the Postscript, which is much nearer to Tolstoy than to Lamarck, and nearer to Blake than to Tolstoy. This makes the Postscript, for me, a Shavian document of the first rank. Now, as I understand it, Creative Evolution is recognised by you as being 'both *mystical* and matter of fact'. You may say 'But it always has been.' I answer: 'Anyhow, it wasn't clear, but now it is.' And what has made it clear — and what the economic materialists (and perhaps your correspondent, Mr. Hennings) would disapprove of — is your collaboration with St. John the Divine!

As Browning said — one word more. I have written this letter in

the spirit of controversy, not of deference. For many years now —
though I have but fifty-two — I have always, in print, argued with you,
but not with less respect or affection than those who have blankly
applauded. I believe in not bothering men. Therefore, even when
your birthday came, I said what I had to say in public and not to you.
Nevertheless I should like to say that your kindness to my wife when
she was a girl has never been forgotten, and that we do not value your
genius the less because we sometimes quarrel about it — she always
casting herself for the feminine part of the devil's advocate. We want
now to send you our homage, and our gratitude for your great work
and life.

PS. Nothing worse has ever been said of you in this house than the old
saying that Shaw's heart is better than his head — and that, I expect,
was originally said by a prophetic Conservative who wanted to reduce
the Surtax.

114. TO MISS JANE GREAVES, *who had lectured on Charles's
novels to a working men's club at Oldham.*

Campden Hill Square
23 November 1946

THANK you for your interesting letter. I think you are mistaken in
supposing that, under Socialism, poverty for many will go. The contrary is my belief. Where all enterprise is stifled and it is useless for
any man to work exceptionally hard because he is not allowed to have
an exceptional reward, general prosperity is unlikely.

Even more important in my view is the sacrifice of human liberty.
The system of the Closed Shop if carried far enough will, in effect, lay
it down as a rule that no man who is not a member of the Socialist
Party is allowed to earn his living. That is plain tyranny. It is the kind
of tyranny against which we fought in the seventeenth and eighteenth
centuries, and I believe that the English will have to struggle against it
again.

[Postscript.] My interest in it springs from my knowledge that all the
liberties are one. If a man is not allowed to be a miner or an engineer

N

unless he belongs to a political union and obeys its rules and subscribes to its party funds, a writer will not be allowed to write freely. So we return to persecution of thought and conscience. I cannot believe that you really desire totalitarianism, and yet it is towards totalitarianism that Socialism is now moving.

115. TO MISS JANE GREAVES.

Campden Hill Square
4 January 1947

A S a novelist I am completely unpolitical. Sometimes, in spite of me, my characters say political things — but I cut them out. The root question that I try to ask is the old Greek question: 'Who am I?' and not: 'What shall I do?' for I think there is no answer to the second question that applies to me *and* to you (therefore I will not, as political novelists do, generalise about action or attempt to dictate it) and think that if I can make you (the reader) ask 'Who am I?' profoundly enough, then *your* right answer to the second question will follow naturally from your *own* answer to the first. You see, I really *do* believe in liberty of thought and imagination. There are a million aspects of truth and a million approaches to it. That is a solitary doctrine in an increasingly totalitarian world. That is why your audience likes Priestley and not yet me. They are like children who like to ask: 'What shall I do, Nanny? How shall I live?' To which Jesus said: 'Seek ye *first* the Kingdom of God' and 'The Kingdom of God is *within* you.' Difficult sayings, just as: 'Who am I?' is a difficult and not a popular question, for no man is, in essence, a member of any group or crowd. He is a *unique* creature with a spark of God in him. That is why he has to 'know himself' before he can know 'how to live'. That is what I am after — but I think you said it better and more clearly. Thank you — and a happy New Year — Socialist or not Socialist.

116. TO MME DELAMAIN, *discussing her translation of the Preface to* The Flashing Stream.

Campden Hill Square
[undated: 1947]

'NO smell of the sixth form' is very English and very difficult.

The 'sixth form' is the top class in the public schools — i.e. the
aristocratic schools, in England. In England, these schools represent
the idea of conventionality, of 'good form', of everything that is stiffly
opposed to originality, queerness or genius. It was this spirit that made
Shelley's life impossible at Eton, and schools have become much more
stolidly complacent since then.

The 'sixth form' is the essence of this complacent conventionality
— the training ground of the kind of men who would despise Verlaine
or Baudelaire.

'No smell of the sixth form' means, therefore: 'free or exempt from
every nuance of stiffly British complacency'.

I wonder what phrase you have used for 'sense of humour'. You will
see that on p. 29, I speak of:

'that acidity of derision and self-derision which is miscalled "a
sense of humour"'.

Many people have missed this. They think that what I am attacking is
balance of mind or a sense of fun.

The real point is that many English sneer at everything and belittle
everything. They are incapable of passion, love, real admiration,
enthusiasm of any kind. And this everlasting 'derision and self-
derision' they are proud of and call 'a sense of humour' and are proud
of being 'able to laugh at themselves too'. Which means, in them, only
that they care for nothing enough to be serious about it.

117. TO CHARLES T. REID, *an Edinburgh lawyer who had queried Charles's use of the word 'England' in one of his* Sunday Times *articles.*

Campden Hill Square

7 March 1947

IT was not disrespect for the Scottish name but rather my love of its poetry and singularity that made me unwilling to cloak it under the word 'Britain'. The words 'Scotland', 'England', 'Ireland' and 'Wales' have a ring that 'Britain' has not. 'It must be remembered', says Fowler in *Modern English Usage*, 'that no Englishman, and perhaps no Scot, calls himself a Briton without a sneaking sense of the ludicrous', and he adds that the attempt to make us stop and think whether we mean our country in a narrower or a wider sense each time we name it 'is doomed to failure'. The difficulty is unavoidable and cannot be got over by quoting the Act of Union. Law cannot give to words a validity against custom. English gentlemen and Scottish gentlemen we know, but a British gentleman would be an odd fish. I can only say that, when I write England, I do not mean Britain; I mean 'England and Scotland' (and Wales and Northern Ireland) wherever the context implies it; and I am sure that the prouder the Scot, the better he will understand me. When Shelley wrote: 'Men of England, wherefore plough' did anyone suppose that he was slighting Scotland or suggesting that there were not Scottish ploughmen? 'We go to plant the Standard of England on the well-known heights of Lisbon,' said Canning, and a modern historian, Guedalla, wrote of the year 1846: 'The major problem was the government of England.' And yet one speaks always of a British Embassy. I have used the English language as it has come down to us, remarkably but not surprisingly loose in this matter. There is authority for great variety of usage; none for consistency. The one thing certainly wrong is abandonment of the great words 'England' and 'Scotland' for the sake of a compromising dullness.

118. TO M. F. GUYARD, *author of* Comment lire Charles Morgan,
a book for French students.

Campden Hill Square
14 April 1947

I HAVE been reading this morning your book about me. It is extremely good and interests me deeply — all the more where I disagree now and then. But I will write again on the book in general. This morning I want to say only one thing, and I have just rushed in from the garden to my desk in order that I may write quickly what is in my mind before I forget it.

You say something terribly exciting to me — something that has suddenly enabled me to grasp, to understand, to *see* a distinction that has always been half-present in my mind but that I have never really *seen* before. Perhaps it will seem less exciting after an hour's thought. That is why I write quickly, while the feeling of discovery is alight on me.

On page 64, you say:

Entre ces trois voies, il n'y a pas à établir de hiérarchie. Toutes trois sont légitimes, pourvu qu'elles conduisent l'homme à se recréer (to be born again), et se recréer, c'est retrouver l'enfance spirituelle, la pureté de cœur, l'unité de l'esprit qui sont pour Morgan une seule et même chose.

As I read that I cried out within me:

'Why does Guyard write: "*se recréer* (to be born again)"? Is it possible that the French language, which has the word "renaissance", has not a verb which exactly translates "to be born again"?'

Then I saw that the two ideas, *se recréer* and 'to be born again', are essentially different and that never before had I *marked* the difference. Again and again I have written:

to renew oneself
to re-create oneself
to be born again

as if they were the same. But they are NOT and Truth itself dwells in the fact that they are not; Christianity depends upon the fact that they are not the same.

'To renew oneself' is active; 'to be born again' is passive.

'To renew myself' is what *I* do, what MAN DOES, and that is something.

'To be born again' is what happens to my being independently of me.

'To renew myself' is my action. But is not 'to be born again' what Christians would call my receiving of grace?

'To be born again' is to receive new life; 'to recreate oneself' is actively to achieve new life.

Therefore the idea of *se recréer* is illusion. I can never recreate myself because I am not God. But I can *receive* new life.

Therefore what *se recréer* really means is to put oneself in a condition to be born again. . . . But I will not go on. This is only the beginning of a long train of thought. But tell me: is it true that in French one cannot say 'to be born again'? Is *se recréer* the nearest possible? If so, it is the most important difference between two languages that I have ever heard of. . . . Forgive me this letter — written in a flash, not thought out.

119. TO MRS. A. MASSIE; *who, after reading* The Judge's Story, *had written 'you show the light your characters live by, as apart from the things they do and say'.*

Cliff Cottage, Laugharne, Carmarthenshire
15 September 1947

YOU will, I think, see what I am driving at, if you think of it in this way.

You have a friend, let us call her Miss A. You can tell me that she is dark or fair, that her voice is deep or light, that she is tall or short, but you cannot so describe her that I can see her and recognise her. *In brief, words will not communicate physical appearance except very approximately.*

Again: you have known Miss A. intimately all your life. You know her opinions, her beliefs, and the way her mind works. You could write down a psychological analysis of her, and that analysis would be accurate as far as it went. But when it was written, you would be dissatisfied with it. You would say to yourself: 'Yes. This is how her mind works. This is the mechanics of her. But it will not convey to

Mr. Morgan that individuality of Miss A. which I *feel* when I am in her presence.' *In brief, words will not communicate a mental condition except very approximately.*

Again: you have not seen Miss A. for many years. You have even forgotten whether her eyes are blue or brown and whether she is taller or shorter than you. You can no longer picture her. You know that, in the intervening years, much has happened which has changed her mentally and physically; her whole behaviour and way of life have altered, and yet, though you can neither picture her appearance nor describe her behaviour, SHE is quite clear to you; she has an identity distinct from any other; she is a unique human being with an individuality that is *not* comprised in her appearance or her behaviour.

To summarise: there is something in Miss A., and in each of us, which is not communicable by description of appearance or by psychological analysis. I do not wish to confuse the issue by saying that this 'something' is the soul. There is also 'something' in a ship, or in an evening, or in a piece of music, which is not communicable by a description or analysis of its parts.

It is this 'something', by virtue of which Miss A. is Miss A. and no one else, and you are you, and I am I, and a ship is a *particular* ship and not the aggregate of its wood and steel, that I am trying to communicate. I am not trying to describe and docket appearances as the Naturalists do; I am not trying ultimately to analyse mental processes as the Psychological Novelists do; I am trying to communicate the FEEL OF THE SPECIAL IDENTITY OF EACH PERSON AND EACH THING. . . . What ultimately matters is that people should gradually come to understand that, within the critical tradition of story-telling and the lucidities of prose, an attempt is being made to communicate, not *my* opinion, not *my* philosophy, but the *feel* of an individuality, the inmost *being* of a man or woman, their own consciousness of being alive as unique persons; and that the English novel is being moved gradually, without a revolutionary break into incoherence, towards poetry — poetic compression (sometimes called obscurity); poetic incantation (sometimes called pretentiousness); and, above all, poetic illumination. If sometimes a reader of a book of mine lets it fall on his knee, and ceases to read, and imagines my characters or scenes for himself, and so begins to re-imagine his own life, then I am content; for, if readers do that now, they will do so in future. Books live in the end because future generations re-imagine them. So I shall go quietly on.

120. TO CHARLES WILLIAMS, *a friend of Oxford days (not to be confused with the author of* The Figure of Beatrice).

Laugharne
18 September 1947

THANK you for what you say about *The Judge.* You have always been kind about my earlier work and I greatly value your judgment. I suppose Mrs. Gorsand is, in a sense, a red herring, though she wasn't so designed. I wanted a distant lady whose pearl of great price Severidge was trying to get from her, and I wanted a job for young Lerrick to do on Severidge's behalf. Hence Mrs. G. And once Mrs. G. was called into existence, my imagination began to play with her to make her alive and interesting, and it seemed not unnatural that her Scottish eye should have an insight into the nature of things. That is all. Many of the idiosyncrasies of Dickens' characters do not, in the end, link up with the plot's dénouement; they exist in themselves and for themselves; so with Mrs. G., but I suppose the fact that, in my book, she is the *only* character not interlocked in the whole plot lays too much emphasis upon her and arouses in the reader expectations which, being unsatisfied, make a red herring of the poor old lady.

I am an exile here because my house in London is being repaired and I have no bed in which to lay myself — probably until December. However, this place is peaceful and I am writing steadily. I am stopping the *Sunday Times* articles at the end of the year and shall be just a book-writer after that, which will be a pleasant independence if I neither starve nor am sent down the mine. I think the time has come for a show-down in our unhappy country. Could we not (like Hampden) go to prison for the crime of importing a book by Balzac?

121. TO LOUIS BONNEROT, *who had dedicated to Charles the book on Matthew Arnold that won him his doctorate at the Sorbonne.*

Laugharne
21 October 1947

THANK you with all my heart for your dedication. It is pleasant to have my name linked in your mind with that of my country, which I love for all the vanishing but remembered things.

What can I tell you about my new story, *The River Line*, except that it is difficult — more difficult technically than any I have attempted. You see, I have chosen a strange form of narrative. The story begins in 1947. An American comes to England to stay with Julian Wyburton and his wife, who *was* Marie Chassaigne. In 1943, at her home at 'Blaise', she concealed the American, Wyburton and two other officers, Frewer and Heron, now dead. The key to the story is that, believing Heron to be a *faux anglais* who had introduced himself into the River Line in order to learn all its connexions and betray it, they killed him, although they loved him personally. In 1947, the American still believes that Heron was false and that the killing, though horrible, was justified. But Heron was *not* false. All this has to be told and discovered in retrospect. The story is really that of a voyage of the American's mind in the past. The *order* of letting out my secrets is incredibly difficult. Old Henry James never set himself a harder task. The advantage, if I can bring it off, is that the two stories — of what happened at Blaise in 1943 and of what the American discovers in England in 1947 — develop *together*. The problem is to keep it *clear*.

[Bonnerot's dedication was as follows:

À

Charles Morgan

Ce livre que j'aurais voulu
Plus digne et de vous et de votre grand pays,
En témoignage de mon affectueuse admiration,
En gage de mon amour pour l'Angleterre,
Aussi fervent, aussi fidèle que votre amour pour la France.]

122. TO MRS. ROBERT MENNELL.

Laugharne
1 January 1948

Pride and Prejudice is a blind spot of mine. It *must* be a good book. But it just isn't about anything that interests me: neither the flesh nor the spirit: just the marriage-market, which I have always considered the most tedious subject on earth. . . .

I want terribly to revisit my old homes at Kenley: Cullesden and Woodhurst — particularly Cullesden, the scene week by week of all my Bible stories. Gethsemane is there, and there Adam ate the apple and God walked in the garden. I know where Joseph's pit was and the lawn where Jesus walked on the water. Oh, the ghosts! the ghosts! The wonderful unwritten poem. I wonder if I dare revisit them. They might vanish. Who lives at Cullesden now? . . .

Sam Courtauld left me a most beautiful pencil-drawing of a nude by Ingres. It is a great joy. You must come to see it when the almond-trees blossom in Campden Hill Square and life begins again. How I hate winter!

123. TO RACHE LOVAT DICKSON, *who was then suffering the rejection of one of his books, but found much relief in this letter.*

Campden Hill Square
31 March 1948

YES, let your mind go slack on it for a bit, and then use me or not, just as comes to you. When *The Portrait* was turned down and I was distracted, Hilda and I were on a holiday at Pardigon. She, with great wisdom, made me *plot* an entirely different novel. Within two days I was writing it. I still have the first 30,000 words, called 'The Reverse of the Coin!'. It did me a lot of good. But don't *withdraw* a book because a publisher says so. Only if, after a time, *you* want to withdraw it because you are on the way to writing a better one.

. . . A certain naïvety on the subject [of love] is essential to the treatment of it. Turgenev's *First Love* and *Acia* are naïve; so is Prosper Merimée's *Carmen*. Naïvety is the good-breeding *and* the poetry of love. The absence of naïvety is just insensitive (or uglily sensual) hard-boiledness.

Of course you are naïf. That you still are, amid your success in business, is what is true and lovable in you. And amusing. But what your friends do — observing that quality in you — is to smile *with* you (even when you haven't yet smiled yourself!) not laugh *at* you.

Anyhow no artist must fear to be laughed at for his sincerities. It is the way of a pretty bloody world.

A sermon, I'm afraid, but an affectionate one — and God knows I am sufficiently sneered at by the Marxists.

Start another book on about April 6th; and, as for this one, follow one of three courses (1) leave it in a drawer until you have had a holiday or got drunk, (2) send it to another publisher at once, (3) send it to me.

124. TO LOUIS BONNEROT, *acknowledging a gift of Chateaubriand's* Mémoires d'outre tombe *from the students of Caen. (Charles's exhaustion was the consequence of an eventful autumn: in October his daughter, Shirley, had been married to the Marquess of Anglesey; in November he had received an honorary degree at Caen, and then — at the Bibliothèque Nationale, Paris — a promotion in the Légion d'Honneur.)*

Campden Hill Square
23 November 1948

I WRITE this from bed, where I have been since my return from France on 18th. I am not ill, but completely exhausted. I seem to want nothing but sleep. In France I was exhausted, too, and felt very ill at lunch with the Lalous before the ceremony at the Bibliothèque Nationale. At your own house, j'ai dû sentir que ma triste disposition formait un contraste trop fort avec l'éclat qui environna votre table. Je crains même qu'il ne se soit fait apercevoir quelquefois dans le peu de moments qu'il m'a été permis de passer avec vous, et je réclame là-dessus votre indulgence.

Now you will understand how I have been spending my time in bed — reading Chateaubriand and stealing (and perilously adapting) passages from *La Harpe*. Even so I am very doubtful of *environna*, which alas is mine and for which *La Harpe* bears no responsibility!

All this is really intended only to tell you and your students that your gift of the *Mémoires d'outre tombe* has held me spell-bound, and to say how grateful I am. Everyone who writes about Chateaubriand says he was egotistical and ambitious, generally with the implication that he was cold-hearted and false. For example, when he has told the story of the English girl, Charlotte Ives, who fell in love with him in 1795 he wonders what would have happened to him if he had married Charlotte. 'Mon pays aurait-il beaucoup perdu à ma disparition? . . .

Est-il certain que j'aie un talent véritable? ... Dépasserai-je ma tombe? ... Ne serai-je pas un homme d'autrefois, inintelligible aux générations nouvelles? Mes idées, mes sentiments, mon style même ne seront-ils pas à la dédaigneuse postérité choses ennuyeuses et vieillies?'

At that point, Sainte-Beuve wrote: 'Non, mais fausses.'

I think Sainte-Beuve was unjust. Chateaubriand was simply a man who had not the gift of colloquial ease. It was in the nature of Napoleon to climb thrones; it was in the nature of C. to build sentences, paragraphs, chapters, volumes, like palaces. He was *superb*. He linked the classicism of the eighteenth century with the romantic era. What would have been false *in him* is simplicity. He was, in his style, true to himself. Therefore his style was not false. Even more important is the fact that the defect of his character is not cynicism or cold-heartedness, but a shy, sentimental desire to be loved. A dangerous desire; the Germans have it (see: Vercors, *Le Silence de la mer*); but dangerous in the Germans because they think they can compel love. Chateaubriand had no such delusion. I am sure that it was foolish of Sainte-Beuve, and would be foolish of us, to be prompted, by the *stateliness* of Chateaubriand, to suppose him false. Have you not a phrase: *un faux bonhomme?* At least Chateaubriand was not that. Today, in literature, there is almost a cult of the *faux bonhomme*. Men are praised for naturalness and sincerity because their grammar is vile and their syntax worse — anyhow, they *were*. But that is a dying fashion. Chateaubriand *has* come back, hasn't he? Anatole France will. Anatole France is a good instance for *me* to choose. I do not like the temper of his mind. He is sneering and destructive. But to despise him is childish and absurd. That I happen to disagree with him does not matter. He could imagine and he could write; *therefore* he will come back. For even more powerful reasons, Chateaubriand cannot be put aside — one of the reasons is that, when once you begin to read him, you cannot stop. O to be *readable* a hundred years hence! And is not that exactly what Chateaubriand was saying in the passage upon which Sainte-Beuve makes his too bitter comment? ... What would your students think of all this? ... In any case tell them how much I am valuing their gift and how grateful I am to them — and to you.

125. TO LOUIS BONNEROT.   *Written from the house in*
Pembrokeshire where Charles and Hilda had found a writers' retreat.

Felindre, Llanrhian
28 December 1948

A LITTLE note to send our love to you at Christmas time and to say
how glad I am about the Sorbonne lectures. I am sure it is a step towards your going to the Sorbonne in your own right, which will do
the Sorbonne a lot of good. . . .

Without writing a vast essay I don't know what more to tell you
about myself and the seventeenth century. John Inglesant was what
first attracted me. Then at Oxford, when I was studying the Civil War
period, I read far outside the set books, attracted by Quietism and by
my conviction (which has never changed) that England was never a
better or a happier place than in the early years of Charles I.

126. TO H. L. MICA, *a Dutch reader of* The Voyage, *who found it
inconsistent that Barbet in that novel should be at once a contemplative, a lover of peace, and a soldier.*

Campden Hill Square
15 July 1949

AS I understand it, there is nothing inconsistent in the idea of a contemplative and peacefully-minded man performing the normal duties
of a citizen. Jesus himself said, 'Render unto Caesar the things that are
Caesar's, and unto God the things that are God's.' The point arises
also, in the context of another religion, when the question is discussed,
in the *Bhagavad Geeta*, as to whether the prince should go into battle or
not. The god advises him to do so. This is one of the classic passages
on this much debated subject, and a very beautiful one.

I do not see how one can support a refusal to fight in a just war unless
one is prepared to base oneself upon the text, 'Return not evil' and is
also prepared to carry this to its logical conclusion in the Tolstoyan
doctrine of total non-resistance. This means that one must abstain
from using force to protect a child whom one sees being murdered in

the street. This is a position which I cannot adopt, and I think it is altogether inconsistent to object to the profession of a soldier, unless you are prepared to object to the use of force in all circumstances.

127. TO ST. JOHN ERVINE, *with reference to his play* Private Enterprise, *produced in 1947 and published in 1949.*

Campden Hill Square
20 July 1949

I BEGAN a letter to you days ago and then was called away by a gent from Porlock and the pages have gone amissing, so now I start again.

First about your play. I don't see what was wrong, even from the strictly theatrical point of view. It *is* propagandist certainly if by 'propagandist' one means 'written to persuade' and, as you are aware, bless you, your 'persuasions' are sometimes pretty fierce. No doubt it made the Left angry. But there is a great deal of Ibsen that makes me angry in my opinions and the fact that I disagree with him doesn't prevent me from valuing and enjoying his play. But you see, what is happening in the modern world is that men's minds are coagulating. They are losing the power to make distinctions. If they reject a dramatist's opinions, they reject his whole play. 'I think this man Ervine is wrong' leads to the conclusion: 'Therefore his play is bad'. It is a hopeless *non sequitor*, but a ruling one. I think your characters live and that your plot (though weighted in the balance) is sound. I can't believe anyhow that the play is not good theatre with a clear — though hot — head working on it. As we are in the process of telling each other what each wants the other to write, I will say that, just as you want me to write a long book, so I want you to write a play in which you screw down your safety valve — a meditative, remote play about completely unspectacular people trying to find a way to live and endure amid the encroaching barbarism; loving and lovable people, *gentle* (though not necessarily 'cultured') — a kind of sturdy, courageous *Cherry Orchard*: English or Northern Irish. The implication being that the barbarians are barbarians because they listen only to their own shouting and never to the voices of the gods. However — you see, my view of you is that you are a poet and that neither your business (nor, God knows, mine) is with politics. We let off our politics through our safety valve and that decreases our poetic pressure. I am preaching to you the sermon I ought to preach to myself. I know that. But, then, you mean, and always have meant the devil of a lot to me. And I want you to write the very great HERMIT's masterpiece which is in you to write, if you would screw down the safety valve and let the pressure accumulate.

As for *The River Line*. Of course if the killing was voluntary, not compelled, then everything falls down, and Marie and Julian were murderers as you say. But my whole point — and I prove it minute by minute — is that they *had* to do what they did. You say you would have asked: 'Why?' You couldn't because:

(*a*) you were sworn to obey absolutely

(*b*) there was *no time* for investigation

(*c*) to have waited OR to have sent Heron on over the Spanish frontier was to imperil dozens of lives right back through the line.

But if I didn't make that clear and persuasive beyond doubt, then I know the thing falls down. . . . I wonder whether that will carry weight with Nora[1] as she goes forward. I hope so, and I'm very proud of her approval of the beginning.

The tide of reviews seems to have turned. Howard Spring (who happens to be able to sell books himself!) is all-out favourable; so is the *Liverpool Post*; so is Yorkshire; and even the *Manchester Guardian* is favourable with qualifications. I await the *New Statesman* and the *Spectator*. Of course if L. A. G. Strong does the *Spectator* I have little to hope for, and the *New Statesman*, though kind to my essays, is in the habit of pretending that my novels have not been published.

You will be satisfied by my next book — anyhow by its length. It will be a whale and God knows when it will be done. . . .

Whatever happens about plays and books, it has been good to have letters from you. I wish we were more easily within reach.

[1] Mrs. St. John Ervine.

128. TO RUPERT HART-DAVIS.

Campden Hill Square
25 July 1949

I AM most grateful for what you say of *The River Line*, and confess that the Jamesian influence is one of which I was altogether unconscious, but I can hear dangerous cadences in the sentence you quote. What I think I have to be careful of is a tendency to over-stylize my dialogue. Of course, the stylization is deliberate and is done with the object, particularly in the shorter books, of preserving an even texture. After all, as Somerset Maugham pointed out in his preface to one of his plays, dialogue cannot be, and ought not to be, completely naturalistic, and every author has to decide for himself how to treat this problem. However, as a result of your letter, I will think it out afresh, and I am very grateful to you for having warned me of the danger.

I think what I really mean is that one has to choose what degree of non-naturalistic selectiveness one will use. It seems to me very odd that Quennell should head his article: 'Oh for a nice loud voice.' He would not ask loudness of Henry James or of Jane Austen. Loudness, as such, isn't a quality that can be *demanded* critically. However, it is of no use to worry about enemy criticism, though I love to have your friendly kind which makes me ask myself the right questions.

129. TO T. WARNER ALLEN, *with reference to* The River Line.

Campden Hill Square
27 July 1949

I WAS made very happy by your letter. You saw the book as I saw it, and tried to communicate it. It is being attacked by people who not only don't know, but are by their natures incapable of knowing what it is about. Even the *Church Times* says it is 'sub-Christian' because in the view of the *Church Times*, there is no sin, therefore no guilt, and therefore no need of purgation except when sin has been deliberately committed. The Greeks knew better: so did Jesus; so did Aquinas; so did Jeremy Taylor. If there is no sin without the will to sin, then there is no Grace without our deserving it; and it is the root of

Christianity that Grace, like poetry and like love, comes not by our
own deserving.

But at least the *Church Times* knew that the book was about the
Grace of God, whereas Mr. Peter Quennell and Mr. Daniel George
ain't never 'eard o' sich a thing.

130. TO MRS. P. WOODIWISS, *who had declared herself 'bitterly
disappointed' in Charles on hearing that* Sparkenbroke *was to be
filmed.*

7 September 1949

I AM sorry that you disapprove of the idea of a film of *Sparkenbroke*,
and I appreciate your reasons for doing so. In fact, I have signed no
contract for a film, but negotiations are in progress and I shall not
hesitate to conclude them if they are satisfactory.

My point of view is that it is an author's duty to write his books at
leisure, in his own way, and without consideration of the market. This
rules applies to all artists. Whereas in the past artists had great patrons
who made possible this leisure and independence, it is now necessary,
as there are no longer any Princes of the Renaissance, for an artist to
endow his own independence. As long as he gives none of his time to
the film, and regards it as an endowment and nothing more, he is, in
my opinion, doing the best he can to preserve his integrity. There is no
need for anyone who has read the book to go to the film. Meanwhile
the artist, after he has paid nearly three-quarters of the product of the
film to the exchequer, can live a little while on what remains. If you
will provide me with the patronage of the Medici or with the sanity of
the Victorian age, I will not sell any more films!

In any case, it may be well to remember that *Hamlet* has been filmed,
not discreditably, and that to my own knowledge — for he told me so
— Thomas Hardy was delighted when he heard that a film was going
to be made of *Tess of the d'Urbervilles*.

o

131. TO RENÉ LALOU, *who was conducting an enquiry among English writers for* Les Nouvelles Littéraires*: his questions being addressed to T. S. Eliot and Stephen Spender, as well as to Charles.*

Garrick Club
October 1949

I WILL confess to you that, in spite of all I have said about the tendencies of the novel, and in spite of all that Eliot and Spender may so wisely say, we are all at sea. We say that we believe that such-and-such a thing will happen, and we rationalize our opinions, but, in truth, we do not know.

My inward belief is that art is not the result of social conditions or of anything that we are capable of estimating. The great movements of art are the result of individual genius, and individual genius is the result of something that we cannot estimate and do not understand. I ask you: what social conditions produced *Tolstoy?* One night after dinner Shelley's father went to bed in accordance with his habit, and, to his own astonishment and embarrassment, the result was *Percy Bysshe Shelley.* That is all. That is how literature is changed — *not* by the organization of coteries, not by the obsessions of politics, but by the divine chance of what happens when Shelley's father goes to bed with Shelley's mother.

Sometimes it seems that the conditions of life govern literature. The wonder and the brilliance of the Elizabethan age *seems* to have produced Shakespeare. But is it true? I doubt it. Of one thing I am certain: that a life of drabness produces nothing except, by chance, the salvation of exceptional genius. No one knows what will happen in literature. The world is so weary of evil and so sceptical of good that neither the threat of evil nor the hope of good produces any response or effect. Individual and personal genius is the only power, the only hope. Tell me tonight what man will go to bed with what woman and what miracle the gods will work, and I will tell you what the future of the novel will be. But it is dishonest to discuss 'tendencies' until we know what personal miracles the gods have up their sleeve.

132. TO THE COUNTESS OF IDDESLEIGH, *whose daughter had become a nun.*

Felindre
16 June 1950

I THINK I am glad your eldest child has done as she has done — though I could have wished that it had been not a teaching but a contemplative order. The contemplatives are the life-blood and perpetual renewal of your Church — the supreme force that exists nowhere else in the world: there are other teachers and workers. Nevertheless, a *religieuse*, like an artist, must follow her own vocation and, if your daughter is called to teach, she must teach. Contemplation is the poetry of faith and poetry of a special kind, and I think your daughter, in choosing a teaching order, may be exercising a humility which is far better than the arrogant self-deception of one who claims to be a pure contemplative without having that exceedingly rare gift. In any case, she has not chosen the world for herself, and that is great wisdom and charity. I think if my own daughter or son had chosen an enclosed order I should have been glad. I see no other hope for the world except in those perpetual prayers.

You will think this odd from one who is not a Catholic, but so I feel.

133. TO THE LIBRARIAN OF KIRKHAM COUNTY LIBRARY, *who had asked for a message on the advantages of reading, for the centenary of the Public Library Service.*

August 1950

ALMOST everyone who is not a fanatical totalitarian acknowledges the value of preserving what is called 'an open mind'. It is less easily and less frequently understood that to preserve an open imagination is even more important. Our imaginations have a tendency to stagnate. The supreme value of all works of art, whether they be books, pictures or music, is to enable the imagination to flow again and to remain in fresh and vigorous movement. The same truth may be stated in another way. We may liken men's minds to the earth and a work of art to the seed that is planted in it. The purpose of great art is not to compel or, I think, even to persuade or instruct, but to impregnate the minds of men so that each man's mind, according to its nature, may bring forth the richest fruit of which it is capable.

There is, therefore, great danger in supposing that only those books are valuable which give obvious instruction, in some political or economic form, to what is called 'a social conscience'. They may corrupt or poison the mind as easily as books which are evidently evil. I am convinced that the greatest need of our time, if the world is to be liberated from the prisons of ideology, is writing, whether in poetry or in prose, which by its beauty and impact sets men's minds free and enables them to re-imagine their material and spiritual lives.

134. TO M. P. MALINOVSKY, *who wished to discuss* Sparken-broke.

27 November 1950

YOUR questions are extremely subtle and extremely interesting. . . .

Detachment is obtained by an individual by means of his withdrawing into his interior life. This is not 'escape' but the attainment of a greater reality hidden within the outward appearance of ordinary life.

He may be confused and withheld from the attainment of this inner reality by his attachment to another person or persons. In most cases solitude is an aid to detachment, as the religious masters of the contemplative life have always believed. Nevertheless, it is my belief that the love of two human beings can in *certain special cases* lead to this detachment. Where this happens and personal love is transmuted into spiritual love, there is a perfect marriage of true minds, but this did not happen, even in the case of Héloïse and Abélard, though clearly Dante thought that it would have happened in the case of Dante and Beatrice. My feeling was when I wrote *Sparkenbroke* that Mary and Piers were ultimately incapable of it. She was of immense value to him as a catalytic agent, but if they had remained together through the ordinary rough and tumble of life they would have failed each other.

135. TO STEWART HUNTER.   (*The novel mentioned
became* A Breeze of Morning.)

Campden Hill Square
8 January 1951

I HAVE finished a novel about the same length as *The River Line*,
which is perhaps in a category with *Portrait in a Mirror*. Its date is
1906, and its subject a love story seen through the eyes of a scholarly
and imaginative boy just old enough to fall in love himself (at a distance) with one of the grown-ups. My idea is that he is, so to speak,
isolated by the fact of being so young, and resembles one who, walking
in a dark garden, looks in through lighted windows into other people's
lives. I want a title. 'The Face at the Window' otherwise perfect
sounds too much a thriller. 'The Lighted Window' or something like
it has been too often used. At present I hesitate between 'The Window'
and 'When I Was Young'. The disadvantage of the latter is that it
might sound like a book of memoirs.

136. TO DR. ORLO WILLIAMS, *who had been made a Fellow
of the Royal Society of Literature, Charles being on its Council.*

Plas Newydd, Anglesey
25 January 1951

I WAS very touched by your letter and pleased by your acceptance.
You will have had an official notification by now.

I return to London tomorrow and shall hope that your domestic
distresses will by then have passed by and relieved you of the anxiety
and disturbance that such things entail — above all nowadays when
no one any more has a smooth household machine that goes on quietly
turning over whatever happens. The longer I live the more I sym-
pathize with Talleyrand on the subject of *La douceur de vivre*. It is all a
question of servants — lots and lots and lots of servants. Without
them, no one has time to meditate, and without meditation civilization,
however active, dries up.

I had an odd experience the night before last. My daughter and her
husband are in London and I had been sitting alone by a wood-fire.

As I went up to bed I tried to turn off the lights. The room is very big and there are eight switches, each governing a group of lamps, and I always forget which is which. By chance, the last switch I moved turned *on* the wireless in a by then dark room — and someone played Chopin. I can't tell you the effect on me — somehow a sudden wild conviction of good in the world.

137. TO MISS HELEN McCANN, *of the* Irish Times; who had *greeted* Liberties of the Mind *as a challenge to atheistic communism, and suggested to Charles that the Church of Rome was likely to be the chief or only effective bulwark in this matter.*

22 March 1951

I SHOULD have greatly valued your letter in any case, but I value it the more because it comes from a member of the Church of Rome. Of course my book has its political and aesthetic aspects, but underlying everything is my conviction that, as Tennyson said, a wave of spiritual evil is passing over the world. Materialists, when they are Communists also, are conscious instruments of this evil. But many materialists who are not Communists but men of goodwill are unconscious instruments of it. It seems to me to follow that all of us, who are not materialists, have become allies in spite of our own differences of doctrine. For that reason, though I am not a Catholic, the assault on the mind of the Cardinal[1] struck at me just as if I were a Catholic, and it is a great encouragement to me to know that you were generously willing and able to see my book as I intended it to be seen — that is to say, as a spiritual witness to an all-pervading evil to which as yet great numbers of people in the West are blind.

It is possible that my book is, in a certain sense, before its time, and that though some may be aware of its importance the great majority may remain unaware of its urgency. But if Catholics take the view of it which you have taken, it will be an immense encouragement to me and a compensation for the fierce attacks which will no doubt be directed against it from the materialistic Left.

[1] Cardinal Mindtzenty.

138. TO MISS E. M. ALMEDINGEN.

Plas Newydd
23 May 1951

I HAVE been reading *Adam Bede* for the first time. I am not at peace with George Eliot's mind. It is terribly feet-on-the-earth, and (*vis-à-vis* Hetty Sorrel and, I suspect, all physically beautiful women) it is spiteful. But how SOLID George Eliot is! Her story and her character-drawing is wonderfully firm and sure — like good architecture which makes you continuously aware of its foundations. I don't greatly enjoy the book but I respect it and try to learn from it.

139. TO FR. CONOR HENNESSY, S.J., *who had sent to Charles an appreciation of* The Judge's Story, *suggesting also a possibly intended ambiguity in his use of the word 'legend' in* The River Line.

Campden Hill Square
5 June 1951

IT matters greatly to me that you should have written as you did. . . . To write is a solitary task and your encouragement has been of great value.

I had not thought of 'legend' in the sense of *légende*, but what you say is true. I mean by legend a story which is not self-regarding but opens up a territory of the imagination beyond itself — in other words, which enables the map of experience to be interpreted. But I had not thought of it in terms of maps until you gave me the idea. Thank you.

The other problem — of what we should find if we were able to penetrate to the core of our being — is one of which you could certainly teach me more than I know. The question is one that I ask and ask in all my work: 'Who am I?' For six years now, as a background to shorter books, I have been struggling with a novel to be called 'Darkness and Daylight'. It is an attempt to say that

(1) the fear of death is an empty fear,

(2) the fear of the complete annihilation of the material universe (by nuclear energy, for example) is an empty fear because (Emily Brontë)

> *Though earth and man were gone,*
> *And suns and universes cease to be,*
> *And Thou were left alone,*
> *Every existence would exist in Thee.*

Therefore I think that what we should find at the core of our being is not (as some say, I think dangerously) God indwelling in us, but that essence of ourselves which IS in God.

I have tried also to think of it in this way — at the risk of metaphor, which is never fully applicable.

Each man is aware of existing in many distinct manifestations. He is, let us say, 'Charles'; he is 'Morgan'; he is still a child; he is a grown man; he is a writer; he is (in survival from the past) a naval officer; he is a political animal; he is a creature who believes that a member of an enclosed and contemplative order is engaged in the supreme earthly activity; and yet, if it comes to war he is an intransigent fighter. He is all these, and many more. None of them is his final I, his absolute identity. All these manifestations of himself are little ships with names, buffeted about on the surface of the sea. But always, at the bottom of the sea, where there is no buffeting, his final I lies, looking up at the little ships.

Of course this explains nothing to others and is no answer to your question. But it helps me, when any one of my little ships is in trouble, to be aware of my own nameless identity, in the still depths of the sea, looking up and regarding them all. I think we are entitled to talk to ourselves in parables.

In the catechism which I learnt as a boy, it is written: *a* soldier[1] of Christ, THE child of God, and *an* inheritor of the Kingdom of Heaven. I am not scholar enough to know what has been written, theologically, about that THE. It may even be an accident of translation; if so, it is a divine accident. It is the THE which I should find at the core of my being if I had vision enough.

---

[1] A misquotation. For 'soldier' read 'member'.

140. TO EDWARD POWLEY, *who had sent Charles a book of his poems.*

Campden Hill Square
8 July 1951

I THINK that many writers today really do not know what scansion is. . . . To me, poetry is an emblem of spiritual order. Observance of form — a new form; if you like, but still not formlessness — is an outward and visible sign of the inward and spiritual grace; and I am grateful to your poems because they sing and because they lock.

You share many of my admirations and loves: Hardy: Inglesant:[1] the sea: and France, I think. Nevertheless I am, as I was in 1917, in full disagreement with you and Bonar Law and Asquith and Devlin on the subject of the Russian revolution. I do not believe that freedom comes by the murder of kings, and Inglesant would have agreed with me.

But disagreement on such a matter does not touch the pleasure I have had in your poems. They *touch* me at so many points. . . . 'The Study Window' and the poem about Hardy in the Abbey greatly moved me. It was, I think, in the dining-room not the study, that I sat with him by the fire nearly thirty years ago, but Max Gate haunts me, and I shall never forget my last sight of him with a lantern swaying in his hand as he lighted me out of his garden on my way back to Dorchester. You have communicated the pride and the modesty of that great man, and I share your indignation at the cutting out of his heart and the disposal of his body. And yet . . . and yet, I wonder. Would he have refused Abbey burial? More powerfully even than other artists he had a desire for recognition and a sense of having been neglected and spurned. He told me, with astounding naïvety, that he was glad *Tess* had been filmed because the film would call attention to the book. He never altogether transcended the mood of *Jude the Obscure*. His honorary doctorate at Oxford meant much to him. Abbey burial might well have appealed to him as one of the more triumphant of Life's Little Ironies.

[1] *John Inglesant*, by J. H. Shorthouse.

141. TO HILDA MORGAN, *with reference initially to a legend which Charles considered for a time as theme for a possible novel.*

Plas Newydd
18 January 1952

I HAVE made some progress with 'The Double Headed Jewel', but I am not happy about it and in the meantime have been plunging into the subject of Ephesus. By tradition, Nicodemus went 'to Asia Minor' after the death of Jesus and I always wondered where. Why not to Ephesus — a great city then, dedicated to the religion of Diana or Artemis, in which St. Paul spent three years. I like the idea of a Christian centre in the midst of a highly civilised Greek City under Roman rule — Paul violently proselytising and Nicodemus, having known Jesus, living quietly within himself. And there is (in Greek and Latin but never translated into English) a Greek novel written about A.D. 200 by Xenophon of Ephesus which is summarised in the January number of *History Today* and which tells an Ephesian love-story and gives an account of the great Ephesian processions etc. There is very rich material for a long-term novel on Nicodemus — but my trouble is that I want a short-term one to go on with meanwhile.

142. TO DR. STEPHEN PASMORE, *written very soon after the death in France of his friend, Jacques Delamain.*

Campden Hill Square
26 February 1953

THANK you for what you so kindly say about *The River Line*. As regards the paragraph (*River Line*, page xxi) beginning 'It seems to depend upon a power to make certain distinctions . . .' I am thinking of the distinctions which lie at the very root, not of manners and taste, but of spiritual civilisation.[1] We must be able to distinguish between the beauty of appearances (which is possessed by innumerable great

[1] The passage from *The River Line*, quoted here, runs: 'Power to receive the gift of interior quiet . . . is within the reach of the simplest among us as it is of the subtlest scholar. It seems to depend upon a power to make — or, I would say rather, to accept as axiomatic — certain distinctions . . .' Dr. Pasmore had asked the meaning of the word 'distinctions'.

works of art) and the special interior beauty which is discoverable in some of them — e.g. Michelangelo's 'Pieta' or Bellini's 'Agony in the Garden'. The same distinction, I think, applies to the manifestations of nature. The French soldier of whom I spoke on page xxii was Jacques Delamain, who wrote *Why Birds Sing*, and was an almost saintly bird-watcher. He went very far into the interior of things. He was able to pass through the bombardment of his trench to the song of the swallows, and to pass yet further from the song of the swallows (considered as an outward and audible music) into the essence of their song, considered as one of the voices of God. . . . It is, I grant, a difficult paragraph. Perhaps I have not made it any clearer. The distinction I have in mind is actually the distinction between a green tree and what Andrew Marvell meant by 'a green thought in a green shade'.

143. TO MISS VERONICA WEDGWOOD.   *Written upon Charles's election as President of the International P.E.N. Club, Miss Wedgwood having been President of its English Centre since 1951.*

Plas Newydd
20 June 1953

YOUR letter, which came after a little delay to this distant corner of the world, was a great pleasure to me. . . . In all the affairs of P.E.N. I shall be as impartial as the Speaker himself, and that won't be difficult to me, for the moment I begin to think in terms of pens and inkpots I become 'indifferent' — using the word in the sense of the Prayer Book when it asks that the Judges may 'indifferently administer Justice'. Indeed this 'indifference' — the fact that my stories are not *engagés* — is what makes those who are hot for certainties accuse me of aloof romanticism. However that may be, it will at least help me to keep calm, as a chairman, when others become excited. . . .

I hope you will sometimes keep me up to the mark if I appear not to be doing what I ought to do. What I should really like to do is to get the P.E.N. to think more in terms of art and scholarship and less in terms of journalism and politics. There are people — particularly in Europe — who regard it as an organisation to be 'captured'. I believe it ought not to be capturable. . . .

I hope you will ... come and dine one evening and let me sit at your feet — as indeed I do in this house for *The Thirty Years' War* is my bedside book.

144. TO MISS E. M. ALMEDINGEN, *who had written of some inept criticism of* War and Peace *which appeared in Russia soon after its publication. She wrote:* 'One owl-minded "critic" took Tolstoy to task for putting the word "awfully" — njasno — in Natasha's mouth, since such a word would not have been used in 1820.'

Campden Hill Square
4 September 1953

I WAS fascinated by your comments on that passage in *War and Peace*. Because, of course, I do not know the Russian word, I have always taken the word 'awfully' for granted. It seemed to me exactly right and I do not care a damn whether it is an anachronism or not. Oddly enough, I wrote about that particular passage in my essay on *War and Peace* in *Reflections in a Mirror*, First Series, page 195. I was talking about Tolstoy's sudden improvisations and I said:

> He was bound to improvise because it was through the complex network of his improvisation (as it was in Turgenev through the strict channel of premeditated form) that his vitality flowed. Tolstoy's divagations from his tale can be as infuriating as his later tracts — but infuriating they are, never flat, never toneless; and how often, after a sentence or two, irritation passes, the deserted narrative is forgotten, the divagation establishes itself, the wisdom (or the perversity) of the improvisation carries the reader away! Pierre, it will be remembered, had a habit, extremely Tolstoyan, of talking and thinking about one thing while Natasha was talking and thinking about another:
>
> 'Do you know what I am thinking about?' she asked. 'About Platon Karataev. Would he have approved of you now, do you think?'
>
> Pierre was not at all surprised at this question. He understood his wife's line of thought.
>
> 'Platon Karataev?' he repeated, and pondered, evidently sincerely

trying to imagine Karataev's opinion on the subject. 'He would not have understood . . . yet perhaps he would.'

'I love you awfully!' Natasha suddenly said. 'Awfully, awfully!' Now how did Tolstoy know that she would suddenly say that? The knowledge was part of the unselfconscious intuition which enabled him to risk, as no one else would have dared to risk, a sagging of his reader's interest. Like Pierre, he could risk anything as long as he was true to his own improvisations. They are not what the reader expects or desires, but they are, even in their faults, a passionate expression of Tolstoy himself. 'I love you awfully!' Natasha exclaims, and indeed there is nothing else to say.

I wonder whether you have read this morning an article on Olivia Manning in the *Times Literary Supplement*.[1] If you can translate that into comprehensible English you are even more skilled than I believe you to be. What is all this nonsense about caterpillars and cocoons? And why, because Miss Manning is 'in', should Edith Sitwell necessarily be 'out'? I simply do not understand this process of the ins and outs. One might as well say that Homer went out when Tolstoy came in! There is no end to this fashionable absurdity.

145. TO LE COMTE VICTOR DE PANGE, *author of* Graham Greene, *in the series* Classiques du XXe siècle.

Campden Hill Square
18 September 1953

IT was kind of you to send me your book of Graham Greene. There are several books of his that I have not read — for I can read nothing that is, even indirectly, a *roman policier* — but I am fascinated by your analysis of his later work. There has always seemed to me to be, in this work, a suggestion that, as Mauriac says, 'pour lui le Christ n'habite pas les purs'. That is a perilous doctrine. It is as if one were to say that sin is necessary to salvation. I cannot believe that Greene intends that, and yet his work seems often to imply it. Your conclusion throws much light on this subject and is of great value and interest for that reason, and yet I still ask myself whether Greene's perpetual emphasis on the *angoisse* of the modern world does not obscure the operation of

[1] A review of Olivia Manning's novel *A Different Face*.

the Grace of God. I believe that there are many happy and serene men and women who are not ravaged by sin, who are continuously aware of Grace, and who above all are inwardly tranquil in the knowledge of His mercy. They are not hypocrites, they are not complacent, but they are not greeniens because they do not believe that the *only* effective truth of Christianity is that Christ died to save sinners. They believe that He lived and lives, and that they may (here on earth) live in Him. You find in Greene's work *un témoinage de nos temps d'angoisse.* That is very true, and the *témoinage* is brilliant. But is not *angoisse* dangerously fashionable? *Angoisse* and *peur* are only aberrations of the human soul. I think that both as men and Christians we have to guard ourselves against becoming too much interested in our fashionable disease. . . .

Thank you for your very distinguished book.

146. TO R. KINGSLEY READ.

30 October 1953

I AM glad that *A Breeze of Morning* pleased you. It is very far from the present anti-romantic school of 'social consciousness', but I have always been far from it both in matter and in style. To be, as you say, 'evocative' has always been my purpose — to tell a story in such a way that the reader re-imagines it for himself; and to do that one must use language for the sake of its overtones and echoes, relying on the reader to respond. The difficulty is that the basis of that response is dying. I am apt to assume that certain phrases — such as 'perils and dangers' or 'Lighten our darkness' — phrases, I mean, from the Bible or the Prayer Book evoke memories in everyone's mind, but it is ceasing to be true. The common language is dying; one can no longer allude to the most familiar Biblical or classical stories without encountering a gaze of complete blankness. Therefore it means much to me that 'perils and dangers' reached your heart.

147. TO MISS D. STANSFIELD, *who had been 'profoundly moved' by a performance of* The Burning Glass *at Stratford-on-Avon, but was concerned as to how Mary Terriford could accept Tony Lack's suicide without the loss of her own integrity.*

8 February 1954

THANK you for an extremely interesting letter. I will try to answer it as well as I can.

The first point to note is that by the time Mary was aware of Tony's action, he had already taken the poison. She was therefore what the lawyers call 'an accessory after the fact', not an accessory before it. This, however, is a small point for she did 'accept' his action without protest and the basis of your problem remains.

The simple explanation is the one you give, namely, that his knowledge of the Burning Glass would never have been safe while he lived — 'and so she held herself back and let him die'.

Still, the religious question remains. It may reasonably be said that her acceptance of his suicide was the action rather of an ancient Greek than of a modern Christian. This is true, but I am a Christian Platonist rather than a Christian *pur sang*. It is not to be forgotten that Socrates himself committed suicide. If we believe, as many Christians appear to believe, that this present life on earth is the only testing stage in the life of the soul, then it would follow that we are not entitled to release ourselves from it. But my feeling is that this life is only one room in a great and mysterious house; that all in this house is God's; that to pass out of this room into another is not the act of finality which some suppose it to be, and that if a man is impelled by his conscience to turn the handle of *this* door, it is not for us to prevent him.

I had this in mind when writing the Prime Minister's speech in which he speaks of having 'the bitter courage to say goodbye'. If you say that this point of view is rather Greek than strictly Christian, I cannot dispute it with you. In any case, I greatly appreciate your and your friends' careful insight into my play.

148. TO SIR CARLETON ALLEN.

Plas Newydd
18 March 1954

HOW pleasant to have a letter from someone who thinks. Although the greater part of the Press has been with me, the Left has been fierce. They see *The Burning Glass* as a snooty play in which everyone has money enough and assumes, in the manner of the English 'upper classes', that my 'intellectual cosh-boy', Hardlip, is unpleasant. I didn't think that my play was about class at all. . . .

Although I have, as a Conservative, some sympathy with mastodons, I agree that to set a canon 'gainst scientific development at any given point is impossible. Your alternative — or, rather, your balancing compensation — of tackling the 'intangibles and imponderables' of the human mind would be all right if it could still be effective. I think we have gone too far; I don't believe that your 'crucial enquiry' can be effective upon a popular mind besotted with *hubris*. There *is* no way out until the gods have hit our civilization hard enough to bring the survivors to their knees. There are plenty of warning symbols — the Flood, Sodom and G., nearly all Greek tragedy, the conversation of Jesus with Nicodemus about being born again. I cannot believe that any development of psychological science can now help us much. It is necessarily powerless against the juvenile picture-papers — the whole attitude of mind that they represent.

But if there is a solution it can only be on your psychological lines — if you will allow that the religious intuition, right or wrong, is a part of your psychological material. I confess that my play does not offer a general solution. All I have tried to do is to ask the right question. My reward comes when wise men like you write to me unprompted. . . .

Nevertheless the spring is here. Outside my window someone is mowing a lawn which slopes down to the Menai Straits and on the water Conway cadets are plashing about with oars. Perhaps someone is preparing to play Jacques in Wadham Gardens.[1]

[1] Played by C. A. during C. M.'s presidency of the O.U.D.S.

149. TO A. NICOL, *thanking him for a translation from Catullus made by a young University lecturer in Manchester, who had referred to C. M. as 'obviously a professional classical scholar'.*

25 March 1955

YOU must not allow your young lecturer to repose in the error of supposing me to be a professional classical scholar. Being a Naval Officer I learned enough Latin and Greek to get into Oxford when both languages were compulsory, but that is all. My translation of Catullus[1] was a long and elaborate process in the course of which I took a great deal of learned advice from people like Helen Waddell and, on the question of pure Latinity, from Barrington Ward of Christchurch . . . Personally I do not think your lecturer's translation is nearly impassioned enough. *Di magni, facite ut* . . . implies, I am sure, that Catullus felt it was extremely improbable that the lady would be faithful. He thought that the gods would have a hell of a time with her. My phrase: 'God, make it come true' gives the angry irony which I am sure is implicit in Catullus. I think your lecturer is on the wrong track with 'guileless and pure'. He is making Catullus look forward to a quiet domestic security which was not in the nature of Catullus. . . .

I wonder what your lecturer thinks of the Latin elegiacs which appear in *A Breeze of Morning* as a translation of certain verses of Gray.[2]

---

[1] The translation in *Sparkenbroke* runs:

> *Thou dost propose, beloved, this our love*
> *Joyful and deathless. God, make it come true!*
> *Bring her to swear it, knowing all her heart!*
> *So against Time may yet sufficient prove*
> *This timeless pledge of loving constancy.*

[2] The concluding lines are given in *A Breeze of Morning*:

> *dat solitas campus fruges; parvisque volucris*
> *deliciis 'grato sim tibi grata' canit.*
> *nil ego proficiens surdas suspiria in aures*
> *do, magis et, vanum est quod mihi flere, fleo.*

The sonnet by Gray ends:

> *The fields to all their wonted tribute bear;*
> *To warm their little loves the birds complain:*
> *I fruitless mourn to him that cannot hear,*
> *And weep the more, because I weep in vain.*

P

There is an amusing story attached to them which at least proves diligence in this poor bloody author! The boy in my story was going up to sit for a scholarship at Eton. I went to Eton, dug out the paper which was actually set in that particular year and then wondered how to get a translation which could reasonably have been composed by a brilliant boy. I asked the Eton Master in charge of the Classical Sixth to set Gray's lines for translation by his pupils and I offered a prize of a pound a line to the winner — which, I may say, is more than the *Sunday Times* pays for poetry! The prize was won by Willink, the son of the former Minister of Health who is now master of Magdalene College, Cambridge.

150. TO MLLE KITTY DE JOSSELIN DE JONG.
Written from the home of Dr. and Mrs. Harold Dearden, after the P.E.N. International Congress at Vienna.

Wye Cliff, Hay, Hereford
11 July 1955

I AM glad P.E.N. is over. I stayed in London about ten days to settle up various pieces of business and then came to this distant country-house to write. It is full of very young and charming children who don't bother me at all, for I have two rooms over what used to be the stables and I only go into the house for meals and after the young have gone to bed. The river Wye — honestly I believe it is the most beautiful in the world — curls round the bottom of the estate and the stretching views from the terrace and lawn (whither I shall go in half an hour to drink a large cold cocktail before dinner) are enchanting. . . . Like so many country houses in England, this one has 'come down in the world', but, unlike so many it is cheerful and happy and normal — everyone working and swimming and laughing: a little like Tchekov's *Cherry Orchard*, but without the complexes and the melancholy. I have done less work than I ought — not because I have been lazy but because the necessity to use this machine (though I use it easily enough) requires an adjustment of my whole method of composition. But I shall learn. . . . You see the trouble with a typewriter is that you cannot do easily what I like to do — keep on writing bits in the margin and cancelling other bits. Of course you can revise afterwards, but that isn't the same thing.

151. TO MLLE ELYANE DARGAND, *a student of the University of Lyon who had chosen* The Voyage *as the subject of her thesis.*

30 August 1955

I WILL help you as much as I can, roughly following the order of your questions.

1. If *The Voyage* is perhaps less well known in France than some of my other novels, it is because it appeared in England in 1940, and the French translation could not appear until long afterwards.

2. Do not be misled by what you call *le côté protestant* of the book. There is no argument protestant or catholic in it. It is true that Thérèse was the illegitimate daughter of a priest, but that is entirely accidental and of no importance. Do not, I beg you, regard it as a criticism of the Catholic Church.

3. You ask me what I think of the book. It is in some ways the liveliest that I have ever written. It marks a departure from the slow-moving, meditative, philosophical novels which preceded it. It contains a much quicker dialogue than they do, and a much more varied scene. My purpose was to lay emphasis upon the variety and vigour of character and to treat my theme more *dramatically* than ever before.

4. The germ of the book was as follows. While I was writing *Sparkenbroke*, some time in 1933 or 1934, there appeared in *The Times* a paragraph from *The Times* correspondent in Paris, giving an account of a legal case then proceeding in one of the provincial courts of France. A gaoler had released his prisoners and had continued to receive from the authorities money for their upkeep. One of the prisoners, on reaching Paris, had complained that he had been driven out of his prison, and claimed board and lodging to which as a prisoner he was entitled. The gaoler was therefore charged with embezzling public funds. I noted this as an amusing incident and several years afterwards asked *The Times* correspondent where he had got it from. He said from one of the popular daily papers, perhaps *Le Matin*, but he could not accurately remember. I searched the files of several French newspapers without success and was never able to discover where the incident occurred or what was the outcome of it. My French friends said it was unbelievable that there existed in France a private prison in which such an incident was possible. I therefore threw my story back into the past. Then, when the characters of Barbet and Thérèse

appeared to me — he a provincial wine-grower, and she a *diseuse* — it was natural that I should choose as my scene the Charente country, because my *traductrice*, Germaine Delamain, lived in Jarnac, and her husband, Jacques Delamain, was one of the greatest experts in France on two subjects: cognac and birds. (He wrote the famous book, *Pourquoi les oiseaux chantent*.) I stayed with them to study the country-side, the making of cognac, and the art of the *tonnelier*. As for Paris, I had a little in mind the career of Yvette Gilbert, though of course Thérèse was not intended to be in any way a portrait of her and indeed pre-dated her by several years. I followed every movement of my characters on the contemporary maps of Paris and studied with great care the contemporary newspapers, particularly *L'Illustration*. You will see that it was chance and not protestantism which carried my country scenes into a protestant area.

5. There is of course a link in the idea of singleness of mind between Barbet, and Piers and Lewis, but they were intellectuals, and Barbet was an intuitive and simple saint. He never doubted and they were always doubting. . . .

I hope all this may be of use to you. It comes with my good wishes.

152. TO HILDA MORGAN.   (*Charles had now begun work on his last novel*, Challenge to Venus.)

Campden Hill Square
4 October 1955

I AM finding myself quietly melancholy here — rather lonely some-times, but that is because I am deliberately not seeking company and go out as little as possible, so that I can get on with my story. This evening I shall have to go out at six. There is an opening of a Proust Exhibition which I must attend in courtesy to the French Embassy and because Harold Nicolson is to speak. . . .

For the most part I just tap and tap at this machine and, in the intervals, read Mrs. Gaskell's *Life of Charlotte Brontë*. What a good book it is! I don't believe Mrs. G. or anyone else at that time grasped what a giant Emily was, though they do seem to have seen that, when the three sisters' poems were published together, hers were the best — but they didn't know by how much they were the best. But what impresses me is the extraordinary truth and decency of the book. It is so true that it is often truer than it knows. Nothing catty or unkind is ever said of Charlotte. All her fortitude and strength are made clear and Mrs. Gaskell liked and admired her — and rightly; and yet one receives somehow the impression that Charlotte could be very arrogant and tiresome. And again, though little is told of Emily or Anne, the impress of each character is wonderfully firm. I think it is because Mrs. G. never hedges, is never afraid of what some fashionable clique will say about her, and gives her own judgment quite simply and straightforwardly. No damned Henry James about it! And how fierce and how dignified she can be when she slashes at the anonymous reviewers of *Jane Eyre* who made flippant guesses about the nature of the woman who wrote it. Also I have enjoyed the book because Charlotte in a long brilliant letter says exactly what I feel about Miss Austen. She is writing to G. H. Lewes, who was besotted about Miss A.

I had not seen *Pride and Prejudice* till I read that sentence of yours, and then I got the book. And what did I find? An accurate daguerreotyped portrait of a commonplace face; a carefully fenced, highly cultivated garden, with neat borders and delicate flowers; but no glance of a bright, vivid physiognomy, no open country, no fresh air, no blue hill, no bonny beck. I should hardly like to live with her ladies and gentlemen, in their elegant but confined houses. . . . Miss Austen is only shrewd and observant. . . . You say I must familiarize my mind with the fact that 'Miss Austen is not a poetess, has no sentiment, no eloquence, none of the ravishing enthusiasm of poetry' — and then you add, I *must* 'learn to acknowledge her as one of the greatest artists, of the greatest painters of human character, and one of the writers with the nicest sense of means to an end that ever lived'. This last point only will I ever acknowledge.

Can there be a great artist without poetry? What I call — what I will bend to as a great artist cannot be destitute of the divine gift. But by *poetry*, I am sure, you understand something different to what I do, as you do by 'sentiment'. It is poetry, as I comprehend the word, which elevates that masculine George Sand, and makes out of something coarse, something Godlike. It is 'sentiment', in my sense of the term — sentiment jealously hidden, but genuine, which extracts the venom from that formidable Thackeray and converts what might be corrosive poison into purifying elixir. If Thackeray did not cherish in his large heart deep feeling for his kind, he would delight to exterminate; as it is, I believe he wishes only to reform. Miss Austen being, as you say, without sentiment, without poetry, maybe is sensible, real (more real than true), but she cannot be great.

Them's my sentiments. I didn't mean to go on quoting at length but when I saw the name of your Thackeray at the foot of the page I thought that Charlotte's views of him would amuse you. Also, when Charlotte says of Miss A. that she is more real than true, I think that is one of the most profound pieces of literary criticism that I have ever read.

153. TO HILDA MORGAN, *with further mention of* Challenge to Venus.

Campden Hill Square
27 October 1955

I HAVE had two good and long letters from you and have myself been very neglectful. I am in the midst of a real battle. It's not that I'm stuck. Once I am over the present hurdle, I have a pretty clear run ahead, but this present chapter — the one that you suggested should be interpolated between the encounter at the cocktail party and the first meeting on the bastion when she turns away from him — is being very troublesome. I want to use it to make the reader interested in the girl and aware of the psychological background of her character, and I am finding it very hard to avoid saying either too little or too much.

154. TO MME DELAMAIN.

Campden Hill Square
10 November 1955

AFTER a very long interval, I am now near the end of a new novel with an Italian setting. It is not long — perhaps eighty per cent. of the length of *Portrait in a Mirror* and I do hope that you will feel inclined to undertake it when the question of French translation arises. At present it has no title. In French I should call it 'L'Usurpatrice', but there is no English equivalent of that. The English word 'Usurper' does not indicate what I wish to indicate — namely that my heroine incurs the vengeance of the gods because she has, like Psyche, usurped by her extreme beauty (and arrogance) the prerogatives of Venus. The English language will not indicate that my Usurper is feminine. It has been suggested that I should use the Latin word 'Usurpatrix' in all languages. It is a bold idea but I hesitate a little in face of it.

If you are able to forgive me for having left your last letter so long unanswered, do please let us have more news of you. Any letter from you recalls happy times and happy memories of Jacques. A few days ago at dinner I met again an old Oxford friend called George Delaforce, a wine merchant whom I think you know. He spoke of Jacques with touching affection, and people who did not know him often speak to me about his books on birds.

155. TO GEORGE BRETT, *President of the New York Macmillan Company.*

Campden Hill Square
23 November 1955

I SHALL now send you my new novel knowing that, when you publish it, you will give it all the support you can. I think, as far as I can judge, it has very good prospects in the American market. *A Breeze of Morning* was handicapped by the fact of its being about a very young boy (and Americans differ from Englishmen more when they are very young than in the later stages of their lives) and by its being concerned with Latin scholarship. The new novel has none of these disadvantages. Its period is 1949, its scene is a hill-town in Italy, its principal characters are an Englishman 29 years of age, who is staying in the hill-town on his way back to his business job in Aden, and a young Italian princess aged 25. They become lovers physically almost at once, almost by chance, and without design. By the ordinary circumstances of this world — nationality, religion, background — they are divided and for a thousand reasons marriage between them is 'unsuitable' and almost impossible. Their going to bed together is physically an overwhelming

success but — and this is the point — it has a different effect upon
each of them. It makes him fall enduringly and idealistically in love
with her, but it makes her, who has never before in her life had such a
lover, desperately in love with him physically but not at all with a view
to marriage. This is the problem which I have to work out. My idea is
that physical love when passionately shared can never be a casual thing
without consequence, and I am asking what happens when the effect
upon the man and the woman differs.

156. TO ST. JOHN ERVINE, *thanking him for a copy of his book*
Bernard Shaw, His Life, Work and Friends.

Campden Hill Square
5 August 1956

ALTHOUGH I was not slow in reading, I have been slow in writing
to thank you for your very noble and generous gift of your book to
Hilda and me because I am secretaryless and can't easily write with my
own hand; disliking this machine as I do, I have a tendency to postpone
everything except those urgent business letters which have to be
written at once. Still, the pause has given me a chance to browse over
many parts of your book again. At first reading, it held me so closely
that I even took it off with me to read in a dentist's waiting-room —
than which there could be no greater proof of a reader's interest in a
book.

There may be exceptions — Swift perhaps — but I think it is
generally true that we write better of what we love or admire than of
what we hate. It is certainly true of you, and the truer in this instance
because, though you admired Shaw's work and loved the man, you
didn't by any means share all his opinions and are able, when need
arises, to confute them. Shaw has always been a difficulty for me. The
little I knew of him personally I liked and admired; it was impossible
not to like and admire so much freshness and keenness and vigour and
enterprise of mind. Nevertheless he was, even as a man, in some way
too strident for me; it was like sitting in a room with all the doors and
windows open with a powerful wind howling in the passages. And in
the theatre — or in the prefaces — I could seldom get away from the

feeling that I was in the presence much less of an artist and a story-teller, which is what I happen to enjoy, than of an orator and a pamphleteer. It follows that, though I admired the astonishing skill of the onslaught, it remained for me an onslaught. Sometimes I was be-guiled into ceasing to resist — *You Never Can Tell, Arms and the Man, Heartbreak House, The Man of Destiny, Back to Methuselah* — but nearly always my resistance remained intuitive and active; I didn't ordinarily believe what he was saying, I wasn't beguiled into a suspen-sion of disbelief, and I had no kind of confidence that he would not at any moment, for the sake of rhetorical effect, turn round and cock a snook at what had appeared to be a passionate expression of his own faith. I don't mean that I felt him to be at long term insincere, but I felt that, at short term, he was so often self-contradictory and perverse and spectacularly journalistic that much of his work would be blown away by the gusts of his own mannerisms. I still think so. His work — or a good part of it — will continue for a long time to hold the stage, and for even longer he will have his place in history because he had so great an influence upon the thought of his time — the influence of a kind of supreme intellectual *agent provocateur* — but that cannot prevent me from disagreeing with him about all the fundamentals: his view of God and the nature of saintliness, his view of the relative bearing of poetry and intellect upon truth; his attitude towards women, his collectivist view of society which seems to me to have been just as perverse when he was collaborating with the Webbs as when he was throwing in his lot with the openly confessed totalitarians.

And that, really, is the mystery which you present and study. The essence of biography is the discovery of the basic tension and conflict of a character. How was it that a man so rich in variety and humour, so generous and benign in his personal life, so able to earn the enduring loyalty of Mrs. Shaw (and your portrait of her is superb and a key to the whole book) — how was it that such a man could be at the same time intellectually harsh and cruel? I don't think you would admit the word 'cruel' but it is implicit in your book — and I think it is the book's strength and honesty — that there was, not only at the end but from the very beginning, an element of cruelty in Shaw's intellectual processes, just as there seems to me to have been on your evidence an element of inhumanity in his sexual processes. Perhaps the key-word was 'clowning'. He seems never to have been able to resist it. It pro-duces many of the most brilliant as well as many of the most infuriating scenes in his plays. And it is a revelation to me that the sofa scene in *The Apple Cart* had an origin in his personal life. Oddly enough, when I last saw that play — at the Haymarket with Coward and Margaret Leighton — the effect was heightened by mere chance. When Margaret Leighton was rolling on the sofa, her ear-ring became caught in the cushions. When the time came for her to get up, she couldn't. I was in a box just above her and could see the disaster before Coward, who had moved across the stage. He hastened back to rescue her but could do nothing. If her ears had been pierced, there might well have been no remedy and the curtains would have had to be brought down. But she was wearing screwed-on ear-rings and with considerable courage — and I imagine pain — she wrenched the thing off and played the rest of the scene carrying it in her hand.

One of the misfortunes of using this machine is that, when one uses it at all, one uses it too much, and this letter is too long. But it is at least evidence of how much your book has interested and stirred me. It has made me think out the whole Shavian problem all over again. It asks all the right questions and supplies, as far as any biography is ever likely to do, the evidence from which just answers may proceed. For that reason and because it is written with such extraordinary liveliness and energy, it will, I am sure, endure. The curious conflict between a kind heart and a ruthless intellect is made brilliantly clear. You have provided posterity with what it needs to browse on, and it will browse and question and provide its own conflicting answers for generations to come. Thank you for so much enthralled interest and pleasure.

Hilda, whose admiration for Shaw is much less reserved than mine, joins with me in affectionate gratitude.

157. TO LE COMTE VICTOR DE PANGE.

Campden Hill Square
23 August 1956

I WONDER if you would very kindly help me with a problem. I am afraid that this looks like a long letter, but if inspiration comes to you, your reply need not be more than half a dozen words.

My new novel, *Challenge to Venus*, which is to be published in London and New York on February 21st, is already in the hands of my

French translator, Madame Delamain. She asks for help in a difficulty which, for me, whose French is so little colloquial, is insurmountable. My hero, an Englishman named Martin Lyghe, is called by all his friends 'Fiery'. There are two reasons for this. The first is the ordinary commonplace one that, as a boy, he had bright red hair. The second reason is that although in the ordinary conduct of life he is conventional and conforming, and hates to be thought in any way eccentric, he has always had a habit of proceeding now and then to a sudden conclusion or decision which he has arrived at not by a rational process but by a visionary process. For example, when at school he and certain other boys went for a run and were lost in a fog on a moor, he suddenly became quite certain of the way home and led his companions there. For another example: he suddenly arrived at the answer to a mathematical problem without going through the normal steps of calculation. (This once happened to me and I always remember it.) For another example: during the war, when landing on the coast of Italy with his men, he attacked and destroyed single-handed a German machine-gun nest because he suddenly *knew* that no bullet would touch him and that he would infallibly succeed. In other words, he sometimes, like a fiery horse, takes the bit between his teeth.

For these two reasons his friends have nicknamed him 'Fiery', and, in order not to be pompous about his moments of certainty or vision, they say jokingly that he has a habit of 'going in off the deep end'. My translator asks how on earth to translate 'Fiery' and how to translate 'going in off the deep end'. There must, I think, be some convenient phrase in French which means to 'take the bit between the teeth', and I think that would serve the purpose. The problem of the nickname itself remains. There is, I believe, a French word — something like *rouquin* — which is the ordinary nickname for boys with red hair. But that will not do, because it does not in any way carry the other significance. Can you possibly suggest a French nickname which is not pompous or pretentious, but affectionately derisive, and which corresponds to 'Fiery'? If you can't, I shall have to abandon the nickname altogether in French and just call him Martin, but I should be sorry to do that. My French translator is admirable but she is no longer young and masculine nicknames such as boys or young men might use among themselves do not come easily to her. But something which was exactly right for my purpose might arise in your mind. If it did, I should be extremely grateful.

158. TO LE COMTE VICTOR DE PANGE.

Campden Hill Square
18 October 1956

ALAS, Madame Delamain rejects 'Flambard'. She says that it gives
an impression of boastfulness which is inconsistent with the character
of my hero. And now, I myself, having looked it up in the dictionary,
find that 'Flambard' does carry the meaning of 'swank'. It is quite true
that this will not do. My hero, on rare occasions in his life, acts suddenly and impetuously because he is possessed by a sudden visionary
certainty, but in all other respects he is normally a quiet and modest
man to whom the word 'Flambard', as I now understand it, would be
inapplicable. I am beginning to think that there is no nickname in
French which gives the idea of fieriness — in the sense in which the
saints (especially Jeanne d'Arc) were sometimes fiery — without
giving also an impression, which is most undesirable, of panache. My
Englishman is by no means a Gascon. I begin to think now that in the
French translation it will be necessary to omit the nickname altogether,
and to use his ordinary Christian name of Martin.

159. TO ST. JOHN ERVINE, *in reply to a letter of advice on com-
bating 'writer's cramp'.*

Campden Hill Square
24 July 1957

OF course I do, in practice, what you suggest — I do my first draft on
a typewriter, and there are plenty of good writers who prefer it that
way. But I don't. I never have been a chap who wrote at full tilt and
then came back and revised. I can't, so to speak, let it go for the time
being. I write exceedingly slowly and re-read and revise continually,
paragraph by paragraph and sentence by sentence, as I go along, with
the result that my first draft, when finished, is damn nearly final, and if
I give out 500 pages of manuscript to be typed, there are probably at
least as many manuscript pages of rejections. Then of course I revise

the typescript and the galley proof and the page proof with the utmost
care, but there are seldom any changes, except of tiny detail, in those
stages. Everything for me happens in first-draft, and all the best that I
have written has been written under a kind of spell of concentration
and privacy and silence which is made impossible by a machine and by
the need to twist back and adjust etc. if I want to re-read and interpolate
and inte^r line. For example that beastly 'r' — and even now it's not put
in properly. No doubt, if I can't cure my hand, I shall adjust to the
change, but it is for me not just an inconvenience but a revolution.

Bless you and thank you.

160. TO MLLE KITTY DE JOSSELIN DE JONG.

Campden Hill Square
18 January 1958

THANK you for your long and very good letter which was most
encouraging to receive. I won't discuss it now because to tell you the
truth *Challenge to Venus* is a subject which at the moment is tedious to
me because I am contemplating new work.

I was sorry that my son, Roger, did not have the pleasure *and education* of meeting you. I say 'education' because when I was less than his
age during the First War, it was people of your kind in Holland who
educated me — particularly the remarkable lady who was born Loudon
but was then known as Madame Elout de Soeterwoude. She afterwards
became Mrs. Wake-Cook. She knew the literature of four languages
and spoke them all like a native. You could not tell she was not
English and certainly no Frenchman could tell that she was not French.
The same I believe was true of German and Italian — so that, with
Dutch, makes five. Nothing is better for a young man than the company of foreign ladies *de l'ancien régime*.

About the possibility of a visit to Holland, in many ways I am, as
you know, tempted, but I am reluctant to undertake the labour and
expense of a journey just in order to deliver a *conférence*. I think perhaps it would be better for me not to come now but to await the other
possibilities at Leyden which we once discussed. Probably nothing will

come of that and I am not counting upon it. But still it would be pleasant if it did happen.

The final sentence, quoted above, referred to the possibility that Charles Morgan might one day be honoured by Leyden University.

So with a salute to a friend and writer, and a last look backward to the formative years in Holland, these letters end. Less than three weeks afterwards, on 6 February 1958, Charles Morgan died in his home at Campden Hill Square, as he would have wished, in his workshop.

APPENDIX

GEORGE MOORE died in Ebury Street two weeks after Charles's letter to Louis Gillet,[1] on 21 January 1933, aged eighty, and Charles was appointed his biographer. It was Moore's desire that his biography should be not a 'tomb-stone in two volumes' but 'a true novel', based upon 'a novelist's complete knowledge and intuitive understanding of his subject'.

Charles had been introduced to George Moore in 1928 by Henry Tonks (The Slade Professor of Fine Arts). These two were old friends, and when Moore was looking for his ideal biographer he asked Tonks if he knew who was writing *The Times* light leaders, 'for whoever it is can write English'.

The result was Charles's first visit to Ebury Street, visits repeated over a space of five years, during which the older writer poured out his reminiscences. Many were already embodied in Moore's *Memoirs of my Dead Life*, and Charles was eager for fresh material. One name mentioned as being of supreme importance was Lady Cunard. The most valuable source, said George Moore, was a series of his letters, beginning in 1895, to this lady, who, before her marriage to Sir Bache Cunard, had been Maud Alice Burke, the daughter of wealthy parents in San Francisco. Without these letters there could be no complete knowledge.

The story of Lady Cunard's response and Charles's abandonment of his task is told in the following letter to Rupert Hart-Davis, who edited such letters as remained.[2] Presumably Lady Cunard had destroyed the greater part.

[1] No. 49, 7 January 1933.
[2] *George Moore: Letters to Lady Cunard, 1895–1933* (1957).

TO RUPERT HART-DAVIS.

20 August 1956

WHEN Moore asked her to let me have them, she said: '*All*, G.M.?', and he answered: 'Yes, Maud, all.' (She wanted him to call her Emerald, but he wouldn't. Did he ever in the letters?) I undertook not to publish any letter or any part of any letter without her specific permission. Nevertheless, she refused them to me both in his lifetime and (in spite of the direction in his Will) after his death. I therefore abandoned the biography, although I had been working on it for years, because he had told me again and again that it would be impossible to write the completely *true* biography which he wished to have written unless I had access to these letters. He attached so much importance to them that when she first refused to let me have them, he made a special visit to her in order to persuade her. When I saw him next, in order to receive an account of this interview, he began by chuckling to himself and saying that he was afraid that, for the time being, he had made matters worse. 'But', he said, 'I couldn't resist it. I walked up and down the room with her and tried to persuade her, and when she went on being stubborn I said: "Now, listen, Maud. Every woman has to go down to posterity on some man's arm, and you must choose. Either you must go down to posterity on my arm or on the arm of that nasty little chemist who beats two beats in a bar."' Then he continued that I need not despair; that I did not understand women and that she would yield in the end. She would have to yield because he had told her to in his Will, and had left her all his pictures! In fact, as you know, she never did yield. Within a few days of his death, I was drinking some sherry before dinner at Claridge's when she happened to come in with a companion. I went over to speak to her and asked whether I might some time come to see her. She was very polite, said she would be delighted, but was it anything in particular? I said: 'Yes — about George Moore.' She then said something which astonished me — presumably in order to give her companion the impression that her link with G. M. had been less intimate than it was. She said: 'You will know, Mr. Morgan; I have been told that he has left me all his pictures. Is that true?' I replied that I believed it was. She then said: 'How interesting. What pictures had he?' Seeing that she had been in and out of his house for forty years, and that his pictures included Manet's

224

portrait of his wife, Monet, Berthe Morisot, Burne-Jones, and Ingres, I should have thought she might have noticed them. To say nothing of the Aubusson carpet.

There, my dear Rupert, is the whole story, except the luncheon party with Lord Crewe of which I have probably told you, but I am afraid it is private. Perhaps after Sir Thomas Beecham and I are both dead, it may amuse someone. Meanwhile, it gives you a bit of background.

[Postscript.] I wonder what has happened to the pictures. There was a charming Conder. Also two (? three) pencil drawings by Ingres. One was from his hand — the others reproductions. I wonder whether she spotted the original.

The story of the luncheon party: Lady Cunard wished the biography to be written during Moore's lifetime and under her direction. With this end in view she invited Charles to lunch with her, giving him to understand that it would be a *tête-à-tête* concerning the letters.

To his surprise the occasion turned into an elaborate repast, served on gold plate in the company of twenty-five guests, including Lord Crewe.[1] In the course of the meal the hostess beat the table with the handle of her knife, announcing that she had a question to put to Lord Crewe. Did he agree with her that the life of George Moore should be written at that present moment. To that Lord Crewe replied quietly, 'Well, Emerald, since you have asked me, I do not think that any man's life should be written during his lifetime; least of all, that of our dear friend George Moore.'

It is reported that Lady Cunard — who, perhaps, had wished to discomfort Charles in public — was very angry. Over the matter of the letters she never yielded.

[1] The Marquess of Crewe (1858–1945). One time Viceroy of Ireland, Secretary of State for India, and British Ambassador in Paris.

INDEX

(See separate index of letters under LETTERS)